HOME AWAY FROM HOME

Cross Cultural Theologies

Series Editors: Jione Havea and Clive Pearson, both at United Theological College, Sydney, and Charles Sturt University, Australia, and Anthony G. Reddie, Queen's Foundation for Ecumenical Theological Education, Birmingham.

This series focuses on how the "cultural turn" in interdisciplinary studies has informed theology and biblical studies. It takes its leave from the experience of the flow of people from one part of the world to another.

It moves beyond the crossing of cultures in a narrow diasporic sense. It entertains perspectives that arise out of generational criticism, gender, sexual orientation, and the relationship of film to theology. It explores the sometimes competing rhetoric of multiculturalism and cross-culturalism and demonstrates a concern for the intersection of globalization and how those global flows of peoples and ideas are received and interpreted in localized settings. The series seeks to make use of a range of disciplines including the study of cross-cultural liturgy, travel, the practice of ministry and worship in multi-ethnic locations and how theologies that have arisen in one part of the world have migrated to a new location. It looks at the public nature of faith in complex, multicultural, multireligious societies and compares how diverse faiths and their theologies have responded to the same issues.

The series welcomes contributions by scholars from around the world. It will include both single authored and multi-authored volumes.

Published

Global Civilization
Leonardo Boff

Dramatizing Theologies
A Participative Approach to Black God-Talk
Anthony G. Reddie

Art as Theology
The Religious Transformation of Art from the Postmodern to the Medieval
Andreas Andreopoulos

Black Theology in Britain
A Reader
Edited by Michael N. Jagessar and Anthony G. Reddie

Forthcoming

Bibles and Baedekers
Tourism, Travel, Exile and God
Michael Grimshaw

Working against the Grain
Black Theology in the 21st Century
Anthony G. Reddie

Another World Is Possible
Spiritualities and Religions of Global Darker Peoples
Edited by Dwight N. Hopkins and Marjorie Lewis

HOME AWAY FROM HOME

THE CARIBBEAN DIASPORAN CHURCH IN THE BLACK ATLANTIC TRADITION

Delroy A. Reid-Salmon

LONDON   OAKVILLE

Published by Equinox Publishing Ltd.
UK: Unit 6, The Village, 101 Amies St., London SW11 2JW
USA: DBBC, 28 Main Street, Oakville, CT 06779

www.equinoxpub.com

First published 2008

British Library Cataloguing-in-Publication Data

A catalogue record for this book is available from the British Library.

ISBN-13   978 1 84553 383 0 (hardback)
             978 1 84553 384 7 (paperback)

Library of Congress Cataloging-in-Publication Data

Reid-Salmon, Delroy A.
    Home away from home : the Caribbean diasporan church in the Black
Atlantic tradition / Delroy A. Reid-Salmon.
        p. cm. — (Cross cultural theologies)
    Includes bibliographical references and index.
    ISBN 978-1-84553-383-0 (hb) — ISBN 978-1-84553-384-7 (pb) 1. Caribbean
Americans—Religion. 2. African diaspora. 3. African Americans—Religion. 4. Black
theology. I. Title.
    BL2565.R44 2008
    277.3′082089969729—dc22
                                        2007039491

Typeset by S.J.I. Services, New Delhi
Printed and bound in Great Britain by Lightning Source UK Ltd, Milton Keynes, and
Lightning Source Inc., La Vergne, TN

Dedication

I dedicate this book to my wife Elaine, whose camaraderie, courage and confidence serve as source of inspiration and hope in pursuing and completing this project. I will forever be indebted to her for her gentle and kind rigor, singleness of purpose and generous spirit from which I drew strength during flagging and difficult times.

My daunting task and seemingly impossible achievement could only be accomplished because of the ideal spouse and friend Elaine is.

Contents

Acknowledgments

This book is the product of years of research which began with a Black history forum at Grace Baptist Chapel which led to my David Jellyman Lecture at the 151st General Assembly of the Jamaica Baptist Union and culminated into my dissertation at the University of Birmingham, UK. I am grateful to all the people who have stimulated my thinking during the adventure of doing this research and writing. Many thanks to Sonji M. Anderson for sharing the vision and working with me to bring my perspective of the Caribbean diaspora into reality, and my academic advisor, Robert S. Beckford, for his insights and advice.

It is a great blessing to have a supportive community. Grace Baptist Chapel has been such a community for me. This church has not only provided the space and time for me to write this book but has given me generous support and expressed deep interest in my intellectual work. I am appreciative to the Board of Officers for its leadership of the church in order for me to complete the writing of this book. This Board is a model of leadership who has taught me the value of trust, delegation, honesty, solidarity and love.

In turning this manuscript from a dissertation to a book, I am especially thankful to Anthony Reddie for his brotherly advice, invaluable insights, consistent encouragement and critical engagement, as well as Augustus Davidson, Pearline Bloomfield, Ewart Simms, Jeniffer Taylor, Voris Walker, Winsome Williams, the members of Wednesday Evening Prayer Meeting, but in particular Roy Thomas for his unique support and Hyacinth Thomas for her special gifts, Lunet Davidson for her acts of solidarity and the many friends who have buoyed me with fervent prayer, deep confidence and a living hope.

During the research phase of this project, the friendship and kindness of Delta Anderson played a great role. Likewise, thanks to Raymond Anglin who facilitated my field trips in Florida, and Samuel and Maeve Vernon who accommodated me during the beginning of this research and to Delroy Hall, Dulcie Dixion, Lynnette Mullings for their encouragement to write and to Jean Campbell for her initial proofreading of this book.

To my parents, Joyce Salmon and Sylven Salmon, I say thanks for believing in me, nurturing my intellectual development and always supporting my academic pursuits. My deepest appreciation to my siblings, Aggrey, Phillip, Jennifer and Gary for their confidence in me, but especially Kevin, whose support of me and my work is far more than I deserve. I am equally thankful for the special support of Chantee Lewis, Monica Lewis and Cherry Wilkins. Finally, I ask for the forgiveness of those who have supported me during the writing of this book but whose names I have not mentioned. I acknowledge their support.

Above all, I thank God for helping me to have done this work which I give to God as an offering and gift for the people of God.

Introduction

This study seeks to define the theological identity of the Caribbean diasporan church by examining how Caribbean people[1] understand themselves as a people of God. By people of God, I am referring to the community of faith that is called into being in response to the invitation to follow Jesus Christ as Sovereign and Emancipator. The biblical witness describes this community of faith as those who are:

> no longer foreigners and aliens, but fellow citizens with God's people and members of God's household built on the foundations of the apostles and prophets, with Jesus himself as the chief cornerstone (Eph. 2:19; NIV).

Using the experience of this community of faith as a source for theological discourse, I argue that this experience is a theological act that is embodied in the practice of the faith community. Central to this theological inquiry are my own cultural history and diasporan experience as well as the socio-political and theological thought in Caribbean intellectual tradition which have all influenced my interest in Caribbean diasporan ecclesiology. This chapter reflects on the importance of the Caribbean diasporan experience and provides the structure of the book which consists of aspects of my personal diasporan journey, a definition of the term diaspora within the context of the Black diasporan experience, the significance of this study, the methodology the study employs and the delineation of each chapter.

My Cultural History

My cultural history shapes my interest in Caribbean diasporan theology. I am a Jamaican who has been living for more than twenty-five years in the United States of America. While I obtained my formative theological education in Jamaica, my theological development took place in America and in the United Kingdom. I began my diasporan journey in America deeply influenced by the history and culture of Jamaica. Although I was not aware of it at the time, Freedom Fighters such as Tackey, Cudjoe and national heroes such as Nanny of the Maroons, Sam Sharpe, Paul Bogle and Marcus Garvey[2] all influenced me. These persons inspired me and stimulated my interest in Black liberation and the pursuit of Black intellectual thought and theology. Learning about them and their struggles,

I became conscious both of the importance of resisting all forms of oppression and that their lives and history are a part of my heritage. The pursuit of emancipation is an aspect of my cultural heritage that contributed to both the formation of my identity and the tradition in which I stand.

This early exposure helped me in my intellectual exploration of the meaning of the diasporan experience. During my first years of living in the United States, I recall going into my room regularly and standing at full attention before the mirror singing the national anthem of Jamaica. I did this to nurture and to remind myself of my national identity and to keep myself connected to my national homeland. The words of the Jamaican national anthem are as follows:

Eternal Father Bless our Land,
Guard us with Thy mighty hand,
Keep us free from evil powers,
Be our light through countless hours;
To our leaders, great defender,
Grant true wisdom from above;
Justice, truth, be ours forever,
Jamaica land we love.
Jamaica, Jamaica, Jamaica land we love.

Teach us true respect for all;
Stir response to duty's call;
Strengthen us the weak to cherish,
Give us vision lest we perish;
Knowledge sends us, Heavenly Father,
Grant true wisdom from above;
Justice, truth, be ours forever,
Jamaica land we love;
Jamaica, Jamaica, Jamaica land we love.[3]

I was sure that as soon as I completed my studies, I would return to my home country. As the years passed I saw that this dream of returning to my national homeland was becoming a remote possibility and it troubled me. I was putting down and growing roots in America but was greatly restless. I began to ask questions and seek the meaning of living in America. I was determined that if I was going to live in America, I would need to go beyond merely acquiring an education and pursuing economic interests. After attaining these goals, one may still experience the desire to return home. Herein resides the tension between the notions of remaining in the host country as home and returning to the national country as home that the reader will note runs throughout the course of this study.

I have grown to appreciate living in America. It provides the opportunity for me to live outside of my native country and so gives me the experience of learning about other peoples and cultures which I may not have had,

had I not lived in America. The experience also puts me in direct relationship with the other members of the Black diaspora which has helped to shape my perspective of diasporan life. For example, my Jamaican experience is limited and insular but living in the diaspora engenders a more open and inclusive understanding of life and the world that allows me to understand my particular identity within the context of a global and diverse world. As such, my national diasporan identity is understood as an element of the general Black family and also that I belong to something greater than my own nationality.

Along with the appreciation of living in America, there are factors that could negate this joyful life. The problems of racism and the nature of Black life in America are two factors endemic to American society. Racial oppression is not an American problem but a human problem. In the United States, it was not only African Americans who suffered racial oppression but all Black persons. It made no difference whether you are a Caribamerican[4] or an African American. American racial policies make no difference in this regard. For this reason it should be noted that the Trinidadian, Stockley Carmichael, otherwise known as Kwane Ture, played a central role in the Civil Rights Movement of the 1960s.[5]

It was in this regard that the father of the academic study of Black theology, James Cone, challenged me to consider seriously the issue of Black theology in relation to the Caribbean diasporan community. After reading his A Black Theology and Black Power, Black Liberation Theology, and God of the Oppressed, I visited him at Union Theological Seminary to discuss the possibility of pursing postgraduate study in Black theology. Cone asked me:

> Why do you want to study Black theology? If you want to study Black theology, do not study about African Americans. You are not an African American. Find an area about the Caribbean people and make that your area of theological expertise.[6]

By this time, I was aware of the emergence of the Caribbean diasporan community and church but did not think of this as a source for theological discourse. Yet I was struggling to discover the meaning of the Caribbean diasporan experience in American society. I discussed this struggle with my friend and colleague, Baptist pastor and theologian, Neville Callam. He said to me that I needed to understand myself as a missionary where I live.[7] His advice became the perspective I used to inform and guide my life in America. This also means my resident home is a mission field. I did not, however, perceive America to be the mission field but rather the Caribbean diasporan community.

My experience as a pastor in the United States of America is another factor that led me to pursue theological reflections on the Caribbean diasporan experience. The Caribbean diasporan church is a growing community of faith. For example, Caribbean diasporan churches are established, houses of worship are built and congregations are growing. This phenomenon of growth implies that the church is an integral part of American society and makes a vital contribution to community and societal development. As a result of this growth, both the nature and character of American religion in general and Black religion in particular are changing. Theologians, however, have not yet recognized or explored this Caribbeanization of American Christianity.

This became evident to me in my preparation to deliver the 2001 Jamaica Baptist Union's David Jelleyman Lecture, "Ministry to the Caribbean Diaspora: The American Context." During my research for this lecture, I discovered that although there are a growing number of Caribbean diasporan churches, very little scholarship has been done on the church as a subject for theological discourse. Exceptions include the sociological work of Ira Reid's *Negro Immigrant*[8] and Irma Watkins-Owens' *Blood Relations: Caribbean Immigrants and the Harlem Community, 1900–1930.*[9] This experience revealed the great need for theological scholarship in this area of learning and ignited my passion to explore what it means to be a Caribbean Christian in American society. More specifically, I was consumed with the passion to know the meaning of the diasporan experience. This involved my consideration of the theological significance of the Caribbean diasporan experience and the role and contributions of Caribbean Christians to American society.

In addition to my cultural identity and theological perspective, the Caribbean intellectual tradition was also a factor in my journey to discover the meaning of the Caribbean diasporan experience. The Caribbean intellectual tradition is the analytical framework Caribbean diasporan thinkers such as Marcus Garvey, Claude McKay, Egbert Ethelred Brown, C. L. R. James and others established in order to develop ideas, promote learning and forge a new perspective of Black identity and existence and to confront the ideological and material realities of society in the quest for a just world.[10] I came to American society with a clear sense of national and racial identity, knowing that I am Black, meaning that I am a person of African descent, but not African American. This required that I establish my own cultural place and path in American society. This consciousness set me on a journey to define my identity and purpose in America. Central to this pursuit was my interest in understanding my life and faith from the perspective of my Caribbean religious heritage within the context of the Caribbean diasporan experience.

The Caribbean intellectual tradition is significant to my theological formation because it provides the framework and model for my intellectual development. This tradition is also significant because it decolonizes and deconstructs Euro-American hegemony of intellectual life. In this regard, the centrality of liberation in Black theology has helped me to recognize the prejudices in Euro-American theology and its domestication of religion. As such, an aim of this study is to provide a theological interpretation of the Caribbean diasporan church and to demonstrate its contribution to society. Theology is essential to the identity and purpose of the church. Theological scholarship, however, has thus far devoted scant or no attention to Caribbean diasporan religious practice. I want, therefore, to provide a doctrine of the church that will guide and assist the Caribbean diasporan church to have its own contextualized understanding of the Christian faith. By a contextualized faith, I mean having a faith of our own, of our own culture and in our own racial identity which Caribbean theology describes as "Fashion me a People"[11] or what Caribbean cultural and intellectual thought refers to as "Inward Stretch Outward Reach."[12]

The Caribbean Diaspora: A Theological Perspective

Diaspora has an evolving meaning. In relation to this study, attention is given to three changes in the meaning of the term. First, the term diaspora means to sow, scatter, disperse, disseminate.[13] It is used in reference to the dispersing or scattering of the Jewish people during the Old Testament era. R. S. Sugirtharajah, of the University of Birmingham, United Kingdom, defines diaspora as the dispersion and deportation experience of the Jewish people who lived out of Palestine.[14] The term is also used to describe the Christian experience during the first century. The Christians understood themselves as God's new people through whom God's promises were going to be fulfilled (1 Pet. 1:1-3). In this regard, Sugirtharajah writes:

> The Christian Church is seen as the wandering pilgrim and a dispersed community, in the sense that they are the instruments to fulfil God's eschatological purpose. The home they were striving for is not an earthly home but a home which is above and yet to come … on earth. Christians living in dispersion would function as the seed in disseminating the message of Jesus.[15]

Sugirtharajah is careful to note that these Christians were not exiles in the contemporary understanding of the term. As the people of Christ, they had a sense of catholicity about their faith and life. According to Sugirtharajah, they knew they were living in a distinct way which had wider global and salvational significance.[16] He goes further in making a very important observation about the amnesia of the Christians after they became part of the status quo or members of the dominant culture.

> After acquiring institutional status, however, the early Christian movement slowly forgot this notion of a sojourning, wandering people of God with transnational connection.[17]

He calls for a closer attention to this changing posture:

> Once a marginal community and seen as a perfect paradigm for provisional sojourning spirit, the Christian community had gradually lost its subalternity, moving into the centre.[18]

The meaning of diaspora is, nevertheless, not limited to the biblical understanding. A second change occurred which transcends the biblical paradigm to include the indescribable genocide of the Atlantic Slave Trade that began in the sixteenth century. It was a forced migration of Africans from their homeland to the so-called "New World" consisting of Europe, North and South America and the Caribbean.[19]

One of the consequences of this legalized slavery is the formation of various Black diasporas. The diversity of the Black diaspora is a result of the variety of homelands from which the people originated which reflected different societies, ethnic groups and cultures. They were also transported to a wide variety of destinations.[20] In other words, their origins and destinations formed the foundation of what constitutes today the Black diaspora. They are homogeneous, however, in the sense of having a common origin, formation and experience which are Africa, the Western world and oppression respectively.[21]

In recent times the term diaspora has undergone a third change in meaning. It changed from identification with the biblical people and the Atlantic Slave Trade to an interpretive account of the experience and meaning of the migration experience. As a signifier of this change in the meaning of diaspora, diasporan scholars created in 1991 the journal *Diaspora: A Journal of Transnational Studies*. In the inaugural issue, the founding editor, Khachig Tololyan, comments: "terms such as immigrant, expatriate, refugee, guest worker, exile community,"[22] are elements of diaspora.[23] Diasporan people are becoming a community but are in the middle of nowhere and are on the margins of the dominant society. Diasporan thinker, William Safran, concurs:

> The segment of people living outside their homeland and have a collective memory, vision or myth about their original homeland…believe that they are not fully accepted by their host society and feel partially alienated from it and where the true home is the ancestral home, where there is commitment to work for its development and whose identity is defined by this sense of home.[24]

Safran correctly observes the ambivalence and ambiguities of diasporan existence by pointing out some of the dangers that diasporan communities face such as alienation and marginalization which have the potential to weaken ethnic identity. He disregards, however, the centrality of faith in the diasporan experience. This experience, I contend, shapes and defines the identity and way of life of the people that they are able to sustain through faith.[25] Faith playing such a pivotal role in the Caribbean diasporan experience makes theological reflection essential to the meaning and purpose of the diaspora. Theological reflection seeks to answer the question of identity and purpose and to assist the church in developing a contextual understanding of the Christian faith and its relationship to experience.

In this regard, attention is given to a theological interpretation of the Caribbean diaspora. Exile being the dominant motif, George Lamming, in his *The Pleasures of Exile*, depicts this exilic existence. The title of the book indicates the author's self-understanding and the relationship between identity and locality. Life in exile is a perennial struggle between death and life, separation and reconciliation, oppression and emancipation, rejection and belonging, hate and love. On the one hand, life is undesirable and, on the other hand, it is pleasurable.

What, then, is exile? Exile denotes displacement, oppression, homelessness, alienation, sin, remorse, shame, marginality, emancipation and hope and also a place of ambiguities and contradictions. It is not clear if it is a place of choice or coercion. When will emancipation take place and on what basis can the exiles live in hope? The oppressor is identified but who is the liberator?

Lamming leaves these questions unanswered. Contrary to the biblical understanding of exile[26] as a place of captivity and coercion, for Lamming, exile is a place of choice. He writes:

> I do believe that what a person thinks is very much determined by the way that person sees. The book is really no more than a report of one man's way of seeing, using certain facts of experience as guide.[27]

Also, exile for Lamming is a good place. It is a place not of sorrow but of celebration. He writes,"…to be an exile is to be alive."[28]

Lamming's use of the exilic metaphor does not take into account the ambiguities and ambivalences of the diasporan experience. It furthermore advocates an assimilationist posture for the diaspora and this opens up the danger of sanitizing the diasporan people whose actions over time can reverse by their becoming oppressors. For example, in the case of the biblical figure, Nehemiah, he and his colleagues administered one of the most brutal treatments to the natives of the country (Ezra 9-10; NIV). They administered anti-family and racist policies that sought to dissolve inter-racial marriages and families. This biblical example reflects some of the limitations of the exile appropriate paradigm for defining diaspora.

Another significant proponent of the exilic paradigm of the Caribbean diasporan experience is Black British theologian, Joe Aldred. Writing about the origin and patterns of a Black British theology, Aldred uses the exilic experience of biblical Israel, with particular reference to the life of Joseph, as a model for constructing a Black British theology.[29] Aldred shares a similar view of exile with Lamming although they represent two different intellectual traditions. The former represents the religious and the latter represents the literary. Where they differ, however, is in Aldred's grounding of the Caribbean diasporan experience in the biblical tradition.

Aldred argues that the Caribbean diasporan people identify with biblical Israel through their experience. For Aldred, three factors which connect both groups of people and through which the Caribbean diasporan community identifies with biblical Israel are: the quest for a better life, marginalization and the hope of returning home.[30]

The strength of Aldred's theology is his assessment that exile is not the ultimate destination of the Caribbean diasporan people. As Aldred observes, "The track record of exile leaves little reason for hope, but the longing for home appears to be unquenchable."[31]

While this is a significant observation, Aldred does not offer a theology that is grounded in the Caribbean diasporan experience. His point of departure is the biblical tradition. Despite the merit of this source, it does not offer any prophetic critique of the system and structures that created and maintained exilic existence.

I commend Aldred's effort to relate the Caribbean diasporan experience to the biblical tradition because it provides a theological framework for interpretation of the experience. This practice engenders theological reflection on diasporan issues and their impact and implications for the diasporan people. Yet, failure to relate this interpretation of the experience contradicts the demands of an authentic diasporan theology.

Consequently, the exilic paradigm is an uncritical interpretation of the Caribbean diasporan experience. It domesticates the Caribbean diasporan theology and gives a reformist portrayal of a complex existence regarding the relationship between faith and experience. Notwithstanding this contention, I regard the limitations in Aldred's interpretation of the Caribbean diasporan experience as an indication that a Caribbean diasporan theology is yet to be developed.

Responding to this attempt to develop a Caribbean diasporan theology, Black theologians understand the Caribbean diasporan experience as a source for theological discourse. Black British theologian, Robert Beckford, advocates this meaning of diaspora in his book, *Dread and Pentecostal: A Political Theology for the Black Church in Britain*. Arguing against the use of the Exodus event and exilic paradigm and further contending that the experience of African Caribbean Christianity and social context are factors in theological discourse, Beckford concludes that the diaspora is a source for doing a Black theology.[32] With particular reference to the British context of the Caribbean diaspora, but significant to the Caribbean diaspora in general, Beckford states:

> The Black settlers arriving in post-war Britain from the West Indies were also conduits of an African Caribbean Christianity. African Caribbean Christianity is a part of and related to this diasporan experience. Therefore, a Black Church serious about its context must take seriously the issues that emerge from the experience of this diaspora.[33]

How is the diaspora a source for doing theology? Any authentic Black theology seeks to address the issues that emerge from and within its context. Beckford explores six areas of concern or issues that emerge out of the Caribbean diasporan experience.[34] These issues are: "Dispersal from an Original Centre, Maintaining a Memory, Never accepted by their Hosts, The Ancestral Home as a Place of Eventual Return, Restoring the Homeland and Group Solidarity."[35] These issues, however, are merely criteria for defining and analyzing diaspora and thus are not a theological interpretation of diaspora.

Beckford's interpretation of the diaspora is, at the same time, an initial attempt to give theological meaning to the Caribbean diaspora. He recognizes that the Caribbean diasporan church in whatever context, Europe or America, is an integral entity of the Black diaspora. Beckford correctly contends:

> It must therefore take seriously the historical fissures, memories, and adjustments that have influenced its emergence. Without careful analysis its theology runs the risk of two limitations. These are historical amnesia – forgetting where we have been and political naivety – unsure of what we must do.[36]

Though I contend that the diasporan experience should be employed as a source for theological discourse, Beckford, like Lamming and Aldred, gives a theological interpretation of the Caribbean diasporan experience. I propose, however, to use the term diaspora as a theological framework to interpret the Caribbean diasporan experience. Given that the Caribbean diaspora is diverse and complex, using the term diaspora as a theological framework provides an appropriate tool for articulating a theological understanding of this experience and identifies a dimension as well as an emerging tradition in Black theological discourse. With this perspective, I understand the term diaspora as a theological belief. As such, the Caribbean diasporan church is a community of faith that has emerged from the Caribbean diasporan experience in its encounter with the Christian religion and is the embodied expression of this belief.

The doctrine of ecclesiology normally concerns internal church issues and doctrinal subjects but Caribbean diasporan ecclesiology concerns the relationship between faith and experience. This relationship is lived out in the Caribbean diasporan church which functions as an agent and symbol of emancipation of individuals, community and society to protect from oppression and dehumanization. The church is the major context within which the relationship between faith and experience is experienced and understood and which reflects a contextualized faith and defines the church as an alternative and diacritical emancipatory community of faith. I specifically contend, however, that Caribbean people brought their faith into the diaspora with them and it is this faith that defines them as Christians.

The Book's Method

In undertaking this theological task, I use the method of textual critical interpretation.[37] I employ the term textual critical interpretation to describe the process of examining the Black theological sources, literature, cultural practices and personal experiences as a means of constructing a Caribbean diasporan ecclesiology. Through the use of the Caribbean diasporan experience, history, heritage and culture as sources for theological discourse, I have aspired to remain consistent with the contextual character of Caribbean emancipatory theology. In this respect, the method stands in the Black theological tradition especially, with particular emphasis on emancipation as the essence of Black Christian religion.[38]

A later chapter discusses that Black religion utilizes its own heritage and culture as sources for theological discourse, but the Caribbean diasporan experience has not been explored as a source for theological reflection. I regard this neglect as the exclusion of the Caribbean diasporan experience so as to maintain both Euro-American and African American theological imperialism. As a challenge to this hegemony, I employ a textual critical methodology. Pursuing this theological task, however, was an irksome and difficult endeavor because the resources were scant, scattered and incohesive. Notwithstanding these challenges, I explored various written texts about the Caribbean diaspora drawn from archives in the United States of America, Great Britain and Jamaica including church documents, reports, magazines, journals and letters. My exploration also includes other primary texts such as personal correspondences and a vast range of secondary texts to which I have given a close and critical reading in search of the particular understanding of being a people of faith that may emerge from these texts and to inform, shape, and sustain the practice and embodiment of a Caribbean diasporan faith.

The textual critical method, nevertheless, has limitations. For the purpose of this study, attention is given to two limitations of this methodology. As a text-based approach in pursuit of learning, this approach does not include the total life and experience of the people nor give an objective account of the people's experience. The texts this study employs reflect the perspectives of the authors. With this bias, the textual critical method expresses a particular point of view and privileges the perspective of both the writers and this researcher. This practice of subjectivity, however, is not unusual but characteristic of any approach to learning. This admission is not a disclaimer but a demonstration of the nature and value of a contextual faith and theology, and that the sources of this theology are expressions of the people's experience.

The other limitation of this methodology is the inability of texts to capture and contain experience fully. Texts are fixed but experience, in general, and the diasporan experience, in particular, is elusive, dynamic and evolutionary. The fixity of texts demonstrates that the textual approach is seeking meaning of that which is transitory. The discovery of meaning in a text, therefore, is only a glimpse, a partial view of the meaning we seek to discover. It is seeing through tinted glasses as the biblical writer attests: "Now we see but a poor reflection as in a mirror..." (1 Cor. 13:12).

These limitations do not devalue the textual critical method because the evolutionary character of the Caribbean diasporan experience resonates with the Christian Protestant tradition. This tradition advances the notion of the church as *ecclesia reformata semper reformanda*, "the church reformed, is always in need of being reformed."[39] The Caribbean diasporan church is in the process of becoming, en route, always looking ahead (1 Pet. 1:1-13). The ecclesia, the Caribbean diasporan church, therefore, is an evolutionary, dynamic and counter-cultural community of faith forged out of the diasporan experience.

The goal of the critical textual approach, nevertheless, gives a contextual interpretation and manifestation of the Christian faith with particular reference to Black theology. It takes into consideration the patterns and practices of the Caribbean diaspora's religious experience and identifies the theology that emerges from the text rather than to impose a theology on the text. Another way of expressing the issue is that, as a theological methodology, this textual critical approach excavates the theological themes and probes the interiority of the Caribbean diasporan's experience in light of the Christian faith. The method interrogates the text, asking questions such as what motivated the people to embark on a diasporan journey? What beliefs do their religious and cultural practices and social acts express? What do these practices and acts tell us about their God, self and community?

The Chapters of the Book

In pursuit of the above mentioned concerns, this book conforms to the following pattern. Chapter 1 contends that the Caribbean diasporan experience is a dimension in Black theology. Underscoring the belief that Black theology must wrestle with the Black diasporan experience within the context of Euro-American hegemony and Black migration and identity, the chapter addresses the absence of the Caribbean diasporan experience from Black theological discourse and calls for the development of Caribbean diasporan theological scholarship.

Chapter 2 examines two forms of Caribbean diasporan identities identifying the diversity of self-understandings that have emerged throughout the diaspora and the theological implications for the Caribbean diaspora. The Caribbean diasporan identities demonstrate both the heterogeneity of the Caribbean diaspora and Black diaspora. With the emergence of distinct Caribbean communities and particularities of heritage, culture and history, this study challenges the notion of a monolithic Black Atlantic identity. I argue therefore that no single identity can fully describe and define Caribbean diasporan people.

Chapter 3 identifies a third form of Caribbean diaspora identity. I propose the term Caribamerican to define the distinct community of Caribbean people who are living in North America. The chapter argues that the Caribamerican identity premises self-understanding on ethnicity.[40] The Caribamerican identity is inclusive of the cultural and cosmopolitan identities but it departs from and is independent of African American identity.

I further contend that in the absence of any concrete manifestation of a Caribbean diasporan identity and that no single identity can fully describe and define Caribbean diasporan people, the term Caribamerican encapsulates the communal consciousness and collective identities of the Caribbean diaspora in North America. In view of the communality and diversity of the Caribbean diaspora, I advance the notion, then, that the Caribbean diasporan church could be regarded as the single most prominent institutional, communal and collective representation of a common Caribbean diasporan identity.

Chapter 4 explores the theological foundations of the Caribbean diasporan church. The chapter proposes the notion that Caribbean Christianity is formed out of two different religious traditions, namely African-derived religions and European Christianity. In promoting this idea, I attempt to demonstrate that this dialectical religious tradition is a foremost dimension of Caribbean Christianity which reflects the nuances in the people's lives and in their faith.

On this premise, I argue that the dialectical religious tradition of Caribbean Christianity constitutes the theological foundation of the

Caribbean diasporan church. In this regard, the chapter offers a discussion on the nature and significance of the dialectical religious character of Caribbean Christianity in constructing a theology for the Caribbean diasporan church.

Chapter 5 analyzes the theological heritage of the Caribbean diasporan church. I advance the view that faith is the basis of the Caribbean diasporan church. Arguing that the church premises its existence and identity on biblical and doctrinal foundations, I propose that Caribbean theology and the theological doctrines of the Incarnation of Jesus Christ and the event of Pentecost constitute the theological heritage of the Caribbean diasporan church. This heritage, I contend, demonstrates the distinctive character of the church, differentiates the church from other communities and institutions and provides a theological framework for the mediation of the faith of Caribbean diasporan people.

Chapter 6 traces the theological origin of the Caribbean diasporan church. The chapter focuses on the socio-historical contexts of the church's development. I consider in depth the pre-suppositions that guided and govern the people's self-understanding as they embarked on their diasporan journey. I pay careful attention to the pilgrim motif as the theological framework that the people used to forge meaning out of their diasporan experience.

Chapter 7 addresses the development of the Caribbean diasporan church through the formation of communities of faith. This formation of churches represents a change in the interpretation of diasporan experience from pilgrim to missionary as the people became settled in the society and planned to extend their stay in the host country. They recognized the importance of addressing the needs of and providing the appropriate leadership for the emerging diasporan community.

Caribbean diasporan Christians established churches as an expression of theological autonomy and self-determination. The chapter argues that this represents both an alternative to African American Christianity and marks a new era in American Christianity. I examine also how Caribbean diasporan church is able to be a faithful witness to Jesus Christ in a changing world. In summary, the chapter explores the historical tradition from which the church originated, the self–understanding as a people of faith informed by a pan-Caribbean identity and undergirded by the perception of themselves as missionaries.

Chapter 8 considers the role and contribution of the Caribbean diasporan church in the resident homeland. I employ the Jeremiahic tradition as the theological framework for defining this role. Paying attention to the moral, intellectual, political and institutional contributions that the church has made to the resident homeland, I contend that the Caribbean diasporan church is the Christian theological voice and symbolic expression of diasporan peoplehood. In advocating this argument, I then identify three dominant practices of the Caribbean diasporan church. These practices, I argue, demonstrate how the church fulfilled its prophetic mission in the society.

Chapter 9 is a discussion of the distinctives of Caribbean diasporan ecclesiology. I consider aspects of and propose a future direction for a Caribbean diasporan ecclesiology. I argue that a Caribbean diasporan experience is central in constructing a Caribbean diasporan ecclesiology as an essential partner in the Black Atlantic intellectual discourse and as a feature of a Black Atlantic Christian theology. This approach breaks a new frontier in Black theology and provides a theological account of the Caribbean diasporan experience. In particular, I present aspects of this theological account and the relationship between faith and experience as manifestations of a contextualized faith.

This study concludes with offering a further challenge to the notion that Caribbean diaspora exists due to the search for a better life. Instead, I argue that the diasporan experience is a theological response to the human quest for the hope of the realization of a life of justice, peace and freedom. The diasporan experience is an element of the people's history and an expression of this quest for hope. The diasporan scholar, Elizabeth Thomas-Hope concurs:

> Migration was one of the few means open to the former slaves whereby they could demonstrate their new freedom and at the same time, display their abhorrence of a system that bound them for so long to one place.[41]

Therefore, the Caribbean diasporan experience is a pursuit in the realization of this vision of freedom which I will argue the Caribbean diasporan church has come to symbolize.

This study, therefore, does not only explore the theological meanings but also confronts Euro-American theological hegemony which I argue neither engages nor provides the framework for interpreting the Caribbean diasporan experience. Ultimately, I argue for a more inclusive Black theology that reflects the Caribbean diasporan experience. The exploration of this new and additional perspective in Black theological thought is the task that we now undertake.

1 The Caribbean Diasporan Experience in Black Theological Discourse: A Neglected Sibling

The Caribbean diaspora is a constitutive element both in Euro-American society and the African American community but African American theology has never before used the Caribbean diasporan experience as a source for theological discourse. Put differently, African American theology neither considers the Caribbean diasporan experience as an appropriate starting point for theological inquiry nor does it address the issues and concerns of the Caribbean diaspora despite the Caribbean diaspora being in existence in America for just over a little more than one hundred years. The diaspora began with the migration movement of 1899 when 412 Caribbean people entered the United States in pursuit of the hope for a better life.[1]

It is not possible to determine with certainty the reason for this neglect of the Caribbean diaspora's experience in African American theological discourse but what is certain is that the Caribbean diasporan church is an integral entity of the American society but no mention is made of its existence or role in the society by African American theology. Thus, this chapter calls attention both to this neglect in African American theology and the state of and need for Caribbean diasporan theological scholarship.

The Neglect

In the first major text on Black Theology, *A Black Theology of Liberation*, theologian James Cone emphasizes the inclusive nature of African American theology but overlooks the diversity of the Black Christian community. Cone attributes this lack to his training, experience and concern for African American liberation. He not only was unable to see the wider world as included in the quest for liberation but he overlooked Blacks who are not African Americans. With his characteristic honesty, he writes:

> When I first began to write about black theology, my concern was limited almost exclusively to the political and social struggle of black people in the United States. In addition, my graduate studies in theology and history as well as my

personal travels, did not include the Third World...because I did not encounter them either intellectually or existentially.[2]

Cone realizes the impact this has had on his theology. Although his concern is not the Black Atlantic diaspora but oppressed people in developing countries, he testifies:

> Unfortunately, black theologians have not always been sensitive to class oppression or the role of U.S imperialism in relation to the Third World. Sometimes we have given the impression that all we want is an equal piece of the North American capitalist pie.[3]

Cone goes as far as to argue for African American theology to be more than merely inclusive; it should be universal. By this, he means that this theology should speak not only for all humanity but that it must also engage with the universal struggle for emancipation. The significance of this claim demands that I quote Cone at length.

> I am firmly convinced that black theology must not limit itself to the race struggle in the United States but must find ways to join in solidarity with the struggles of the poor in the Third World. The universal dimensions of the gospel message require that we struggle not only for ourselves but for all. For there can be no freedom for any one of us until all of us are free. Any theology that falls short of this universal vision is not Christian and thus cannot be identified with the man Jesus who died on the cross and was resurrected so that everyone might be liberated into God's coming kingdom.[4]

Cone premises African American theology in dialogue with other theologies on the universality of the gospel in solidarity with the oppressed of the world. How, therefore, does one account for Black unity in light of the exclusion of other oppressed Blacks? Writing about inclusion, Cone contends:

> Black Ecumenism and the Liberation Struggle is important, because it connects the movement for unity among the churches with the struggle for freedom in the larger society... The ecumenical perspective that connects the unity of mankind with the liberation of the world's poor does not diminish our focus on black liberation. Rather, it enhances it, not only because the vast majority of the world's poor are colored but also because economic exploitation is a disease that requires the cooperation of all victims if the world is to be transformed. The vocation of the poor is to struggle together for the transformation of their history...[5]

Cone's claim of unity through the common struggle for liberation represents the inclusive nature of a Black theology of liberation but it is unclear if a similar claim can be made concerning the inclusivity of African American theology. Cone, for example, relates Black theology to developing countries and identifies African Americans as a third world people, or preferably, developing world people, but he does not include the Caribbean or the people of the Caribbean diaspora.[6]

The Black theology in dialogue initiative, which was the attempt to foster relationship with others of the developing world,[7] is another example of African American theology's neglect of the Caribbean diasporan experience as a source for theological discourse. While African American theology seeks to be in dialogue with other theologies of liberation, the goal of this dialogue is ultimately the de-centering of Euro-American theology. Otherwise put, Euro-American theology is not the dominant theology for Black people. With liberation as the essence of the gospel, African American theology calls for a reading of the Bible in light of the culture and experiences of the oppressed and the affirmation of their culture.[8] The dialogue was facilitated through the formation of international ecumenical organizations as an expression of solidarity, to encourage reflection and to engage in conversation.[9] This dialogue, however, does not include the Caribbean diasporan church, which is an integral entity of the same society as African Americans.

The universal dimension of the Christian gospel is also emphasized in the works of James Deotis Roberts. He differs from Cone, however, by emphasizing African American theology in dialogue with liberation and Euro-American theologies. He grounds his theology in the particular context of the African American reality and at the same time embraces a universal dimension of the Christian faith. He writes:

> We have in mind an approach that is contextual in reach and outreach. It is a means whereby the theologian seeks to know where he or she stands in a community of faith. But such an approach may also have ethnic and cultural traits. This inner understanding, identity, or commitment does not nor should not lead to self-righteous narrowness. It should lead instead to a profound cross-cultural and ecumenical encounter with those who stand outside the particular context of one's decision and life of faith. The goal is to get to know others in their context and in the depths of their commitment to the end that mutual understanding and enrichment may take place.[10]

Migration leads to changes in the society but there has not been any theological reflection on it. Roberts recognizes this issue but only sees it as a problem. He observes:

> We face in our midst the influx of large numbers of people from Third World countries. These people compete for jobs in a diminishing market. They are often willing to take menial jobs at low wages. This makes a bad situation worse. It puts the domestic poor against others coming from the outside. We have not solved our race problem, and this additional mix of non-white peoples is taking place in a situation of jealousy and strife.[11]

American Black theologians are indifferent and have ignored the issue of migration. Roberts admittedly argues:

This multicultural and interethnic situation is explosive and it confronts us daily. The churches and seminaries seem to show a lack of sensitivity to what is going on outside their walls ... For the most part theology and theologians have been indifferent to these changes and new challenges. They have carried on with "business as usual" so far as theological reflection is concerned.[12]

While Roberts emphasizes the universal dimension of the Christian faith, his call for dialogue is among African Americans, the various Christian religious traditions and world religions. He recognizes the changing character of American society and also of Black religion but does not acknowledge these non-African Americans as members of the African American family.

This insularity of African American theology is challenged by Dwight Hopkins. He is one of the first major African American theologians to broaden the focus and orientation of African American theology. The book, *Black Theology USA and South Africa: Politics, Culture and Liberation*, is the starting point of a more inclusive African American theology. The one faith, common experience of oppression and need to bear witness to the gospel are bases for the unity of both groups of people. Hopkins writes:

Blacks in the United States of America and in South Africa are brothers and sisters of the African diaspora. They share a specific and similar relation to the gospel – the good news of holistic liberation, systemic and individual, political and cultural. Such faith and theological claims in both communities, coupled with demonic and heretical white racist confrontations provide the basis for a comparative theological study... Thus the joining of black theology in the United States and South African counter-parts, results from common life experiences with the gospel and a need to witness before all Christians.[13]

While I concur with Hopkins in his effort to cultivate a more inclusive African American theology, the basis on which he forges the relationship between Black theology USA and Black theology South Africa focuses on South Africa but also is applicable to other people of African origins. Hopkins' work complements Cone's and Roberts' as their notion of liberation is directly related to African Americans. Like his predecessors, however, Hopkins does not take into account the faith of other African diasporan people while at the same time he claims the kinship of African peoples.

Hopkins' effort is inclusive but it ignores the diversity of the Black diasporan community, which, in this context, refers to the people of the Caribbean diaspora. Nevertheless, in his most recent work, *Being Human: Race, Culture, and Religion,* he provides an interpretation of the human being but it is understandably through the lens of the African American experience. He advances a diverse and contradictory notion of the human being which challenges dominant Euro-American interpretations and at the same time redefines this doctrine. He declares:

One amazing reality – or miracle of the human–divine interaction is the persistent creative genius of global dark-skinned peoples. Millions have, in the midst of a damning definition of white skin privileges, appropriated both racial categories and a re-interpreted Christianity to model a theological anthropology of individual renewal and structural transformation toward the practice of freedom – that is to say, a new self and a new common wealth.[14]

Probably the most recent manifestation of this neglect of the Caribbean diasporan experience is represented in Anthony Pinn's *Varieties of African American Religious Experience*. Pinn argues assiduously for diversity and variety of the Black religious experience. Pinn asserts:

It is my contention that African religious experience extends beyond the formation and practice of black Christianity. That is to say, historically African Americans have participated in a variety of traditions, such as Yoruba religious practices (attention to the orisha or deities), Vodoo (Vodou), Islam, and humanism.[15]

Judging from the usage in African American theology, the term Black refers exclusively to American Blacks. While Pinn is on a crusade to demonstrate that Black theology, by which he means Black theology in America, must go beyond African American theology, he seems to forget that African Americans do not constitute the total Black community in American society. Perhaps by Black he means exclusively African Americans. In which case, he has the right to speak for this particular community. The problem, however, and this is misleading, is that he advocates the notion of the variety and diversity of Black religious experience when in reality that merely means the African American religious experience.

This study does not contend with Pinn's claim of not limiting the Black religious experience to African American Christianity, but argues that the American Black community is diverse. In other words, while there is no homogenous but rather an heterogeneous Black community, African American theology, if it is going to function as an authentic expression of Black faith and religious practice, must take into account this heterogeneity within its own context. I furthermore contend that if African American theology is going to be in dialogue, be inclusive and to practice the universal dimension of the faith, it must consider the experience of the diasporan Blacks that constitute its immediate context.

In a major departure from Cone, Roberts and Hopkins, Pinn does not regard liberation as the essence of the Christian faith. While Pinn is advocating for Black humanism, he is aiming to bring this philosophy under the rubric of Black Christianity. Engagement with this claim is beyond the scope of this study. However, where Pinn's humanism is of concern, is in the promotion of the diversity and variety of Black religion without acknowledgment of the diversity of the Black community. Pinn, probably, does not establish an account for the difference between Black religion and Black theology. The former describes the way of life of Black people in response to a Divine or Supreme Being as seen in the diversity of Black religion. The latter is the interpretation of the faith about God in relationship to Black people. All Black religions have their theology and all Black theology is an expression of that particular Black religion.[16] This important distinction must be made so as not to confuse or equate both.

The neglect of the Caribbean diasporan experience and religious thought and practices in African American theology is also represented in Womanist theology. Delores Williams' *Sisters in the Wilderness* illustrates this neglect. This is an American theology in the liberation tradition which concerns the theological interpretation of African American women's experience. Williams delineates in this volume four essential features of this theology which she believes are: an autonomous identity, a dialogical nature, a critical theory of oppression and an organically related Black theology.[17] Williams proceeds to define the tasks of Womanist theology as follows:

> While its aim is discourse and work with black women in the churches, it also brings black women's experience into the discourse of all Christian theology, from which it has been previously excluded. Womanist theology attempts to help black women see, affirm and have confidence in the importance of their experience and faith for determining the character of the Christian religion in African–American community.[18]

Liberation is the central motif of Womanist theology. The essential features, however, are definitive and distinguish it from other forms of liberation theologies. In this respect closer attention should be given to the essential features of Womanist theology in order to demonstrate its point of departure from African American Black theology. With particular reference to its autonomy and organic relationship to Black theology, Williams declares:

> Womanist theology, however, also branches off in its own direction, introducing new issues and constructing new analytical categories needed to interpret simultaneously black women's and the black community's experience in the context of theology.[19]

Consideration must also be given to its critical function and dialogical nature. Williams asserts:

> Womanist theology challenges all oppressive forces impeding black women's struggle for survival and for the development of a positive, productive quality of life conducive to women and their freedom and well being. Womanist theology opposes all oppression based on race, sex, class, sexual preference, physical disability and caste.[20]

As far as the dialogical nature of Womanist theology is concerned, Williams argues that:

It welcomes discourse with a variety of theological voices – liberation white feminist, Mujersita, Jewish, Asian, African classical and contemporary "male–stream," as well as non-feminist, non-womanist female voices. Womanist theology considers one of its primary tasks to dialogue with the church and with other disciples.[21]

Of all these significant features, this last one is of particular importance to the Caribbean diaspora.[22] Here we see the ambitious claim of openness to dialogue but no mention is made of either the Caribbean region or of the Caribbean diaspora in American or British society. It is inexplicable that this broad and comprehensive welcome is not extended to those who are not only neighbors but siblings and living in the same society. Womanist theology has not entered into dialogue with the women of the Caribbean. Caribbean diasporan women constitute a vital aspect of the constituency of Womanist theology and share the same context with African American women although their experiences differ.

African American women's experience is not normative for the Black community. If their experience is the definitive source and point of departure, then it can only be an African American Womanist theology. With the exclusion of other Black women's experience, nevertheless, Womanist theology concerns existential issues that resonate with Black women in general. Williams articulates:

> The greatest truth of black women's survival and quality-of-life struggle is that they have worked without hesitation and with all the energy they could muster. Many of them, like Hagar, have demonstrated great courage as they resisted oppression and as they went into the wide, wide world of making a living for themselves and their children. They depended on their strength and upon each other. But in the final analysis the message is clear: they trusted the end to God. Every important event in the stories of Hagar and black women turns on this trust.[23]

The United Reformed Church clergy and educator, Majorie Lewis, argues that as an African American theology, Womanist theology is not an adequate representation or interpretation of Black diasporan women. She proposes "Nannyish T'eology"[24] which is commonly believed to embody the experience of Caribbean diasporan women in British and American societies.[25] Lewis contends: "The concept of 'womanism' is inadequate to represent the perspectives of all Black women across the many locations of the world."[26]

The Baptist pastor, Kate Coleman, differs from Lewis in the usage of the term Womanist to describe the experience of Black British women. According to Coleman, "The parameters of womanist theology make it a particularly useful term in the articulation and development of a Black British womanist theology of liberation."[27]

Coleman, however, concurs with Lewis's claim regarding the source of this theology. Coleman declares:

> As Black British women we cannot simply depend upon the insights of our African-American cousins. Our voices must also be heard if we are to achieve liberation. This will require that we dispense with the essentialized concept of Black womanhood and with the idea of a monolithic Black identity and instead recognize that there are varied and many models of Black womanhood. It is this concept that underlines the notion that the issues that have had an impact upon Black British women are many and varied.[28]

Coleman correctly acknowledges the common experience of Black women in the United States and Britain but argues that the experience is not limited to racism and sexism. The experience is contextual which includes personal, spiritual, social and institutional issues that affect the lives of these Black diasporan women. Coleman claims: "…womanist theology attempts to be contextual, seeking to identify relevant categories of oppression while simultaneously proposes analytical approaches directed at liberation."[29]

Although Coleman is writing about Black British women's experience, her description is reflective of the experience of Black Atlantic diasporan women in general and Caribbean diasporan women in particular. This experience includes, for Coleman, patterns of settlement, economic strength, community cohesion, composition and ethos of black majority institutions such as churches along with their leadership structures.[30]

The agreement between Cooper and Coleman on African American Womanist theology shows the limitation of employing only African American women's experience as a source for interpreting the Caribbean diasporan experience. In recent time, an alternative voice has emerged with regard to this issue. Dianne Stewart, for example, has made a challenging contribution to this debate. She argues for an African-centered Womanist theology using the experience of Kumina women. Writing about African-derived religions, Stewart observes:

> The presence of African-derived religions in the Americas and the Caribbean demonstrate that some religious communities resisted Euro-Christian domination and the cooptation of their images of the Divine under the ubiquitous image of Jesus Christ as the only valid divine revelation.[31]

Stewart continues to argue that the experience of women of African-derived religions, such as Kumina, is a source for Black theological discourse. In her words:

> I see in Kumina and other African-derived religions important resources for constructing an African–derived theology of the cross that promotes the holistic liberation of Black women and Black communities.[32]

Stewart bases her claim on the role of women in Kumina as leaders, participants, preservers and embodiment of the religion.[33] While I do not contest this claim nor disagree with the Womanist perspective of emancipation as holistic, the claim, however, of using the experience of women of African-derived religions as a source for theological discourse is still exclusionary. These religions are not representative of all Caribbean women; thus, Stewart assumes too much on the part of African-derived religions.

It is appropriate for this discussion to note that while Marjorie Lewis and Kate Coleman critique Womanist theology for its limitation to African American women's experience, Dianne Stewart has not only overlooked this limitation but has defined her theology on one particular religion. Here I contend that Stewart has not taken into account the ethnic, religious and cultural diversity of Caribbean diasporan women in her focus on only one Caribbean religious tradition. This limitation is additional exposure of a gap in Black theology but provides the opportunity for a Caribbean diasporan theology. It advocates the need for additional and new theological voices that can speak to and about the varied and diverse needs and challenges of this vast and heterogeneous Black diaspora. In this case, a Caribbean diasporan theology with particular reference to ecclesiology represents an emergence of this voice.

The State and Need for Caribbean Diasporan Theological Scholarship

To date, most studies of the Caribbean diaspora in the American context have been in the fields of anthropology, sociology, history and literature.[34] There is a plethora of studies on Caribbean diasporan life but very little scholarship on their religious practices. The three most substantive texts in this regard are Ira Reid's *Negro Immigrant* and Randall Burkett's *Garveyism as a Religious Movement* and *Black Redemption: Churchmen Speak for the Garvey Movement*.[35] In the case of Reid's work, it describes the assimilation process of Caribbean immigrants but is not a theological interpretation of that experience. As for Burkett, his work is a study about the United Negro Improvement Association as a religious movement but this represents only one particular aspect of the Caribbean diaspora. In this regard, it does not fully represent the religious practices and faith of the Caribbean diaspora.

The most representative theological study on the Caribbean diasporan church is Irma Watkins–Owens' *Blood Relations: Caribbean Immigrants and the Harlem Community, 1900–1930*. This study addresses the relationship between Caribamericans and African Americans and the role Caribamericans play in American society. Of particular significance to this research is my argument that the role of the Caribbean diasporan church is understated and limited to the function of a preserver of culture. According to Watkins-Owens, the churches were "formed to maintain contact and preserve traditions of immigrants from the same town or region" [country].[36] While acknowledging this function of the church, however, I contend that the Caribbean diasporan church is a distinct and alternative community of faith to both Euro-American and African American churches.

These important studies nevertheless provide both sociological and historical insights into the diasporan experience but they are neither theological interpretations of the experience nor expressions of a belief of a Christian faith. Moreover, too little theological attention has been given to this area of scholarly pursuit. Addressing this crucial problem, sociologist Nancy Foner concurs: "Given religion's importance in the lives of West Indians...it is surprising that the church is barely mentioned in the most scholarly accounts."[37] Similarly, Elaine Bauer and Paul Thompson, in their study on the Caribbean diaspora, acknowledge the role of religion in the diasporan experience but only in terms of personal support and as a moral agency.[38] What this indicates is that Bauer and Thompson are totally unaware of the prominence of the Caribbean diasporan church; consequently, they came to an erroneous conclusion concerning the declining significance of the religion in the host countries due to racism and secularization.[39]

With the arrival of Anthony Reddie's *Black Theology in Transatlantic Dialogue*, the landscape of Caribbean diasporan theological scholarship begins to change. Given the dominance and prominence of Caribbean people in the Black church in Britain,[40] I situate *Black Theology in Transatlantic Dialogue* in the Caribbean diasporan theological tradition of Black theology. In concurrence with my claim, which will be discussed in Chapter 3, Reddie asserts that the ancestral heritage and the numerical composition of the Black church in Britain consist of people from the Caribbean.[41] Along with this prevailing perspective, both the church tradition in which Reddie stands and the people for whom he writes are also primarily of Caribbean heritage.[42]

Reddie's *Black Theology in Transatlantic Dialogue* is a constructive evaluation of the development of Black British theology through a comparative analysis with Black theology in the United States of America.[43] Reddie undertakes this task by organizing his work within a thematic rather than a developmental framework. This framework includes the origins of Black theology, the relationship between Black theology and the Black church, Womanist theology, practical theology and a proposed future direction for Black British theology.

This thematic framework is Reddie's attempt to identify and define the general contours of Black British theology and so leaves the micro dimensions of this theology to the specialists in the various branches of Black theology. For example, Reddie acknowledges that as a male, he does not have the right to define Womanist theology. He writes apologetically:

> Clearly, as a black male, it is not my place to tell black women what to do and how they should do it. What I offer instead are some personal reflections on womanist theology, comparing and contrasting the significance, themes and approaches between the United States and Britain.[44]

Notwithstanding this disclaimer, Reddie is careful to devise a new method for doing Black British theology which he calls "Jazz hermeneutic."[45] Reddie considers the element of improvisation in jazz, which he likens to Black homiletics in particular and Black practical theology, as a means of providing meaning beyond the immediate context and of forging a relationship between the Black church and the academy. Reddie expresses this notion as follows:

> The central motif in this particular conception of black theology is one that borrows from the practice of improvisation in jazz music. It is a way of conceiving black theology with a view to developing a more accessible method for engaging in God-talk that is reflective of the experiences of black people and their expressions of faith.[46]

Improvisation, as Reddie describes it, creates a synthesis between the past and the present to create new meanings while grounded in the tradition of the faith.[47] What is unsettling, however, is Reddie's dependence on African American theology. More than just a version of African American theology, a distinct Black British theology is still to emerge. Awaiting this voice, what I am hearing from Reddie's *Black Theology in Transatlantic Dialogue* is an African American voice in a British body. This is unfortunate, given that Reddie is aware of his Caribbean heritage.[48]

Reddie attempts to excuse his overdependence on African American theology by acknowledging that his account is both a journey and it is not normative for Black British theology.[49] In the beginning of the discussion, however, he is very forthright and proud, and correctly so, of using his experience as a paradigm for constructing a Black British theology. He writes: "I want to use my own subjective narrative as a microcosm for the overarching historicocultural and political account of Black people in Britain."[50] The reason he uses this approach is to

provide a context from which we can depart and make further explorations into
the complex meanings and issues that are bound up with the process of
highlighting the central import of black theology, to my own development, and
also that of all black people in Britain and the United States.[51]

Having made this statement, Reddie concludes his creative work with an
acknowledgement of not only his neglect of his Caribbean heritage but
his excessive reliance on African American theology in the development
of a Black British theology.[52]

Reddie's inconsistency in this regard, nevertheless, does not negate
and cannot eliminate the African American influence on Black British
theology but it is not clear why he does not give an account of the role of
Caribbean religion and culture in the development of Black theology in
Britain. Reddie leaves open for one to conjecture that he has very limited
knowledge of his Caribbean heritage. As noted earlier, with the exception
of his parents, he mentioned no other source of Caribbean influence on
his life and intellectual development.

Given the descriptive character of Reddie's excellent analysis of the
relationship between the Black theologies in Britain and the United States,
he may have provided a partial account of Black theology in Britain. The
crucial task of social analysis and the confrontation of issues such as classism,
religious pluralism and the legacies of colonialism including migration,
underdevelopment in the former British colonies and the emergence of
diasporan communities are left unexplored. Above all, I maintain that the
Black British theology that Reddie advances is greatly impoverished without
any engagement with the rich and illustrious resource of Caribbean theology
such as Idris Hamid's *Out of the Depths*,[53] Kortright Davis' *Emancipation
Still Comin'*[54] and Noel Erskine's *Decolonizing Theology*.[55]

Adding to the significance of this work would have been a dialogue
between both African American theology and Black British theology.
Instead, what Reddie provides is a comparative account of these theologies
without any dialogue taking place, as the title of the book suggests.

Notwithstanding these weaknesses in *Black Theology in Transatlantic
Dialogue*, the interdisciplinary nature and the methodology that is proposed
are two definitive factors of Black British theology. Also, this is both the
first study of its kind and so represents the birthing of a Caribbean diasporan
theology within the Black Atlantic theological tradition.

Postcolonial Black British Theology[56] is an additional new voice to
Caribbean diasporan theological scholarship. Whereas *Black Theology in
Transatlantic Dialogue* focuses on the relationship between Black British
theology and African American theology, *Postcolonial Black British Theology*
is an emerging, new but eclectic voice[57] that reflects the nature of diasporan
theological thought as the term "postcolonial" signifies. The term is used
as a paradigmatic framework that defines the theological sensibilities of

Black British Christians and connects the past, present and future, affirms the diversity of a Black diasporan theology and advances this discourse beyond any one particular religious tradition,[58] as the proponents point out:

> Postcolonial Black theology in Britain emerges from the diasporan experiences of Black and Asian peoples and their experiences with and introduction to Christianity. For the bulk of mainly Caribbean people (who have historically constituted the development of Black theology in Britain) this emerging Christianity was one that sought to challenge the allegedly Christian inspired oppressive acts of White imperial power.[59]

Postcolonial Black theology is a counter discourse to white hegemony and represents a point of departure from British theology which encapsulates the diversity and complexity of the meaning of blackness in British society and occupies a significant dimension in Black British theology.[60] But a crucial problem of a severe identity crisis surrounds this theology as the following remarks express in the generic usage of the term "black" and "slavery":

> (1) The roots of a postcolonial Black theology lie in the counter-oppressive struggles of Black peoples in the Americas, the Caribbean, Asia and Britain to challenge the worst excesses of oppressive Christian-inspired supremacist practices through radical reinterpretation of the central tenets of the Christian faith.

> (2) The roots of Black theology can be found in the radical and subversive reinterpretation of Christianity by Black slaves in the so-called New World, during the eighteenth and nineteenth centuries.

> (3) The desire of Black people to form their own ecclesial spaces was the process of a long period of history arising from the "Great Awakening" in the middle of the eighteenth century.[61]

Postcolonial Black British Theology is a specie of Caribbean diasporan theology and incorporates Black history and experiences as one of its constitutive elements, but it does not take into account the differences in the experiences between people of African and Asian ancestries. For instance, Asians did not experience nor were involved in the struggle against slavery. Also, the de-centering of Black ethnicity in order to forge an inclusive Black theology trivializes the Black experience. Blackness in this case is a social construction that is associated with non-positive experiences.[62] As Asian theologian Mukti Barton argues, "non-White people of the world and many are now proudly calling themselves Black in order to counter racism."[63] I insist, however, that Black ethnicity is a central element in Black theology and the Caribbean diasporan theology that I propose affirms African ancestry.

Now that I have established that the Caribbean diasporan experience is a neglected and unexplored area of theological reflection, this study represents a theological contribution to this fertile area of theological discourse. I will demonstrate that although Black theology utilizes culture and experience as sources for theological reflection, the culture and experience of diasporan people have been excluded in Black theological discourse. Along with exploration of what the diasporan experience reveals about God and humanity, this study is an initial attempt to provide a doctrine of the Caribbean diasporan church, add another perspective to and deepen the understanding of the nature of Black theology. As such, it advances the understanding of Black religion and joins the ongoing ecumenical theological discourse.

A further aim of this study is to connect the missing link of Caribbean diasporan religious thought in Black theology. I focus primarily on the Caribbean diaspora in the American context but incorporate aspects of the Caribbean British diaspora. This inter-continental focus forges a Black Atlantic theology which engages a wider and more inclusive theological discourse on the Black diaspora and connects the diaspora through faith and gives theological voice to the Black Atlantic Caribbean diasporan experience. Additionally, a Caribbean diasporan theology within the Black Atlantic theological tradition attempts to articulate a broader and more inclusive vision of the Black experience and demonstrates the diversity of not only the Black religious experience but also of Black Christian theological thought.[64] In so doing, a Caribbean diasporan theology de-African Americanizes Black Christian religion and theology.[65] In one sense it could be argued that this study expresses not only the catholicity of the Christian faith but the catholicity of Black Christianity.[66] As I have discussed, new theological voices are emerging within the Caribbean theological tradition but, at the time of writing, no distinct Caribbean diasporan theology exists. This study, therefore, is an attempt to develop such a theology. However, since diaspora connotes diversity, which is the nature of the Caribbean diaspora, Caribbean diasporan identities can be understood as theological self-understandings. It is, therefore, to this central issue of the forms of Caribbean diasporan identity that the discussion now turns.

2 Theorizing the Caribbean Diasporan Identity: Identifying Ourselves

I explore in this chapter two forms of identity, which, intentionally or unintentionally, define the Caribbean diasporan self-understanding in order to determine the Caribbean diaspora as a distinct community of people. In my initial discussions to explore the topic of the Caribbean diaspora, my conversants expressed disinterest, dismay or even disregard for the subject. I recalled being told bluntly in my earliest discussions that there was no such thing as a Caribbean diaspora. In subsequent discussions, I was asked about the value of referring to Caribbean people living in foreign countries as a diaspora. People also questioned whether this was not a way of separating Caribbeaners[1] from others of African descent. They asked: Is this another attempt to create an ethnic enclave and ghetto? Will not this self-identity alienate us from other people groups? Why is it important to have this identity?

While I did not provide any answers to these questions, I will not dismiss them. They reflect a general public understanding of the meaning of diaspora. Implicit in the response also is a lack of understanding that Caribamericans are a diasporan people. All Caribbean people came from somewhere else to be where we are. Addressing this issue, the sociologist Stuart Hall states:

> The Caribbean is the first, the original and the purest diaspora. These days blacks who completed the triangular journey back to Britain sometimes speak of the emerging black British diaspora, but I have to tell them that they and I are twice diasporised. Furthermore, we are not just living in a diaspora where the center is always somewhere else, but we are the break with those originating cultural sources as passed through the traumas of violent rupture.[2]

The response of my interlocutors to the designation of Caribamericans as a diaspora is an expression of the problematic nature of diaspora. The reasons for this problem may be many but two of immediate concern are the complexity and centrality of diaspora to public life in a rapidly changing world. For example, the certainties, sense of identity and unity that once characterized societies have changed with the advent of globalization.[3] Consequently, alienation, fragmentation, instability coupled with transnational economic, social and communication trends have redefined the nature of identity.[4] Migration policies, trade agreements and economic initiatives, such as the Caribbean Basin Initiative,[5] also contribute to the changing meaning of a Caribbean diaspora. These factors both directly and indirectly transmit culture and as a result facilitate the creation of a Caribbean diaspora.[6] Initially, the concern was with immigrants but with globalization and the formation of new relations, the emphasis has changed to incorporate the emergence of diasporan communities.[7]

The Caribbean diaspora contends with these global forces taking into account hegemonic issues such as migration, relocation, alienation, marginalization and the struggle to live a meaningful life.[8] These issues evoke questions such as: What does it mean to live in a strange land? Who are we, when we are uprooted, dispersed and displaced from our homeland, whether through coercion or by our own volition?

Seeking to answer these questions raises the issue of diasporan identities. Responding to the meaning of diaspora, you will recall that this book employs the term diaspora as a theological paradigm to interpret the relationship between faith and experience. The paradigm comes to theological studies via various routes.[9] As noted previously, I identified some major usages of the paradigm as it developed out of the biblical tradition to posit a different understanding of the diasporan experience. This becomes a source for theological discourse with particular reference to the Caribbean diaspora. This understanding of diaspora is significant because it demonstrates the social, historical and theological factors and motifs that shape a diasporan people.

Regarding the issue of identity, the concern of this chapter is not the formation of identity[10] but the self-understandings that Caribbeaners assume in defining themselves as a diasporan people. With this understanding, I examine the subject of identity in light of heritage, history and culture within the context of the Caribbean diasporan experience from which emerge cultural and cosmopolitan identities.

Cultural Identity: An Agent of Culture

The challenge of living with the ambiguities of diasporan existence is what sociologist Robin Cohen demonstrates in his attempt to define a Caribbean diasporan cultural identity. He examines "whether Caribbean peoples abroad constitute a 'new' post-colonial hybrid cultural diaspora?"[11] In pursuit of an answer to the question, I consider three definitive elements of the Caribbean cultural identity. First, I consider culture as the total way of life of Caribbean people. Second, I explore relational dialogism referring to the evolutionary character of culture which deals with continuity and change. Third, I discuss diversity that reflects the plurality of the Caribbean cultural identity.

Culture

Diasporan identity has not been formed as a result of the transportation of various Caribbean identities to new countries. Rather, these identities have been created in the place of residence. Cohen delineates the constitutive elements of the cultural diaspora as the common history of slavery, colonialism, imperialism, racism and the retention and affirmation of an African identity in terms of cosmology, religious and cultural beliefs and practices, the dialectical consciousness of remaining in the host country and returning to the home country, shared cultural expressions and the trans-national relationships which exist through commercial and social endeavors.[12]

This self-understanding indicates that the Caribamericans are not natives of their resident homeland. They came from diverse countries and nationalities each with its particular cultural customs, beliefs, language and religion to live in a country that does not necessarily understand nor respect these differences. The people, however, have not lost the identity and culture they brought with them. Instead, they employed these two factors as the raw material to fashion a communal identity that emerges out of the dialectical relationship between their native cultures and the diasporan experience. What emerges is the Caribbean diasporan cultural identity.[13]

Cohen's perspective departs from diasporan thinkers such as William Safran, whose definition of diaspora[14] has been discussed in an earlier chapter. In Safran's view of diaspora, there is an emphasis on victimhood which is implicit in the notion of forced movement. For Cohen, diaspora is a voluntary movement in search of a better life. In another departure from Safran, Cohen defines diaspora in terms of its relationship with the homeland based on culture.[15] He argues, for example, that diasporan communities have to go beyond just maintaining memories of their homeland. Instead, they have to also create their own identity based on heritage, history and memory.[16]

Cohen continues to define diaspora using the rope as a metaphor. The fibres of the rope such as dispersal from homeland, memory and commitment to its maintenance, return movements, community identity, ambivalent relationship with the host country and desiring a better life represent motifs of diaspora.[17]

While Cohen's perspective is insightful, he defines diasporan identity only in terms of its African ancestry which he regards as a definitive factor. In reality, as we shall discuss in Chapter 3, Caribbean heritage and diaspora are made of diverse peoples and cultures. Writing of this diversity, Mervyn

C. Alleyne notes that there is neither scholarly consensus nor any one interpretation of Caribbean African heritage. He states:

> There are groups for whom it might be argued that they were stripped of their culture, or at least of some of it. There are other groups and societies who have preserved and consciously recognize African culture and ethnicity, although it is obvious that this culture has undergone some measure of change and is not simply an intact survival.[18]

African ancestry is but one element of the Caribbean diasporan identity. On this issue, Stuart Hall is helpful. According to Hall,

> ...by the recognition of a necessary heterogeneity and diversity, by a conception of identity which lives with and through, not despite difference, by hybridity. Diasporan identities are those which are constantly producing and reproducing themselves anew through transformation.[19]

The Caribbean diasporan cultural identity, however, decentralizes African consciousness and rather than determining identity as fixed, it interprets it as evolutionary.

Hall proposes that this can be understood in two ways. The first traditional way of understanding Caribbean diasporan cultural identity is an African-centered view. It is based on a common heritage, shared culture and collective sense of self that creates the spirit or peoplehood, which, according to Hall,

> provides us as a 'people' with stable, unchanging, continuous, frames of reference and meaning, beneath the shifting divisions and vicissitudes of our actual history.[20]

This perspective, Hall further contends, constitutes the foundation and the "essence of 'Caribbeanness'" and plays a central part in the struggle for liberation. It is still a dynamic, creative and mighty force in the shaping of an identity.[21] It is, however, not the rediscovery of identity but the creation of an identity that becomes a resource for resistance to face the oppressive forces of dehumanization[22] and emancipation of the forgotten and devalued self.

Hall's second interpretation of Caribbean diasporan cultural identity is the construction of an identity both of the past and the future. The essence of it is not a determined past or immutable heritage and culture. For Hall, it is an identity that is

> becoming and being... Far from being grounded in the mere recovery of the past, which is waiting to be found, and which when found, will secure our sense of ourselves into eternity, identities are the names we give to the different ways we are positioned by, and position ourselves, within the narratives of the past.[23]

In light of this observation by Hall, the Caribbean diasporan cultural identity is an identity that is in the process of being made. Hall posits the view that identity is incomplete and is constantly in the process of development. This understanding is consistent with the self-identity of Caribbean society itself, which, according to the Caribbean theologian, Kortright Davis, "is still in the making."[24] In his analysis of the development of Caribbean society, Davis observes that the history of the plantation system, the uncertainty of political independence and the undeniable reality of heterogeneity are indications that the society is in the process of development.[25] The Jamaican historian and cultural critic, Rex Nettleford, writing about this character of Caribbean society, concurs with this view. He captures the essence of the ongoing process in the creating of identity when stating that:

> History does not stand still in its tracks. There are still societies to be shaped, freedom to be consolidated, nations still to be built, whole histories to be constructed.[26]

Relational Dialogicalism

Given that heritage and history are essential to identity, they alone do not adequately define the Caribbean diasporan cultural identity. Identity is too complex to limit it in this way since history is determined by a series of transformative processes. In view of these limitations, Hall creatively argues that Caribbean diasporan cultural identity is to be understood in terms of a "dialogical relationship between similarity and continuity and difference and rupture."[27] What this implies is that no one phenomenon determines the character of the cultural diasporan existence; it is a combination of phenomena which are operating simultaneously.

I must mention that a common ancestral heritage and origin does not mean ancestral homogeneity. The African ancestors came from a diversity of tribes, religions and languages.[28] Also, the people who constitute Caribbean societies came at different periods and under different circumstances. The Africans came as an enslaved people between 1518 and 1870[29] while the Asians came as indentured servants between 1838 and 1917.[30] These two factors, time of arrival in the Caribbean and the circumstances of arrival, are essential to the cultural identity. These factors, according to Hall, represent the "discontinuity and rupture" that define a Caribbean identity. Hall further suggests with this comes the issue of "similarity" and "different." He posits the view that in terms of common history and heritage, Caribbean people are one, but in regard to the relationship to the major political, economic and cultural centers of the world, they are different. Hall states:

> ...the boundaries of difference are continually repositioned in relation to different points of reference. *Vis-à-vis* the developed West, we are very much the same. We belong to the marginal, the underdeveloped, the periphery, the "Other."

We are at the outer edge, the "rim," of the metropolitan world – always "South" to someone else's *El Norte*.

At the same time, we do not stand in the same relation of otherness to the metropolitan centers. Each has negotiated its economic, political, and cultural dependence differently. And, this 'difference,' whether we like it or not, is already ascribed in our cultural identities.[31]

Diversity

The foregoing observation alludes to the notion of diversity as an essential element in a cultural identity. Borrowing the categories Aime Cesaire and Leopold Senghor constructed, Stuart Hall observes correctly that the Caribbean diaspora is made up of an African, European and American or New World presence symbolizing memory, power and space respectively.[32] Concurring with Hall, theologian Kortright Davis describes these diverse factors as "social pluralism."[33] As Caribbean people believe deeply, "it takes all sorts to make a world and that all horses cannot run alike."[34]

Camille Hernandez–Ramdwar offers an illuminating perspective. She argues in defence of the existence and for the recognition of the heterogeneity of Caribbean diasporan identity. She quotes a Trinidadian woman of Chinese, Indian and Spanish ancestry.

> I always believe that as people of the Caribbean we are one…so many people think that if you're from the Caribbean you've got to be African, and if you're East Indian looking then you have to come from India, or if you are like me, you've got to come from the Philippines.[35]

The Harvard sociologist, Mary Waters, in her study on the Caribbean diaspora, notes:

> the culture of the Caribbean peoples that evolve from this mix was a transplanted and syncretic one – a creole culture in that no particular parts were indigenous and the parts of Africa, Europe and Asia that survived were combined and passed on from generation to generation.[36]

So far in this chapter, I argue for the existence of a Caribbean diasporan cultural identity. I premise this identity on Caribbean culture which recognizes and embraces not only the total life of the people but the total population of the Caribbean diaspora. I observe further that this identity is defined not only by Caribbean culture but by a dialectical relationship between the history and existential experience of the diasporan people as well as the racial diversity of Caribbean societies. What is problematic, however, is that a Caribbean diasporan cultural identity presumes a homogeneous identity.

While racial diversity is a constitutive factor of this identity, it does not take into account the diversity of the cultures that constitute Caribbean societies. Unless, however, it is presumed that racial diversity is both incorporated in and inseparable from the culture. Still, it is my contention that each racial group has its own particular culture, but it is not the Caribbean cultural identity. For example, Aisha Khan examines this issue in her study on the Indian culture in Trinidad. While creolization is the focus of her study, she demonstrates how this particular group of people participates in the general society as integral members, yet maintaining their distinctive culture.[37] Race, therefore, is only one factor of the Caribbean diasporan cultural identity. Thus, Caribbean culture could be regarded as monolithic but Caribbean diasporan identity is diverse. This then leads us to consider another form of Caribbean diasporan identity.

The Cosmopolitan Identity: An Intellectual Tool

The cosmopolitan identity is the second form of a Caribbean diasporan self-understanding as represented by the works of Paul Gilroy. The cosmopolitan identity is an intellectual tool for public discourse. The term cosmopolitan describes Black people's common global experience which Paul Gilroy refers to as the Black Atlantic.[38] Both terms, cosmopolitan and Black Atlantic, will be used interchangeably throughout this discussion. The most significant text that delineates this identity is Gilroy's *The Black Atlantic: Modernity and Double Consciousness.*

Whereas culture is the basis for the Caribbean diasporan cultural identity, the Black Atlantic experience is the basis of the cosmopolitan identity while de-centering its African heritage. At the same time, it attempts to be representative of the Black diaspora. Gilroy roots his notion of the Black Atlantic in a European heritage. He writes:

> My concern here is less with explaining their longevity and enduring appeal than in exploring some of the special political problems that arise from the fatal conjunction of the concept of nationality with the concept of culture and the affinities and affiliations which link the blacks of the west with one of their adoptive parental cultures: the intellectual heritage of the west since the Enlightenment.[39]

Advancing his anti-essentialist perspective, Gilroy contends that:

> In opposition to both of these nationalist or ethnically absolute approaches, I want to develop the suggestion that cultural historians could take the Atlantic as one single, complex unit of analysis in their discussions of the modern world and use it to produce an explicitly transnational and intercultural perspective.[40]

Gilroy is arguing against the notion of a unitary or monolithic Black identity. Yet, he is proposing a single paradigm as an analytical tool for interpreting the Black experience. Since there is a diversity of Black identities, so the

Black Atlantic experience may not fully represent all possible Black experience within the diaspora. Nevertheless, Gilroy insists:

> This perspective currently confronts a pluralistic position which affirms blackness as an open signifier and seeks to celebrate complex representations of black particularity that is internally divided by class, sexuality, gender, age and political consciousness. There is no unitary idea of black community here and the authoritarian tendencies of those who would 'police' black cultural expressions in the name of their own particular history or priorities are rightly repudiated.[41]

Thus, Gilroy grounds a Caribbean diasporan identity in the Black Atlantic experience while maintaining a critical distance from an essentialist articulation of Black identity. This has the potential to be an authentic model of Black identity but not without examining its nature. In this regard, attention is given to three definitive hallmarks of the Caribbean diasporan cosmopolitan identity, namely, the transformational, transatlantic and counter-cultural which are considered in turn.

Transformational

As I indicated above, the Caribbean diasporan cosmopolitan identity is the amalgamation of nationalities and cultures which emerges from the process of making sense of life.[42] James Clifford, professor of history at the University of California at Santa Cruz, affirms this claim. He asserts:

> Diaspora communities, constituted by displacement, are sustained by hybrid conjectures. With degrees of urgency, they negotiate and resist the social realities of poverty, violence, policing, racism, and political and economic inequality.[43]

Additionally, the emergence of transnationalism and global changes have redefined and transformed the meaning of national, ethnic and racial identities.[44] Gilroy argues that the Black diaspora in Britain, for example, defines itself by certain local and transnational affinities that serve as a form of defensive mechanism against racial discrimination and political oppression (police brutality) and as a critique of capitalism.[45] This, for Gilroy, is a transatlantic or cosmopolitan movement that is not only interwoven but transcends the notions of race and nationality that he is calling the Black Atlantic experience. It leads to the reemergence of pan-Africanism but not in the traditional form as represented by the Black American church tradition, Garveyism and W. E. B. Dubois. This is a pan-Africanism that focuses on the African continent represented by the rise of national leaders such as Kwame Nkrumh of Ghana, the independence of African countries such as Kenya and prominent advocates such as Padmore and others.[46]

Recognizing this transformative element in Black diasporan life, Gilroy rigorously attempts to revisit this central movement as a paradigmatic phenomenon not by reinforcement but by redefinition. He shifts the focus of the relationship from one between African Americans and Africans to include the Black diaspora of Britain and the Caribbean. Gilroy declares:

> I want to suggest that much of the precious intellectual legacy claimed by African American intellectuals as the substance of their particularity is in fact only partly their absolute ethnic property...the idea of the black Atlantic can be used to show that there are other claims to it which can be based on the structure of the African diaspora in the western hemisphere.[47]

Gilroy realizes the centrality of the Black Atlantic experience in defining a Black diasporan identity. This acknowledgement of diversity and its significance for a Caribbean diasporan identity, however, is problematic. He regrettably does not take into account the differences in the contexts that shape the respective identities. For example, the American, Caribbean and British contexts are all different. The Caribbean diaspora in America came out of a society where they were in the majority. As Winston James notes:

> The black immigrants from the Caribbean entered the United States with what we may describe as a majority consciousness; that is they were accustomed for the most part, to negotiate a world in which they constituted the overwhelming majority of the population.[48]

The issue goes beyond majority consciousness. The Caribbean diaspora in the American context came into a heterogeneous society, while those in the British context came into a homogeneous society.[49] In a study on Caribbean racial consciousness and identity, Constance R. Sutton and Susan R. Makiesky-Barrow attest to this claim. They observe that Caribbeaners in the British context went to Britain without any distinct sense of Black identity, whereas in the American context, Caribbeaners went there with a clear and developed sense of Black identity.[50] Sutton and Makiesky-Barrow conclude:

> Barbadians moving into the relatively homogeneous White society of Britain have rather different experiences than their compatriots going to the racially-divided United States. This experience is essential to define identity.[51]

Sutton and Makiesky-Barrow continue to say:

> West Indians immigrating to New York travel a rather different route to racial consciousness than taken in England. They bring with them a notion not of their likeness to Americans, Black or White, but of their distinctness – as Barbadians, Jamaicans, Grenadians, etc... They arrive with some foreknowledge of White attitudes of racial superiority and with experiences with problems with inequality.[52]

These contextual factors, of a Black majority consciousness, heterogeneity and homogeneity, reveal a major limitation in Gilroy's Black Atlantic identity. Yet, his analysis recognizes the value and significance of the transformational dimension of identity.

Transatlantic

In a definitive manner, Gilroy states unapologetically in the Duboisan tradition, "striving to be both European and Black requires some specific form of double consciousness."[53] For Gilroy, it is to use the Atlantic experience as a unitary paradigm to analyze society with the intention of creating a cosmopolitan Black identity.[54] Decentering Africa, Gilroy in his *Black Atlantic* constructs the cosmopolitan's perspective within the framework of three traditions: the intellectual as represented by W. E. B. Du Bois, Fredrick Douglass and Richard Wright, the cultural as symbolized through Black music, and the historical-experiential embodied through memory.[55] Rather than being simplistic and reductionistic, Gilroy persists in arguing that identity is formed through traveling, and struggles to create a transnational tradition that shapes and defines a Black diasporan identity. According to Gilroy:

> The history of the black Atlantic since then, continually crisscrossed by the movement of black people – not as commodities but engaged in various struggles towards emancipation, autonomy, and citizenship – provides a means to re-examine the problems of nationality, location, identity, and historical memory.[56]

Gilroy's concern, however, is not just the formation of identity but the desire of Blacks to transcend their ethnicity and nationality. He notes:

> Du Bois's travel experiences raise in the sharpest possible form a question common to the lives of almost all these figures who begin as African-Americans or Caribbean people and are then changed into something else which evades these specific labels and with them all fixed notions of nationality and identity.[57]

Wanting to transcend the particularities of one's identity raises questions about having an identity crisis and ignoring also contextual realities of diasporan existence such as marginalization, alienation, exile, relocation and displacement. Central to a Black Atlantic identity, like the cultural identity which has been discussed previously, are ruptures and recurring discontinuities that constitute the pattern of Black existence as symbolized by slavery and the slave ship. Without discounting the indescribable horror of slavery, Gilroy astutely points out that it is through the slave trade that Western societies achieved economic and cultural hegemony. Gilroy contends:

> In particular, [the desire to put Euro-American modernity against slaves] is formed by the need to inflict those forms of rationality which have been rendered implausible by the racially exclusive character and further to explore the history of their complicity with terror systematically and rationally practiced as a form of political and economic administration.[58]

In further clarification of this transnational identity, Gilroy uses the ship[59] as a symbol to show the nature and dimension of this identity so as to describe the movement and evoke the memory of the slave experience as elements of this identity and essential to understanding the experience of a Black Atlantic identity. He writes:

> I have settled on the image of ships in motion across the spaces between Europe, America, Africa and the Caribbean as a central organizing symbol for this enterprise and as my starting point. The image of the ship – a living, micro-cultural, micro-political system in motion – is especially important for historical and theoretical reasons... Ships immediately focus attention on the middle passage, on the various projects for the redemptive return to an African homeland, on the cultural ideas and activists as well as the movement of key cultural and political artifacts: tracts, books, gramophone records and choirs.[60]

In seeking to demonstrate that identity is far from static, Gilroy, therefore, asserts that diaspora involves history, movement and dynamism. He admits that although using this symbol conjures negative memories of a painful and inhumane past, Gilroy insists that the ship is a significant symbol of unity among Black people,[61] communication with the wider world and relationship with the past.[62] As such, Gilroy urges:

> For these reasons, the ship is the first of the novel chronotopes presupposed by my attempts to rethink modernity via the history of the black Atlantic and the African diaspora into the western hemisphere.[63]

Michelle Stephens joins Gilroy in arguing that the ship is a metaphor for Black organization and reflection of the quest for Black identity.[64] Obviously, Stephens does not help to redeem Black identity of this negative portrayal but rather perpetuate it. Stephens demonstrates this perspective in stating that:

> The Negro ship of state at sea without a rudder images the black peoples of the African diaspora in America in a state of political limbo, as a floating colony perpetually drifting somewhere between slavery and freedom, yet bound together, sharing a common transatlantic history and destiny.[65]

The case can be made that while the ship is a negative symbol in Black intellectual discourse, these scholars are not using it as such. I maintain, nevertheless, that the metaphor represents the evils of slavery, in that the ship was the means of transportation of the Africans into slavery and comes to represent oppression and not emancipation. Consequently, no positive employment of the metaphor can undo the inhumane event, erase the painful memory nor minimize the brutal legacy of slavery.

A Counter-cultural Critical Theory

The cosmopolitan diasporan identity is not without its limitations. Although a proponent of this perspective of identity, James Clifford, in a very penetrating and thorough analysis of Gilroy's Black Atlantic, observes that the Black Atlantic identity cannot become the ideal model for any Black identity given the complexities of nationalities, cultures and ethnicities. A Black Atlantic identity, moreover, is diverse and not homogenous.[66] This difference is already noted and further mention is made later in this chapter. It is worth noting, however, that while Caribbeaners and African Americans share a common racial identity, they have a distinct ethnic identity.[67] In other words, Caribbeaners regard themselves as Blacks but give precedence to their particular national or ethnic identity. The immigration experience and institutional socialization are significant factors in this difference. As political scientist Reuel Rogers writes:

> First, by virtue of their immigration status, Afro-Caribbeans define themselves from a different frame of reference than their native-born counterparts. Second, African Americans' sense of racial identity derives from their socialization within a set of institutions to which Afro-Caribbeans may have little or no connection.[68]

The Black Atlantic is not an adequate model of Black identity.[69] While the paradigm addresses the issue of the Black diasporan identity, Gilroy understands it as a critical theory of society. The goal, according to Gilroy,

> is to conjure up and exact the new modes of friendship, happiness and solidarity that are consequent on the overcoming of racial oppression on which modernity and its antinomy of rational, Western progress as excessive barbarity relied.[70]

This raises questions about Gilroy's claim that the Black Atlantic is not a counter discourse but a counter-culture. He urges that it is a counter-culture that intentionally and, in protest, creates its own moral and intellectual history[71] and also as an

> expressive counter-culture not simply as a succession of tropes and genres but as a philosophical discourse which refuses the modern occidental separation of ethics and aesthetics, culture and politics.[72]

This study avers, however, that the Black Atlantic is an alternative to the dominant cultural self-understanding as well as one of the responses to the meaning and formation of a Caribbean diasporan identity. Whether it is a critical theory of society or a counterculture, the Black Atlantic represents a significant break from the normative Euro-American binary construction of reality. It is a defiance of the dichotomic mode of life that characterizes diasporan existence. The Black Atlantic postulates even further that an integrated holistic belief is an essential feature of Caribbean diasporan identity. Gilroy writes:

> The memory of slavery actively preserved as a living livening intellectual resource in their expressive political culture, helped to generate a new set of answers to this enquiry. They had to fight – often through their spirituality – to hold onto the unity of ethics and politics sundered from each other by modernity's insistence

that the true, the good, and the beautiful had distinct origins and belong to different domains of knowledge.[73]

In contrast to the cultural identity theory, the cosmopolitan identity is a tool for critical engagement with contemporary society. As a method for public discourse, however, it has not provided any social analysis of society that is needed to resist and overcome oppression nor provide any vision of what the society ought to be. The Guyanese historian and public intellectual, Walter Rodney, attests to this assertion. For Rodney, Black intellectual engagement with the society includes an attack on white supremacy, an exposure of social myths and solidarity with the oppressed.[74] As a further departure from the cultural identity, the cosmopolitan identity does not engender community formation for which and through which it is mediated.

In concluding this chapter, therefore, I wish to reiterate that the discussion delineates two forms of Caribbean diasporan identities. It should also be noted that cultural factors constitute Caribbean diasporan identities. These identities include the Caribbean diasporan cultural identity which functions as an agent of culture. In this regard, diaspora preserves and mediates culture with the understanding that culture represents the totality of a people's way of life.

The other identity is the Caribbean diasporan cosmopolitan identity. This form of identity understands diaspora as an intellectual tool that analyses and interprets the Caribbean diasporan experience. What has not yet been identified, however, is an identity that could be regarded as representing a distinct and inclusive Caribbean diasporan community. Making this case is what constitutes the content of my next chapter.

3 Forging an Identity for the Caribbean Diaspora: Knowing Ourselves

The previous chapter identifies two forms of Caribbean diasporan self-understandings, namely, the cultural and cosmopolitan. These identities are not mutually exclusive but inter-related through a common cultural heritage and are the product of a common diasporan experience, but we must also acknowledge their differences. The cultural and cosmopolitan identities decentralize Black ethnicity but nevertheless they center identity on the Black Atlantic experience and function both as a source and tool for contemporary Black intellectual discourse. Also, neither the cultural nor the cosmopolitan identity fosters the formation of or embodies any particular Caribbean diasporan community.

Leaving aside the limitations of these two different but mutually related identities, I wish to identify another form of identity that has emerged out of the diasporan experience to constitute a distinct Caribbean community that I am calling Caribamerican. I must, however, underscore that the Caribamerican identity premises self-understanding on ethnicity, concretizes in the formation of a community and departs from and is independent of African American identity. The argument, then, can be made that in the absence of any concrete manifestation of the Caribbean diasporan identity, the Caribamerican identity, while inclusive of the cultural and cosmopolitan identities but accentuating Caribbean ethnicity,[1] has become the collective representative identity of the Caribbean diaspora.

Inherent in the term diaspora, as previously discussed, are notions and practices such as movement, migration, exile, alienation, marginalization, dislocation but also settling down, forming communities and putting down roots and so forth. These experiences must be historicized. Furthermore, the term diaspora as mentioned earlier in Chapter 1 encompasses these realities and together they form a link and source for contextual intellectual engagement. This need for the historicization of experience and contextual analysis initiates the emergence of a pan Caribbean or, as will be termed from now on, a Caribamerican diasporan community that the Caribbean diasporan church represents.

Many studies demonstrate that the Black church, of which the Caribbean diasporan church is a specie, is an expression and forum of Black identity.[2] But with the exception of Nicole Toulis' work concerning the Caribbean diaspora in Britain, with particular reference to the Black British Pentecostal church tradition, to date, no available study addresses the historicization of Caribbean diasporan identities.

Toulis examines the formation of identity through the church. With the church as an agent of identity formation, she maintains that the relationship between faith and ethnicity is complex and conflicting. The Black church, Toulis argues, is a "powerful forum for the construction of new identities which are used to negotiate the dominant, and often injurious, representations made about African-Caribbean people..."[3]

Although Toulis advances the perspective that the Caribbean diasporan church is a forum for identity formation, her argument is too insular. She constructs identity around the dichotomy between the secular and the spiritual. Toulis spiritualizes and dichotomizes identity whereas Caribbean diasporan Christianity attempts to historicize and cultivate a holistic identity. By promoting a dichotomized theology, Toulis mis-represents Caribbean diasporan Christianity as reflected in her assertion: "Rather than define themselves as Blacks in White society, church members identify themselves as model Christians in an imperfect Christian society."[4]

Indeed, Toulis' observation reflects the theological view of one particular Caribbean diasporan church tradition, but her perspective does not represent fully the Caribbean diaspora. In this regard, there must be a distinct Caribbean diasporan identity that gives clarity of purpose and a sense of self in the process of seeking to live a meaningful life. What follows now is an exploration of this Caribbean self-understanding. The focus is on the sources of the identity, three definitive factors of Caribbean diaspora's relationship with African Americans, the encounter with racism and the moral and historical cords of the common good and common history and heritage of the Caribamerican identity. But first, we must define the term Caribamerican.

Defining the Term Caribamerican Identity

Caribamerican is the term I use to designate, identify and define the people of the Caribbean diaspora in the United States of America. West Indians and Caribbean Americans are the names that have been used historically and currently. Regarding the former, it is the pre-independent self-designation when the identity of the people was defined in relationship to the British colonial government. The latter is a post independent self-designation that is used in relationship to both the homeland and resident country. A direct result of this self-designation is that it reflects a dual identity and does not describe a distinct community.

The name Caribamerican incorporates the elements of the above mentioned two terms but signifies and describes a distinct community. As such, the term acknowledges Caribbean people as a constitutive element of American society. Formerly, the Caribbean people living away from their native country were not regarded as a diaspora. Now that this community has grown to become a critical mass of people and other factors which will be discussed in Chapters 4 and 5, they are regarded as a diaspora that the term Caribamerican signifies. Of particular importance is the fact that the Caribbean diaspora is not a Caribbean community in America but an American community of Caribbean people.

The term Caribamerican, additionally, encapsulates the nature of Caribbean society and history and refers to all people of Caribbean heritage inclusive of those born to parents in the diasporan homeland and, at the same time, fully conscious that the Caribbean varies in culture, geography and population and is diverse in race. This issue I have already discussed in regard to the Caribbean diasporan cultural identity in Chapter 2. The term Caribamerican, therefore, describes and designates the people from the countries known as the Commonwealth Caribbean or the former British colonies who have a common history and experience of slavery, British colonialism and American imperialism.[5]

Caribbean ethnicity,[6] which I stated earlier, is the basis of the Caribamerican identity. As in the case of the Caribbean diasporan cultural identity, the Caribamerican identity represents continuity with its historical heritage creation of community and preservation of identity and also as a symbol of Caribbean unity and emancipation in the struggle against injustice to symbolize the meaning of life, values and identity forged out of the diasporan experience. Consequently, in the diaspora, I argue, Caribamerican is an all-inclusive term used to identify and describe the collective identity of Caribbean diasporan peoplehood.

The Sources of Caribamerican Identity

A nascent form of Caribamericanism exists in the formation of relationships through community involvement, employment and marriage. Sutton and Makiesky-Barrow's research supports this argument. They write:

> Employment, housing, and school provide settings for this contact, and though island rivalries and jealousies may be aired, there is also recognition of similarities of background and shared experiences as non-White immigrants, the salience of a particular identity situationally defined.[7]

This interaction provides the context for the formation of the Caribamerican identity. These two social scientists, in a comparative study on the Caribbean diaspora in Britain and America, have this to say:

> Just as England provides a unique context for merging West Indian concerns with broader notions of Black Commonwealth and Third-World issues, New York nourishes a Caribbean consciousness that has not been actively promoted in the Caribbean. This Caribbean consciousness is both a form of separation and a basis for relating to Black Americans with whom West Indians interact and are defined by the wider society.[8]

This acknowledgment of the existence of pan-Caribbean consciousness plays a pivotal role in the formation of Caribamerican identity but neither the cultural nor cosmopolitan identity shows the important matter of the sources of Caribbean diasporan identity. This is relevant because it underscores the centrality of the diaspora's experience in the formation of its identity and the relationship between homeland and resident home. The Caribamerican identity, therefore, is the product of the Caribbean diasporan experience that is shaped by two sources of origin, namely, (1) the pre-existing and (2) the organic. These features are the focus of analysis.

The Pre-existing Source

The pre-existing source of the Caribamerican identity represents the perspective that Caribbean people brought their identity with them to the host country and that it is different from other diasporan identities, as well as from that of the Black identity represented in the resident country. Representing this perspective is the Harvard sociologist, Mary Waters. She argues that, "black immigrants from the Caribbean come to the United States with a particular identity/culture-worldview that reflects their own unique history and culture."[9] In demonstrating the distinctiveness of this Caribbean diasporan identity, Waters is careful to observe its history and experience. She writes:

> This culture and identity are different from the immigrant identity and culture of previous waves of European immigrants because of their unique history of origin and because of the changed contexts of reception the immigrants face in the United States. This culture and identity are also different from the culture of African Americans.[10]

This school of thought helpfully suggests that Caribbean people did not arrive in the host country searching for self-understanding but that they came with their own. This, according to Mary Waters, consisted of a moral value of hard work-ethic, education, monetary investment for the future and pre-conceived notions of the nature of racial relationships in the host country.[11] This value system, however, reflects that economic success is the ultimate reason for the existence of the Caribbean diaspora.

While economic success is part of the purpose of the disporan journey, which social scientist Ransford Palmer describes in his seminal work, *In Search of a Better Life*,[12] this is often not the sole or even the central purpose. Migration takes place as a result of a larger global phenomenon, especially in regard to the need for labor. On one hand, the host country needs the labor and on the other hand, the home country needs employment opportunities for its workers. The migration, therefore, is not a one-sided but a mutual phenomenon. Palmer observes:

> The gravitational pull of a large developed industrial country in close proximity to small developing economies dictates that there will be a flow of workers from the lower-income developing countries to the higher-income developed country.[13]

Palmer recognizes that economic factors were a prime motive for Caribbean migration but suggests further reasons. He claims:

> Caribbean governments have routinely encouraged migration from the bottom to relieve the high unemployment rates among their unskilled labor forces and to ensure remittances in the years ahead.[14]

Moreover, there is a migration tradition established between the Caribbean and both Britain and the United States. This phenomenon is a reflection of a pattern grounded in a long history of established social, economic and political relationships. In support of this claim, Bonham C. Richardson writes:

> Much of the human movement into and through the Caribbean can be directly attributed to the plantation, the metropolitan-focused institution that has dominated the region for centuries.[15]

The Organic Source

The other source of origin of the Caribamerican diasporan identity is the organic. In contrast to the pre-formed source of identity, which is the identity the people brought with them into the diaspora, the organic source of identity is formed out of, or is the product of, the diasporan experience. The organic source of identity is a similar process in the formation of both the cultural and cosmopolitan identities but it differs in terms of the kind of identity that is formed. For example, the cultural identity excludes ethnicity and the cosmopolitan identity transcends ethnicity but the Caribamerican involves and embraces ethnicity.[16]

A major exponent of this perspective is the Caribbean sociologist, Milton Vickerman of the University of Virginia. His work, *Crosscurrents*, provides a useful examination of the emergence of the Caribbean diasporan identity. In his study, he takes a social constructivist perspective in defining ethnicity and delineating its meaning in the Caribbean. He uses Jamaica as the representative model as it is the largest of the Caribbean diasporan communities with which other Caribbean nations identify.[17]

The Caribamerican identity is organically formed. The identity is formed out of a combination of factors including but not limited to the common experience of living in a diaspora involving the systemic constraints of racial discrimination and anti-immigrant hostilities and the persistent practice of alienation and displacement. In addition, there are interactions with other people and involvements in social and civic events such as West Indian Day Parade and Carnival.[18] All these factors erode any differences in order to form a new common identity.[19] Vickerman states it as follows:

> Through a combination of social interaction – such as Labor Day Carnival – and deliberate political mobilization [they] have striven to create a distinct sense of themselves as West Indians.[20]

What this indicates is that the Caribamerican identity is the product of a combination of factors, including history, culture, experience, race and nationality within a particular context. According to Vickerman:

> It takes settlement in metropolitan centers such as London and New York City to form this sense of ethnicity. In these and other cities abroad, Anglophone West Indians confront the difficulties of adjusting to new societies, as manifested in such factors as dealing with regular people of other nationalities, obtaining employment and finding places to live.[21]

The social construction of Caribbean diasporan identity inevitably begins on arrival in the host country. Defining themselves as Black, for example, was not an issue for Caribamericans until the beginning of their diasporan journey. They came from a society where race has a different meaning from that in the United States, for example. Vickerman argues:

> Given this reality, the fact that…West Indians would claim to have discovered their 'Blackness' only after migrating to America appears puzzling, but only until it is realized that they were referring to the social meanings attributed to skin color, rather than to skin color itself.[22]

In the Caribbean, according to Vickerman, race is defined by class rather than by pigmentation and this engenders the ideology of non-racialism[23] and leads to the norm of Black majority rule.[24]

Both sources of origin, the pre-formed and the organic, affirm a Caribamerican consciousness and identity as political scientist, Reuel Rogers, avers in a provocative essay, "Black Like Who?" He argues that the people of the Caribbean diaspora identify themselves according to their national origin and see no contradiction between ethnicity and race. There is, however, according to Rogers, an "exit option" which neither of the other two forms – cultural and cosmopolitan – of Caribbean diasporan identity includes. The "exit option" advocates the belief that if and when life in the diaspora does not work out as planned, one can return to the homeland.[25]

Implicit in this option is a sense of uncertainty, unsettledness and alienation in the resident homeland. This approach, while providing a viable option, fosters a dual identity. However, in keeping with the cultural and cosmopolitan identities, the exit option of the Caribamerican diasporan identity does not engender the sense of belonging endemic to the Caribbean diasporan existence which is essential to the sustenance of the emerging community. This leaves open, therefore, further analysis of the Caribamerican identity. The analysis considers the features of this identity.

The Features

There are two dominant characteristics of the Caribamerican diasporan identity: the relationship between Caribamericans and African Americans, which is otherwise identified as diasporan kinship,[26] and the experience of racism. These are considered in turn.

Diasporan Kinship

African Americans and Caribbean people are kins. The Jamaican anthropologist, Barry Chevannes, advances this idea in his discovery of what it means to be a Black human being. The importance of this relationship warrants that I give the full account of Chavannes discovery. He writes:

> ...when I left Jamaica in 1959 to become a student in a Jesuit seminary deep in the Berkshire Mountains of New England, [I was] the only black person among 200 seminarians and faculty,[who was] treated, even in retrospect, without even a hint of prejudice. Then one Sunday afternoon, the Boston Glee Club put on a concert for the seminary community, and there, as the curtain opened[,] was a black face, the only one among the 60 choristers. My heart leapt and I was disturbed. What difference should a black face make? Why should I find in his presence there such special and evidently personal significance as to create within me this new and troubling emotion? I had never before known such feeling of affinity, and it seemed to me as unnatural as it was spontaneous.
>
> In the reception afterwards I resisted the pull for as long as I could, but it turned out that I too was not unnoticed by him, and so we met, the beginning of a lifelong and fruitful friendship, which was to usher me into the world of being black, into civil rights, Martin Luther King, and the black Boston ghetto of Roxbury.[27]

Indeed, kinship, solidarity or a sense of affinity exists between African Americans and Caribbean people but there is no common understanding of this relationship. Milton Vickerman posits the view that Caribbean people do not identify themselves as African Americans primarily because of the derogatory notion of blackness. He writes:

> Basically, West Indian's relationship with African Americans revolves around the process of distancing and identification, sometimes leading to a synthesis of the two… They want to be viewed by the society as 'West Indians,' an identity which encompasses pride in African ancestry and a focus on achievement.[28]

There is a reverse side to this self-understanding and attitude that Vickerman observes. He notes: "On a negative note, this attempt at identity construction sometimes involves the holding of negative stereotypes of African Americans."[29] Consequently, the people of the Caribbean diaspora employ three strategies for relating to the African American consisting of social distancing, racial solidarity and moral exemplar.[30] These are indications of the complex relationship between these two groups of people. Caribamericans, for example, premise their difference from some African Americans on "work, achievement and culture."[31] Caribamericans, Vickerman argues, "perceive themselves as sober, hard working individuals who possess definite goals and are willing to sacrifice to achieve these."[32]

Social distancing strategy has a degree of inconsistency. The dominant culture does not make any distinction between African Americans and Caribamericans. Both are Black people and the society treats them alike. Trying to forge a distinct Caribbean identity is a very difficult task. Caribamericans, however, apply a number of strategies to forge a separate identity which includes but is not limited to taking an anti-black stance or working in cooperation with African Americans to support a common cause.[33]

Regarding the role-model option, Caribamericans advocate the idea that their norms and values can serve as a pattern for African Americans in dealing with problems and crises. This option is problematic since it raises questions of paternalism and superiority towards African Americans. As Vickerman correctly observes:

> To some African Americans, role modeling appears to be yet another instance of foreigners offering unsolicited advice on how native-born blacks should live their lives.[34]

This observation is significant but it is one-sided. It describes the attitude of Caribbean people towards African Americans. What of the converse? It would have been helpful if Vickerman had pointed out how African Americans relate to Caribamericans. The issue, however, is noted later in this chapter. Regardless of this acknowledgment, Vickerman's observation still implies the lack of mutuality in this relationship between African

Americans and Caribamericans. Indeed, from this perspective, the issue should not center around how Caribamericans relate to African Americans and vice-versa but rather the inter-relationship between both groups of people.

Inasmuch as Vickerman describes the nature of the relationship between Caribamericans and African Americans, he has not provided any solutions or resources to nurture such relationships. What resources can these siblings use to foster and nurture a meaningful relationship with each other? Caribbean theologian Noel Erskine makes a significant contribution to this debate. Erskine acknowledges the ecclesiastical and theological foundations of this relationship. He premised the relationship on the African American Baptist preacher, George Liele, the African American who brought Black Christianity to Jamaica[35] and consequently to the Caribbean. Erskine points out this important event by making the claim that:

> The black American connection with black Jamaica was made in 1783 when some four hundred white families, together with their black slaves numbering about five thousand, left the United States for Jamaica because they were not in sympathy with the new republican form of government, preferring to live under the British rule. Among the black people thus removed to Jamaica were George Liele and Moses Baker, both of whom were to become renowned in black religious affairs.[36]

Liele, among others, established the first Baptist church in Jamaica and carried out ministry among the Black population. Erskine is careful to mention that Liele not only established a church but also developed a church covenant that formed the context and framework for teaching and preaching which unite Caribamericans and African Americans. Attesting to this assertion, Esrkine asserts:

> This indicates that the black church in Jamaica is connected historically with the church in North America not only through Liele, Gibbs and Baker, but also through the church covenant.[37]

With particular reference to the estranged relationship between these two siblings, the solution Erskine presents leads to the foundational principles of the relationship. He emphasizes, however, an anthropocentric rather than a Christocentric basis for the relationship between Caribamericans and African Americans.

Caribbean theologian, Kortright Davis, also provides a framework to understanding the relationship between Caribamericans and African Americans. Davis' concern is to address the tensions in this relationship. He provides a framework for facilitating and nurturing the relationship. Davis states:

The Black Story is thus a most powerful framework through which Caribbeans and Americans, especially those of African descent, can move forward in an intercultural theological process in the struggle for Christian solidarity and the search for more concrete expressions of freedom.[38]

Davis recognizes two factors that are essential to an authentic relationship. He points to mutuality and the common heritage of both groups. Therefore,

[w]e can contribute to each other's freedom by the collective engagement in the discovery of our rich heritage. Most of the tensions that have historically tended to exist between Afro-Caribbeans and African-Americans have resulted from a lack of knowledge about each – from our reluctance to understand each other's historical and cultural struggles and from our insensitivity in communicating with each other.[39]

Davis, like Erskine, is seeking to foster relationships between Caribamericans and African Americans although he employs a different method. While Erskine offers a basis for the relationship, Davis provides the tools to cultivate it. Erskine, on one hand, acknowledges the existence of a relationship and demonstrates the framework that facilitates it. Davis, on the other hand, seeks to facilitate the rebuilding of a relationship which indicates a quest for reconciliation. Davis proceeds to root the relationship in the Black Story and offers the African Soul,[40] religious experience,[41] story telling, history, role models and culture as the connecting elements[42] or "emancipatory connections."[43]

While the relationship between Caribamericans and African Americans is tenuous, the common destiny is, in fact, interwoven. The meaning of the Black experience indicates, even warrants, that more value be given to the forging of an inter-relationship or a pan-Black identity of which the Caribamerican identity is a dimension. Kortright Davis affirms this claim:

The common experience of oppression and slavery, the common struggle for full humanity and economic reliance and the common fight against racism and other forms of social and systemic injustice are all too compelling to engender tensions of mistrust and hostility between Afro-Caribbeans and African Americans.[44]

It is essential that this relationship be forged especially since American society does not make any distinction between Blacks as the Caribamerican identity purports. The African American philosopher and public intellectual, Cornel West, gives the following account of his experience while a professor at Princeton University, in New Jersey.

I left my car – a rather elegant one – in a safe parking lot and stood on the corner of 60th Street and Park Avenue to catch a taxi…I waited and waited and waited. After the ninth taxi refused me, my blood began to boil. The tenth taxi refused me and stopped for a kind, well-dressed, smiling fellow female citizen of European descent. As she stepped in the cab, she said, "this is really ridiculous, is it not?"

Ugly racial memories of the past flashed through my mind. Years ago, while driving from New York to teach at Williams College, I was stopped on fake charges of trafficking cocaine. When I told the police officer I was a professor of religion, he replied, "Yeh, and I'm a flying Nun. Let's go, nigger!" I was stopped three times in my first ten days in Princeton for driving too slowly on a residential street with a speed limit of twenty-five miles per hour.[45]

These incidents reflect the reality of race in American society. For the Black race, ethnicity makes no difference to the experience of racism when it comes to the issue of Black identity. In this regard, the Caribamerican identity, however, makes no difference to white Americans. Though this identity seeks to disregard blackness and adopts the same problematic attitude of non-blacks towards African Americans, Caribamericans are still targets for discrimination. Writing of this discriminatory practice, Mary Waters observes that other people groups such as the Irish, Polish, Italians, Chinese and Hispanics aspire to become white.[46] She reports the society's perception and attitude towards Asian and European immigrants and implicitly towards the Caribbean diaspora as well.

> In the nineteenth century Irish immigrants were regarded as "niggers turned inside out" and Negroes were referred to as "smoked Irish." Yet over time, the category absorbed these European groups by identifying them as "not Blacks". By consciously and assiduously distancing themselves from black Americans these groups became white.[47]

Despite attempts to distance themselves from blackness, racism is nonetheless a reality of the Caribbean diasporan experience. How they deal with it is a matter of great significance which we will now consider.

Encountering Racism

The experience of racism is another dimension of the Caribamerican diasporan identity. Racism as it is experienced in America, Vickerman argues, is a new experience for the Caribbean diasporan community. After discussing the ubiquity of racism in the resident society and its adverse effects on Caribbean diasporan peoples, he observes the creative means used in response to it and the emergence of a Caribamerican ethnic awareness. As noted earlier, Caribbean people have been indoctrinated to de-emphasize the seriousness of racism. In explaining the awareness of the reality of racism, Vickerman states:

> Because West Indians' prior notions of, and experience with, racial discrimination differ substantially from those prevailing in this country, they experience persistent difficulty dealing with this explicit racism.[48]

While Vickerman correctly argues for a difference between homeland and resident home racism, he de-emphasizes the nature of it in the homeland. This in no way minimizes the harsh reality of its existence in the resident home. Recognizing this reality, Winston James and Clive Harris write:

> As to be expected, the harsh realities and perennial winter of British racism, in a number of respects, helped to create an identity – which perhaps under different circumstances would not have developed – among Afro-Caribbeans living in Britain which is more commensurate with their concrete situation and historical experience.[49]

They further add:

> The whole experience of living in a white racist society has helped to forge a Black identity where in many cases such an identity did not exist previously or was not consciously thought about.[50]

Racism, however, is not a new reality for Caribbean people. As will be discussed in this chapter, Caribbean societies have their own form of racism.[51]

It is an understatement to suggest that racism forms the fabric of Caribbean society. Through colonialism, and its offspring, slavery, racism was not only instituted but perpetrated. The Caribbean society was based on race where those who were not white were regarded as inferior, in particular those who were far removed from any resemblance of having a white pigmentation.[52] The accepted ideology and norm were that the Black person was the absolute lowest member of the human family. Based on the degree of one's pigmentation, a system described as "pigmentocracy,"[53] otherwise known as "colorism"[54] as well as "skinocracy"[55] was developed.

"Skinocracy" is the ideology that those who have the closest resemblance to being white, which means physical European features such as having a straight nose, long hair and clear skin, are regarded as superior to being black, while those whose physical characteristics are different, are treated as low class. The African-American Womanist theologian, Emile Townes, writing about Black identity and color, describes this issue as

> interiorized colour consciousness that draws out the various shades of complexion among black folk, hair texture, and physical features. Colorism is a colour grading that ranges from virtually white to brown to black.[56]

Kortright Davis concurs, describing it as an "elite skinocracy." It is this notion that persons of mixed or Negro race who possess Caucasian characteristics are assured of special attention solely on the basis of their physical appearance... People with darker skin have traditionally been accorded lower status than people with lighter skin...[57]

The existence and practice of this evil and dehumanizing ideology created a double standard as well as a way of life that shapes the identity of the victims, namely, the people of African descent. Supporting this claim by Davis, James and Harris state:

In the British Caribbean (with the sole exception of Barbados), one was designated legally white after the category of mustee [a mustee is a child of a pure amerindian and a white man] and became automatically free.[58]

Thus, the experience of racism is not new to the people of the Caribbean diaspora but they encounter it in a new way in their resident homeland. This experience is what helps to devise mechanisms to respond and cope with the problem of racism.[59] A direct result of this creative response to racism[60] is the creation of a new and different racial awareness in the Caribbean diaspora. Describing this development, Vickerman writes:

Over time, continued exposure to racial discrimination causes many West Indians to shift their paradigm from a non-racial one to one that is more explicitly racial. By this, one means that West Indians:(1) come to understand that race permeates all facets of American life;(2) expect to have unpleasant encounters because of race; and (3) often become pessimistic that the United States will become color blind any time soon.[61]

The Moral and Historical Elements

As I have been arguing, Caribbean ethnicity is the basis of the Caribamerican diasporn identity. It stages a confrontation with African Americans, which has created avoidable and unnecessary alienation from each other but at the same time has the promise of reconciliation and mutual co-existence. What follows, therefore, is an attempt to reveal the problematic nature of the Caribamerican identity and try to provide a solution to its shortcomings. In particular, taking the cue from the nature of the relationship between Caribamericans and African Americans, I will reflect on the implicit argument that the Caribamerican identity does not fully define the Caribbean diaspora because of its individualistic nature.

What does this strategy of forging a relationship with African Americans say about the nature of a Caribamerican diasporan identity? It could be understood as opportunistic where one is only seeking personal survival without regard for the welfare of others. Furthermore, with this emphasis on interpersonal relationship, the Caribamerican identity does not address the causes and issues of the structural and systemic practices that mitigate against its own existence. These practices include the reasons for migration, the perpetration of racial injustice, economic exploitation, political oppression and social and cultural degradation. In other words, the Caribamerican identity is far too provincial and parochial. It does not connect the particular struggle of the Caribbean diaspora to the larger struggle of Black people.[62]

These social realities mentioned above are reshaping the self-understanding of the Caribamerican identity. While belief in Caribbean ethnicity as its focal point remains constant, the manner in which the Caribbean diaspora develops ensures its existence changes especially as the population grows. It is possible, for example, to have interaction with fellow Caribamericans without sensing the need for similar relationships with those who are not members of the Caribbean diasporan community. But we must consider that changing immigration laws, which are anti-immigrants, engender hostility towards diasporic existence. And, whereas the increasing size of the diasporan community fosters the cultivation of a distinct identity, the immigration laws coerce those who are not citizens to seek naturalization. Becoming naturalized citizens guards against losing the opportunity of fulfilling the purpose for emigrating from their homeland.[63]

This aspect of the study has been addressing the centrality of ethnicity in the formation of a Caribamerican identity. The emphasis, however, on individual achievements denies the moral value of the common good in the Caribbean religious tradition and decentralizes Caribbean history and heritage. I will, therefore, seek to affirm the value of the common good, and assert the significance of Caribbean heritage as additional essential elements in the Caribamerican identity.

The Common Good

The Caribbean diaspora's emphasis on individual achievements fosters individualism which is inconsistent with the cardinal value of the common good in Caribbean Christian tradition. Individuality, as noted earlier, is one of the practices that the Caribamerican identity engenders.[64] The Caribbean Christian tradition encourages this practice and regards it as a virtue to be cultivated for the common good. Writing about the centrality of the common good in Black Christianity, the African American social ethicist, Peter Paris, observes:

> African peoples agree that…ethnic community is the paramount social reality apart from which humanity cannot exist…community is a sacred phenomenon created by the supreme God, protected by the divinities and governed by the ancestral spirits.[65]

The individual is important to the community but this person is not primary to the whole human community. The idea of the primacy of the individual is alien to Caribbean religious tradition. This does not mean that the tradition does not value individual conscience and liberty and responsibility. It does, but it is within the context of the community that the individual derives these rights and responsibility. A distinction, however, must be made between individuality and individualism. Making this distinction, Cornel West makes the claim that:

> The norm of individuality reinforces the importance of community, the common good and the harmonious development of personality. And it stands in stark contrast to those doctrinaire individualisms which promote human selfishness, denigrate the idea of community, and distort the holistic development of personality. The norm of individuality conceives persons as enjoyers and agents of their uniquely human capacities, whereas the norm of doctrinaire individualism views them as maximizers of pleasure and appropriators of unlimited resources.[66]

In addition, individualism alters the relationship between the individual and the community. The quest for emancipation reflects the spiritual and moral yearnings and beliefs of Black people as observed in the various emancipatory movements from the period of slavery through the time of colonialism to the present era. This is also the case in the formation of the Caribbean diasporan community. The individual-centered orientation, however, does not ground nor relate to this self-understanding of the quest for emancipation nor provide any analysis of the Black condition especially in terms of the migration movement. Writing of the relationship between the individual and the community, Peter Paris provides an instructive observation:

> Consonant with their understanding of their African forebears, African Americans have always known that persons cannot flourish apart from a community of belonging. They have also known that any community that oppresses its members is not community at all but, rather, a seething cauldron of dissension, distrust, and bitterness. Thus they have no difficulty in discerning a moral contradiction at the heart of the American republic: a contradiction caused by the primacy of racism as the organizing principle in the nation's public life… They have never been able to conceive of societal structures or their leaders as morally neutral in the exercise of their duties. Nor…view their resistance to racism in anything other than moral terms.[67]

The existence as a diasporan community warrants that the members of this community know and act as one community in order to transform the society from its unjust and systemic oppressive policies and structures. Individual well-being is integrally related to the one struggle for emancipation. As a diasporan community that is not only marginal but also a minority group in the society, it is essential that the Caribbean diaspora realizes that individual and communal survival depends on the commitment and willingness to work together.[68] It is in this regard that it becomes necessary to examine the all-important issue of Caribbean history and heritage in the formation of an identity for the Caribbean diaspora.

Common History and Heritage

The history and heritage of the Caribbean diaspora is an integral element in the formation of a Caribamerican diasporan identity which has not been taken into account by its proponents. The experience of living in a foreign country is one of displacement, alienation and hostility. When, however, there is the opportunity to discover and become involved with persons and communities of a common heritage and history, there is a liberating sense of affinity and identity. In his classic novel, *Lonely Londoners*, the Trinidadian writer, Samuel Selvon, describes the experience of Caribbean people in the British diaspora of the mid-twentieth century in the following account:

> In the grimness of the winter, with your hand plying space like a blind man's stick in the yellow fog, with ice on the ground and a coldness defying effort to keep warm, the boys coming and going, working eating, sleeping, going about the vast metropolis like veteran Londoners.
>
> Nearly every Sunday morning, like if they going to church, the boys living in Moses [sic] room, coming together for a old talk, to find out the latest gen [news], what is happening, when is the next fete. Bart asking if anybody see his girl anywhere, Cap recounting an episode he had with a woman by the tube station the night before, Big City want to know why the arse he can't win [at] pool, Galahad recounting a clash with the color problem in a restaurant in Piccadilly, Harris saying he hope the weather turns, Five saying he have to drive a truck to Glasgow tomorrow.[69]

What this account raises are not only issues of the emerging formation of a community, the incessant need for relationships, the brutal existential realities of race, class, and the hardships of life but also the merging of nationalities, cultures and experiences to formulate a distinct identity. It is also important to observe that this description of diasporan existence is a recognition and affirmation of Caribbean history and heritage which form the core of Caribbean diasporan self-understanding. Winston James and Clive Harris, who correctly acknowledge this essentiality, state:

There has thus been a pan-Caribbeanization of the cultures of those from individual countries and territories of the region. Languages, idioms, cuisines, music and so on, have scaled their individual boundaries and have become far more generalized, shared and amalgamated within the Caribbean diaspora than within the Caribbean itself.[70]

Advancing this understanding, Rex Nettleford argues that Caribbean heritage includes:

…the severance from ancestral home whether it be from Africa, Europe, Lebanon, India, China, or the indigenous Caribbean itself originally inhabited by Arawaks and Caribs. It constitutes suffering under enslavement, indentureship, and colonialism. It also constitutes *survival* and what exists beyond that survival…[71]

Nettleford's contention is that the elements of the severance from ancestral heritage, the experience of sufferings and strategies for survival[72] are what constitute the Caribbean heritage and form the foundation for building a Caribamerican identity.

While I concur with Nettleford's affirmation of these definitive experiences that shape Caribbean diasporan identity, he defines this identity too negatively. It is at this point I contend that these Caribbean identity proponents such as Robin Cohen, Stuart Hall, Rex Nettleford, Milton Vickerman and others, focus too much on the less than positive aspects of the Black experience. For example, Nettleford observes that Caribbean cultural identity is a form of resistance to Euro-American hegemony. Nettleford asserts:

The migrants' preservation of the heritage of the intangible heritage in the host habitats is a clear means of coping with new environments, especially if they are hostile. It also serves to build zones of comfort rooted in what is known, even as one assimilates the unknown – all the more reason why such intangible heritage must be facilitated and better understood.[73]

Regardless of this penetrating insight, there is a persistent Caribamerican identity crisis if we continue to ignore the resources that African ancestors brought into the diaspora with them. Although the issue of African retentions and change is an ongoing debate among scholars, there is the perspective that the Africans who were transported to the Caribbean brought their own world-view with them.[74]

This world-view James and Harris describe as manifesting itself in the Caribbean diaspora.[75] They ground their view on Barbadian writer, George Lamming's, novel of 1954, *The Emigrants*, in which he articulates this emerging diasporan Caribbeanism.

It is here that one sees a discovery actually taking shape. No Barbadian, no Trinidadian, no St. Lucian, no islander from the West Indies sees himself as a West Indian until he encounters another islander in a foreign territory. It was only when the Barbadian childhood corresponded with the Grenadian or the Guinanese childhood in important details of folk-lore, that the wider identification was arrived at.[76]

Lamming's observation attests to the Caribbean diasporan identity that I have been advocating. This identity is created in the Caribbean diaspora but the Caribbean is at the center of the identity. As a Caribbean-centered identity, it is shaped by a common historical and cultural heritage and common experience. This identity draws from the past and takes from the present to construct a particular identity of fixed and contextual but evolving factors. In this regard, the Caribamerican identity that I articulate is neither essentialist, although it consists of the fixed elements of race, class and gender nor a totally social construction, given the realities of movement, interaction and all that constitute diasporan existence which has been discussed earlier in the introductory chapter. What I maintain, nevertheless, is that Caribamerican identity is evolutionary and contextual. For this reason, I argue that the Caribbean is in the diaspora in the sense that the Caribbean is what informs and defines the Caribamerican identity and, at the same time, the identity is evolving due to the nature of diasporan life. Again, George Lamming's observation concerning the challenge of constructing a Caribbean identity can also be considered in this regard. Lamming observes:

> I do not think there has been anything in human history quite like the meeting of Africa, Asia, and Europe in this American archipelago we call the Caribbean. But it is so recent since we assume responsibility for our own destiny, that the antagonistic weight of the past is felt as an inhibiting menace. And that is the most urgent task and the greatest intellectual challenge: how to control the burden of this history and incorporate it into our collective sense of the future [and peoplehood].[77]

Given this reality, my intent, therefore, is to demonstrate that it is the task of Caribbean diasporan theology to construct out of the continuity, complexity, ambiguity and change of the diasporan experience our own identity, without which, we will not live meaningful lives much more to knowing ourselves as a distinct people. Central to this self-knowledge, however, is the Caribbean diaspora's Christian theological heritage which is the subject for discussion in the following chapter.

4 Standing on Our Own Two Feet: Theological Foundations of the Caribbean Diasporan Church

As previously discussed, diasporan life is complex and adverse. In order to survive, Caribbean people have to forge their own identities. Having explored these identities, I want to ground them theologically. In so doing, I want to demonstrate that the dialectical religious tradition of Caribbean theology is a foremost aspect of the theological heritage and an essential resource for the survival of the people of the Caribbean diaspora. Caribamericans draw on this heritage as a combative and empowering resource in resisting opposition and pursing the realization of our full humanity.

As will be discussed later in this chapter, Caribbean Christianity is formed out of two different religions, namely African derived religions and European Christianity. The nature of Caribbean Christianity reflects the nuances in the people's life and making of their faith. Paying attention to this dialectical tradition departs from the normative theological practices and categories and thus provides a new paradigm for theological reflection. For this reason, I argue that the dialectical religious tradition of Caribbean Christianity is a theological basis for Caribbean diasporan identity. In so doing, this chapter discusses the case, provides a descriptive account, and offers a perspective of the significance of the dialectical religious traditions of Caribbean theology in constructing a Caribbean diasporan theology.

The Case for the Dialectical Religious Traditions

A clarification of the term dialect is essential to the issue in question for this discussion. The term dialect[1] refers to the mutually interdependent relationship between the African centered and European based religions that constitute Caribbean Christianity. The dialectic reflects dynamism, change, continuity and holds these two religions in tension without seeking to accomplish any resolution.[2] Caribbean Christianity, however, is not always understood as having a dialectical tradition. The dominant perspectives are that Caribbean Christianity is dualistic, ethnically based and contextual. While I will not deny these perspectives, this study argues that Caribbean Christianity is made up of two distinct religious traditions which function in a dialectical relationship. Though this relationship is not to be understood as hostile, tensions exist, but rather as vital aspects of a dynamic faith. It is an engaging relationship between two traditions of faith that the term dialectic describes and also identifies as a distinct feature of Caribbean theology.

The perspective that Caribbean Christianity is constituted of two different forms of religion is a dominant understanding in Caribbean theology. Historian Shirley Gordon expresses this view. She defines Caribbean Christianity by arguing for the existence of a Euro-Caribbean Christianity and an Afro-Jamaican Christianity. While the former represents a religion of respectability, the latter represents a religion as an alternative community of emancipation. According to Gordon:

> The European missionary culture provided an acceptable model for those who could improve their circumstances in a colonial society promoting current British social values; they found their self-expression and identity in this setting. For those whom a subsistence living seemed the only prospect Afro-Jamaican Christianity provided a spiritual support; it also offered forms of community loyalty which could be applied to the problems of poverty and their considerable marginalization from the colonial society.[3]

This definitional polarization between these two religious traditions is problematic. It does not address the internal conflicts of each tradition nor accommodate the ethnic diversity of Caribbean society or the diversity of the African derived Caribbean community.

Dianne Stewart, however, is particularly resistant to this dualistic interpretation of Caribbean Christianity. Stewart, in her groundbreaking work, *Three Eyes for the Journey,* argues for an ethnically-based Caribbean religion.[4] For Stewart, Caribbean religion is African derived and theistic. She considers European Christianity as hostile to African religions and cultures and also thinks that European Christianity is elitist, imperialistic and an agent of Western hegemony. She bases her presupposition on the premise that

> theology has primarily been the property of the Western Christian tradition, a discourse that seeks to standardize the Christian faith by its orthodox beliefs and practices and by proclaiming its significance for humanity.[5]

Given this focus, Stewart advocates the notion that Caribbean religion is the product of the engagement between African and Western religions.[6] She acknowledges the Christian influences on these religions but contends that the African-derived religions incorporated elements on Christianity into their practice to form a Caribbean religion.[7]

While I agree with Stewart on the formation of African-derived religions and their role in the society as agents of social change,[8] she rejects their

Christological basis. It is here I would argue that Stewart's rejection of the Christological basis of Caribbean religion is misguided. According to Stewart:

> But to speak of a historic human-divine sacrifice as universally redemptive for human beings is to grant a place of authority to Christian anthropology, Christology and eschatology. The idea that all human beings are in need of Christ's redemption is just that – an idea.[9]

What is striking is that Stewart believes Caribbean religion is theistic but she attributes the cause of suffering and oppression to the universal redemptive claim of Christianity. While I certainly do not share Stewart's view on universal redemption through Jesus Christ, there is some validity in her analysis on European Christianity. As this study will show, European Christianity has been an agent of oppression. But I maintain that the influence of European Christianity is a constitutive factor in Caribbean Christianity.

What is important is that both Gordon and Stewart acknowledge the role of European and African religious traditions in Caribbean society even though they have different perspectives on the nature of Caribbean religion. But by juxtaposing African and European religious traditions, they fail to recognize the particular Christian religion that is created as a result of the encounter between these two religions. Diane J. Austin-Broos' study on Caribbean Christianity gives support to this assertion. In the quest to establish European connections and African origin, the product that is authentically Caribbean is not identified.[10] She calls this creation the "re-contextualizing and new use of practices and knowledge that might be read as merely hegemonic,"[11] thus the contextual Caribbean Christianity.

In delineation a contextual Caribbean Christianity, Austin-Broos considers the issues of African ancestors, water baptism and music to demonstrate how these are interpreted in Caribbean Christianity. For example, biblical personalities replaced the place that was assigned to African ancestors.[12] Thus, "Christianity becomes Jamaican [Caribbean] while bearing as part of its Jamaicanness [Caribbeanness] ranked folk renderings of its origins and its attendant meanings and power."[13]

Austin-Broos interprets Caribbean Christianity through the lenses of the Pentecostal movement. This work is too internally oriented. It focuses on the internally religious practices of one particular movement, Caribbean Pentecostalism. Indeed, this is a Caribbean created religion but it does not fully reflect the nature of Caribbean Christianity. Although I support Austin-Broos' observation of the oversight of the creation of an organic Caribbean religion in the polarization between African and European origins, Austin-Broos constructs her thesis exclusively on one particular religious movement whereas there are a diversity of Caribbean religious movements as well as different religious traditions. In this regard, I insist that Caribbean

Christianity consists of two dialectical religious sources that are inherently diverse.

Winston Lawson defines the dialectical tradition of Caribbean Christianity. In his *Religion and Race: African and European Roots in Conflict – A Jamaican Testament*[14] Lawson discusses the role of the Caribbean church and how its theology and cosmology influenced the growth and development of colonial society.[15] He examines the African origins of Caribbean Christianity paying attention to traditional religions, the problems the church faced and the response of the Caribbean church to its European counterpart. He then concludes that Caribbean Religion is the fusion of the commonalities between European Christianity and traditional African religions. In this regard, Lawson writes:

> Both African and Christian churches united the principles of love, justice and equality with traditional African values and belief. This was emotionally fulfilling and formed their only means of social and political transformation.[16]

Lawson's theological analysis of Caribbean theology reflects the nature of Caribbean Christianity. According to Lawson's observation, Caribbean Christianity is created out of two different religious traditions. The analysis, however, addresses the issue of the conflicts between these two traditions without regarding their differences. By focusing on the conflicts between these religious traditions, Lawson highlights their different purpose and understanding. For example, the European tradition understood the Caribbean church as an institution that served the interest of the socio-political establishment through political and ecclesiastical domination. Noel Erskine supports this perspective.

> Basically the mother country had in mind for black people the type of society known in England, with the middle class, and upper class, through which the industrious and ambitious may rise. The Colonial Office wanted to see mirrored in the Caribbean a rising middle class made up of mulattoes and industrious, but also respectful of the plantocracy and the middle class. They did not want to see blacks acquiring political power.[17]

In contrast to the Eurocentric source of Caribbean Christianity, the Afrocentric source functions as an agent of emancipation. For example, Dianne Stewart advocates this understanding in her analysis of the Africa-based religions when she notes:

> Although Black Christian acquiescence to missionary Afrophobic theology was a developed phenomenon in the nineteenth century, when some enslaved Christians experienced aspects of White religion and Euro-Christian valves as a threat to their Black values to be free…they often resort to critical forms of Black consciousness, which kept their Black demands for social equity and autonomy alive and central in Black religion and culture.[18]

In light of this tension between these two religions, the dialectical tradition of Caribbean Christianity reflects the dialectical nature of this religion. I will examine these two dialectical traditions, not as separate entities but as constitutive elements of a single faith, for without both there is no organic Caribbean Christianity. We begin with the Eurocentric followed by the African religious tradition.

Describing the Tradition: Eurocentric Religious Heritage

The Eurocentric religious tradition is one of the sources that constitutes Caribbean diasporan theological identity. The major representative work on this subject is the church historian, Arthur Charles Dayfoot's, *The Shaping of the West Indian Church.*

> The character of the Church in the Caribbean was also determined, in part, by the long history of the Church through the first fifteen centuries of the Christian era. This development took place in various parts of the Old World, principally Europe.[19]

In this study, Dayfoot's purpose is to provide an account of the institutional formation of the church in the Anglophone Caribbean and its response to contextual reality. The study includes an examination of the historical factors, the external origins, denominational development and the issues and challenges that the church faced.[20]

The Eurocentric source is also expressed in the definition Dayfoot offers of the church as both a Christocentric institution and as a movement. The church, he contends, is not so much institution as movement – one that has visible expression, both in the form of communication and co-operation (and indeed controversy) among believers in Christ, and also as a variety of ecclesiastical institutions. Wherever we can identify Christ-centered worship, proclamation, teaching, fellowship, pastoral help and social concern, the Church is recognized, whatever form of ecclesiastical organization there may be.[21]

The Eurocentric tradition interprets faith through the lenses of European culture, history and religion. One of the dangers of this interpretation is the disregard for the African religious heritage as an integral aspect and feature of Caribbean Christianity. Dayfoot, in his Eurocentric perspective, argues that:

> African Traditional Religion is a modern term to describe the faith of millions of African people south of the Sahara… Since it does not have written scriptures, creeds, historical founder figures or a unified organization, its history is not easy

to trace but oral tradition, art, music, proverbs, myths, prayers, ritual formulas and ceremonies, and basic consistency of ideas, point to its long ascendancy in villages and national areas.[22]

Dayfoot is obviously unacquainted with African culture and certainly he reflects the usual white intellectual superiority over that of Blacks. By arguing that the term African traditional religion is new and appealing to the oral nature of traditional Black culture, he reflects European cultural imperialism as indicated earlier in this chapter. Mary Turner's study of Caribbean Christianity concurs with this assertion. She observes that: "The Missionaries' teachings challenged the slaves' established religious beliefs, denigrated their culture, and attempted to impose new social mores."[23] Turner and other Caribbean historians note further that European Christianity was established in the Caribbean to create a Black version of White culture. In order for this to be accomplished, she argues that,

> the missionaries had to attack the slaves' established culture, to root out their religious ideas, to divorce them from the social traditions and moral assumptions of plantation life, to replace Anansi, the supreme ginal, with Christian the Pilgrim, who fought his way through life.[24]

Although the Eurocentric religious source is inherently adverse toward Black culture, that dimension still profoundly influences Caribbean culture, religion and intellectual life. The Caribbean intellectual tradition, for example, is one aspect of the Eurocentric source of the Caribbean theological identity. In this regard, I will consider the Caribbean intellectual C. L. R. James with particular reference to his significant work, *Beyond a Boundary*.[25]

My use of James as a paradigm of this source reflects his enormous contributions to and continuing influence on Caribbean diaspora's intellectual life. Writing of the significance of James, Selwyn R. Cudjoe and William E. Cain situate James in the Black liberation tradition as one of its foremost thinkers. They note:

> Throughout history, humankind has been blessed with persons who, by their sheer exuberance and intellectual commitment to struggle, leave an indelible mark on their time. The liberation of colonial peoples in Africa and the diaspora has been distinguished by such persons: Toussaint-Louverture and Jacques Dessalines; Fredrick Douglas and W.E.B. Du Bois; Frantz Fanon and Aime Cesaire; George Padmore and Ida B. Wells; Mahatma Gandhi and Ali Shariati; Walter Rodney and Malcolm X.
>
> In this distinguished company of activist intellectuals stands the eminent scholar and revolutionary, Cyril Lionel Robert James. Although Edward W. Said has called him "the father of modern Caribbean writing," James has transcended geography and genre, contributing enormously to our understanding on the colonial question, the Negro question, the Russian question, and the role of dialects in proletarian struggle; and his elaboration on Marxist practice and

theory in America and the world has been surpassed by few. Today, James is even hailed as one of the pioneers in such avant-garde field as cultural studies.[26]

James is known and regarded as an historian and political thinker and not as a theologian. While he may not have espoused any theological thought, I detect in his classic work, *Beyond a Boundary*, that Eurocentric theological thought deeply influenced his life and played a pivotal role in his formative years. For example, theological beliefs influenced his early formative years. Using theological precision and perspicuity, he writes:

> I discovered that I had not arbitrarily or by accident worshipped at the shrine of John Bunyan and Aunt Judith of W.G. Grace and Matthew Bondman, of *The Throne of the House of David* and *Vanity Fair.* They were trinity, the three in one and one in three, the Gospel according to St. Matthew, Matthew the son of Thomas, otherwise called Arnold of Rugby.[27]

While this remark reflects the theological framework that James uses to interpret his life, his Christian and theological perspective are rooted in Eurocentric Christianity. James acknowledges that he came from a religious background. His grandparents and parents were devoted Christians. "My grandfather went to church every Sunday morning at 11 o'clock…,"[28] he writes. In addition, he initially claims to be unsure of the source of his motivation for learning but in his recollection, he attributes it to his Christian background. He gives the following account.

> What drew me to it I do not know… As I dig into my memory I recall that the earliest books I could reach from the window-sill when I had nothing to do, or rain stopped the cricket or there was no cricket, were biblical. There was a series of large brightly colored religious pamphlets telling the story of Jacob and the Ladder, Ruth and Naomi and so forth. There was a larger book called *The Throne of the House of David.* One day somebody must have told me, or I may have discovered it from listening to the lessons being read in church that these stories could be found in the many Bibles that lay about the house, including the one with the family births and deaths. Detective-like, I tracked down the originals and must have warmed the souls of my aunt and grandmother as they saw me poring over the Bible. That, I had heard often enough, was a good book. When the parson read the lessons, I strove to remember the names and numbers, second chapter of the Second Book of Kings, the Gospel according to St. Matthew, and so forth.[29]

The theological concept James uses to define his world-view is a further expression of Eurocentric theological thought on his life. The concept "Puritan" is an example. James defines himself as a "Puritan" and regarded his life as being pre-determined. The term Puritan refers to the morally strict, non-conformist, radical brand of Christianity that originated from English Protestantism in the early seventeenth century.[30] This was the form of the Christian religion that had great influence in the Caribbean.

C. L. R. James shows the influence of this religion in the following account. "The story of my elder aunt, Judith, ends this branch of my children days. She was the English Puritan incarnate..."[31] In another instance he writes, "Josh was no Puritan...who kept...a convent..."[32]

James offers a deeper insight into the extent of the influence of Eurocentric Christianity in the life and culture of the people. He describes himself as a Puritan and related such self-understanding to his immediate context. He writes: "My Puritan soul burnt with indignation at injustice..."[33] He continues to describe it in the following manner:

> Before long, I acquired a discipline for which the only name is Puritan. I never cheated, I never appealed for a decision unless I thought the batsman was out, I never argued with the umpire, I never jeered a defeated opponent, I never gave to a friend a vote or a place which by any stretch of imagination could be seen as belonging to an enemy or to a stranger. My defeats and disappointments I took as stoically as I could. If I caught myself complaining or making excuses I pulled up. If afterwards I remembered doing it I took an inward decision to try not to do it again. From the eight years of school life this code becomes the moral framework of my existence. It has never left me. I learnt it as a boy, I obeyed it as a man and now I can no longer laugh at it.[34]

He concludes:

> My inheritance...Puritanism and cricket came from both sides of the family and a good case could be made out for "predestination", including the house in front of the recreation of the ground and the window exactly behind the wicket.[35]

The Jamesian understanding of Caribbean Christianity is an uncritical acceptance of European Christianity. James, for instance, accepts Eurocentric Christianity without reflecting on its practice of domination. In a penetrating analysis of the domination practice of the established church in the Caribbean, Neville Linton makes this observation:

> Traditionally, the Caribbean church, coming out of a wholly colonial history, did not pay much attention to political issues on the one hand and supported the established powers on the other.
> At various times, however, individual church people – both clergy and laity – have stood up and fought political authorities on matters of principles. This goes back, notably, to the time of slavery. The institutional church, however, has always cooperated with and supported the "legal" authorities and has never questioned the fundamentals of the political system – even under colonialism. The exceptions to this have been a few non-conformist churches, especially in Jamaica and Guyana, which were characterized by their sense of cultural identity with the masses, e.g. the Baptist churches.[36]

Another indication of James' uncritical acceptance of Eurocentric Christianity is the absence of any mention of the conflict within Eurocentric Christianity. He also portrays Eurocentric Christianity to be primarily concerned with personal salvation and the maintenance of the status quo.

Theologian Robert Beckford, writing of the tension within Eurocentric Christianity, argues that there is a tradition of Black resistance within this source of Caribbean Christianity. He observes two inter-related approaches which he defines as the combative and the negotiative. With the combative approach, the church is a place of hostility, struggle, marginalization, identity and prophetic spirituality.[37] The value of this approach is that it offers a critique of racism but, at the same time, it demonizes white people and alienates itself. Beckford states:

> The marginal space occupied by the combative approach re-inscribed the marginality conferred by the church hierarchy on its Black rebels. While the marginality provides degrees of freedom of expression and action, it is removed from the influence of White power structures.[38]

Beckford's second approach to Black resistance is the negotiative. This describes the church as a place of good practice, negotiation, internal change, participation and persuasion. The approach fosters unity but at the expense of addressing difficult issues and making structural changes.[39] For Beckford, the "negotiative advocates often argue that, race does not matter because we are all God's children."[40]

Beckford offers a third approach to Black resistance which he calls the middle ground and describes it as one of patience and pressure. He proceeds to locate this in Caribbean emancipatory tradition.[41] Beckford writes:

> In Caribbean history, the examples of slaves negotiating their freedom are less prominent than the records of slaves who took their freedom from benevolent masters by force or stealth. Consequently, runaways were more commonplace than freed slaves.[42]

Beckford's analysis of the Eurocentric source of the dialectical tradition in Caribbean Christianity acknowledges the tension in the source, but he has not identified this tension within the dialectical tradition of Christianity. Furthermore, although he locates resistance in the Caribbean emancipatory tradition, his "middle ground" approach is reformist and not revolutionary. Beckford's middle ground approach to Black resistance is not revolutionary because it does not seek to change the social structure nor fashion a society based on the values and beliefs of the Black resistors. Consequently, it is not consistent with the Caribbean emancipatory tradition which is revolutionary. It was not just the reformation of an institution or the society that the enslaved Black people sought, but a radical transformation that restructures and reorders the society so as to affirm human personhood, dignity and equality.

This was a goal that the previously mentioned Caribbean Freedom Fighters were prepared to pay with their lives to achieve. The piecemeal conciliatory "middle ground" approach Beckford proposes does not go that far in the pursuit for justice. In other words, the pursuit for freedom by these Freedom Fighters was unconditional and non-negotiable. The Freedom Fighters premised their desire, right and pursuit of emancipation on the gospel of Jesus Christ. The testimony of the venerable Baptist deacon and revolutionary, Samuel Sharpe, who led the historic "Baptist War" of 1831, gives support to this assertion. Sharpe is reported to have said while hanging on the gallows moments before he was executed:

> I depend for Salvation through the Redeemer who shed his blood upon Calvary for Sinners…and follow your Christian duties to work out your salvation. Let me beg you my brethren, to attend to your Christian duties, for it is the only way to go to your salvation. I now bid you all farewell! That is all I have to say.[43]

This account of Samuel Sharpe is not just a personal testimony and belief but a reflection of the revolutionary dimension of a Black Christian religion. Supporting this claim is Mary Turner in her study on Christianity. She affirms:

> Sam Sharpe, ideologue and organizer of the 1831 rebellion, as a leader in the Baptist church and ruler among the Native Baptists, united the Native Baptist traditions of slave leadership and free thought with the radical Christian tradition of principled resistance. Under this leadership, in the ferment created by economic and political pressures of 1831, members of the mission churches and of the independent sects united in key element in a bid for freedom.[44]

I contend further that Sharpe understood the struggle for freedom as the duty of the Christian and that all Christians should be prepared to pay for it with their lives, if necessary. This dimension of faith, along with the African religious influences, is excluded by James and Beckford from their interpretation of the Eurocentric source within Caribbean Christianity. Given this neglect, the discussion now examines the second source that constitutes the dialectical tradition of Caribbean diasporan church theological foundation.

Describing the Tradition: The Afrocentric Heritage

In addition to European religious tradition, the Afrocentric religious heritage is the second source of Caribbean dialectical tradition. Both sources not only form but constitute the dialectical character of the Caribbean of diasporan religious heritage.

Of foremost importance is the understanding that the Africans who were brought to the Caribbean brought their religion with them despite systematic attempts to destroy it.[45] The diversity of the African population indicates that they did not necessarily embrace the same world-view but they did have a common cosmology.[46] The commonly held beliefs were the existence of God, ancestor worship, a holistic universe, life after death and various other religious beliefs and ritualistic acts such as healing, dancing and singing.[47] This does not mean their religion survived in its pristine form. Their religion underwent changes due to the oppressive conditions of slave existence and the hostile response of the religious and political system. The determination to maintain their religion led to it being secretly practiced.[48] The Caribbean historian, Dale Bisnauth, concurs.

> Indigenous African religious ideas did survive the difficulties of estate life... African religious ideas were to undergo significant changes but they remained recognizably "African" in structure.[49]

He summarizes these ideas as "the belief in God, the worshipping of God, life after death, the indwelling of the spirit and the commitment to life."[50]

Additional indication of the Afrocentric source in Caribbean dialectical religious is Kortright Davis' reference to the "African Soul." He carefully points out that:

> By African Soul, we are not referring to a part of, or spark in, the physical anatomy. We are using the term to depict an intangible yet energizing force, an invisible yet effective reality, a formless yet formative source out of which actual feelings, fears, faith structures, and cultural preferences are born and bred.[51]

For Davis, the African Soul is the spiritual matrix, the source of meaning and worth for all that energizes African existence. It is that which accepts the continuing presence of God as the Great Ancestor and therefore seeks to share in God's creative activity.[52] Davis claims the African Soul makes the case for the continuity and connections between Africa and the Caribbean which are reconfigured and modified to forge a contextual expression of faith. According to Davis:

> There are strong continuities between African and the Caribbean in the area of symbolism, proverbial wisdom, music, movement, theodicy, the serial spirit and the myth. The African Soul has subsisted in these principal sub-streams in the history of the Caribbean; but determined efforts have been made to counter its survival.[53]

Given that Davis grounds Caribbean theology in its African heritage and even observes some of the ways in which it is expressed, without elaborating on the distinctives of such theology, he therefore obscures his contention on the African heritage of Caribbean theology. Consequently, Davis does not give an adequate interpretation of Caribbean theology.

George Simpson, nevertheless, attempts to address this oversight by Davis in his very informative sociological study, *Black Religions in the New World*. Simpson examines the various religions of the Black diaspora. The study shows the development of Black religion, the role of Black people in the Euro-American churches and the differences between religions of the various Black diasporan communities.[54]

Maintaining that Caribbean people interpret Christianity from their own religious perspective indicates that as a people of African descent, they did not always identify with European Christianity. As George Simpson notes:

> In the British possessions of the Church of England was the religion of the white settlers and officials... The arduous work of the Non-conformist missionaries, especially the Baptist and the Methodist ...resulted in the conversion of only a small minority of the slaves in the non-Catholic countries.[55]

Despite this struggle for survival, in some of these non-Catholic countries like Jamaica, Black religion flourished. "During this time a re-interpretation of Christianity spread throughout the island and by 1830 the Native Baptist had become another religion competing with the Christianity of the European missionaries,"[56] according to Simpson.

While Simpson focuses on some of the major difficulties in the formation of Caribbean Christianity, George Mulrain explores the process that defines this form of Christianity. Mulrain argues that there are similarities between Judea-Christian and African religious cosmology. Both religions believe in a sovereign God, the existence of spirits, the mediatory role of priests. He asserts that:

> There should be an expression of Christianity wherein God, as revealed in Jesus Christ through the Holy Spirit, is worshipped and adored and wherein some of the African cultural facets which are not in contradiction to the essential gospel message, have been employed to good effect in the communication of that same gospel.[57]

George Mulrain is careful to observe that African cosmology is woven into the fabric of Caribbean society.

> All Christian denominations in the Caribbean, whether they were cradled in European or American culture or otherwise, are affected with the challenge of having now to express their Christianity within a culture in which African cosmology permeates.[58]

The African cosmology of which Mulrain speaks is in reference to the theological perspective that God and human beings exist within one unified social order and are engaged in a mutual relationship.[59] This theological assumption presupposes an organic unity indicating that all aspects of life, the spiritual and the secular, are sacred. As Winston Lawson observes:

> Towards this, earthly existence became a mere forerunner and preparation. It thus rejected African religion's contrary view of the good life consisting of health, prosperity, success, good fortune, happy and fruitful marriages occurring in a community of compassion and concern for each other, here and now and not primarily in the hereafter.[60]

The Jamaican sociologist, Barry Chevannes, writing about the role of African religion in the shaping of Caribbean cultures, describes the nature of Caribbean religion as one reality and not dualistic as in the case of Eurocentric Christianity. According to Chavennes:

> The same world in which we live and breathe is the same world inhabited by God, the Spirits and the Ancestors. This belief produces an approach towards the world which we might call "this worldly", in contrast to the "other-worldly" approach propounded by European religion.[61]

George Mulrain adds further:

> The African world-view maintains that there is the active interest and involvement on the part of the spirit world in the day to day affairs of the people. Human beings are never alone, whether they are struggling or celebrating.[62]

The discussion so far, attends to the theological nature of Caribbean diasporan identity. An additional issue is the significance of this dialectical tradition to a Caribbean diasporan theological discourse.

The Importance of the Dialectical Religious Tradition to Caribbean Diasporan Theological Discourse

What is the significance of the dialectical tradition for Caribbean diasporan theology? I will discuss three ways in which this tradition is significant to Caribbean theological discourse: namely, (1) the alternative perspective to the interpretation of Caribbean theology, (2) a theological framework and (3) a symbol of the dynamism of the Christian religion. In recent times religious scholars such as Dianne Stewart have made a significant contribution to Black theological discourse. In her work that I have noted earlier, Stewart examines the relationship between Christian theology and African derived religions in the Caribbean.[63] A special feature of Stewart's work is that it is not an attempt to address the process of Christianization of the enslaved Africans but to attend to how they survive what she termed "antiafricaness in Christianities."[64]

In advocating her argument, Stewart explores the historical context, the European attitude towards enslaved Africans and, in return, the enslaved Africans' response to Europeans, the legacy and implications of the study for the study of theology. In Stewart's view, African-derived religions are essential to the development of a Caribbean emancipatory theology.[65] Stewart's intent is to provide a Caribbean theology both as an alternative to and beyond the normative categories of Christianity. The Caribbean theology that she advances is theologically African-centered and epistemologically embodied. Caribbean theology, for Stewart,

> maintains critical distance from ideational theology as Eurocentric articulation of faith testimony, which is false when applied to the African-Jamaica religious context... In this contest testimony is enacted, dramatized, and ritualized.[66]

Inasmuch as I share Stewart's critique of the European dimension of Caribbean Christianity in support of her perspective of Caribbean theology, she bases her analysis on the juxtaposition between African-derived religions and Eurocentric Christianity. In this regard, I argue that Stewart ignores the dialectical nature of Caribbean theology and as such she dismisses the Christian dimension of Caribbean theology. Fully aware of the African element in Caribbean theology, the dialectical theological heritage of the Caribbean diasporan theology, which I propose, is essentially Christian based both on the emancipatory nature character of both traditions – Eurocentric and Afrocentric – and the contents of the Christian Faith which I will explore in the forthcoming chapter.

Along with the alternative perspective to the understanding of Caribbean theology, the Caribbean dialectical religious tradition provides a theological analytical tool for interpreting Caribbean diasporan theology. It takes into account the religious diversity of Caribbean diasporan life. As such, it seeks to represent an inclusive, even ecumenical and probably catholic theology of which the biblical witness speaks:

> The body is a unity; and though all its parts are many, they form one body. So it is with Christ. For we were all baptized by one Spirit into one body – whether Jews or Greeks, slave or free – and we were all given the one Spirit to drink (1 Cor. 12:12-13; NIV).

Also, this dialectical tradition challenges the notion of dualistic Caribbean religion which promotes the idea that Caribbean people practice European religion for respectability and African derived religions for identity and spirituality.[67]

I intend to dispel this notion of "respect and spirituality" as the reason for the religious choice and practice of Caribbean people and their ancestors because it reinforces the belief that they were without respect until Europeans conferred it upon them. Furthermore, the dualistic perspective connotes the idea that Black people's self-respect is derived from Europeans. Inherent in this "respect theory" is an implicit form of racism. Otherwise put, the notion is not only racist in character but totally ignorant of the Black illustrious heritage.[68] As theologian James Deotis Roberts puts it:

> We are taken back to classic Africa in the era before Christ in Egypt, Ethiopia and Cush…this ancient and noble civilization as that which belongs to us as a people… We affirm our dignity as a people without downgrading the status of any other people. We categorically reject an inferior place in the human family.[69]

The consensus among Caribbean scholars is that the intent of European Christians in the name of Christianizing the enslaved Africans was to eradicate every residue of Africanism among which was regarded as barbaric and heathenistic.[70] But this effort failed because Caribbean people have created their own distinct religion, as Brian L. Moore and Michelle A. Johnson note:

> The reality, however, was that the people wanted neither to be led nor driven. They wanted to decide for themselves what was suitable and meaningful for them, in accordance with their own world view and moral system. They sought cultural self-determination, not cultural paternalism. Hence they were selective in their adoption of the moral precepts of Christianity.[71]

In the final analysis, the significance of the dialectical religious tradition in Caribbean Christianity for Caribbean diasporan theological discourse underscores the fact that Christian faith is dynamic and must be contextualized in order to have universal significance. As Caribbeaners accepted their freedom, they applied it not only to their personal lives but to their existential reality as an act of protest against oppression and domination. Writing of this engagement in the African American context, Gayraud Wilmore observes:

> The independent church movement among blacks…must be regarded as the prime resistance to slavery – in every sense, *the first black freedom movement*. It had the advantage of being carried on under the cloak of ecclesiastical affairs rather than as an affair of the state or the economy. The movement, therefore, could pass as representing the more or less legitimate desire of slaves to have "a place of their own in which to worship God under their own fig vine and fig tree." But it was, in fact, a form of rebellion against the most accessible and vulnerable expression of white oppression and institutional racism in the nation: the American churches.[72]

Robert Stewart notes also this dynamism in his study on Caribbean Christianity. He contends:

> The frustration experienced by the European churches in attempting to implant a system of religious and moral practice among the ex-slave population that

corresponded entirely with European ideals of religious culture did not mean that the blacks rejected that culture in preference for a secular and amoral society. On the contrary, the other side of the coin of missionary frustration was the triumph of Afro-creole religious practice and personal norms...not a total rejection of missionary Christianity but an adaptation of it on the basis of customs, values and perceptions that began in Africa and were modified in the black's experience of slavery and emancipation...[73]

In this chapter, I have shown the nature of Caribbean religion. This is an attempt to construct a perspective for the theological basis for a Caribbean diasporan theology. As a point of departure from the normative theological categories, I define Caribbean Christianity as dialectical religion. This tradition both makes room for an alternative approach for interpreting Caribbean theology and demonstrates that Caribbean religion is inherently diverse and dynamic. This diversity and dynamism show the tensions between two different cultures, religiously diverse traditions and peoples. But at the same time, this religion demonstrates how people from diverse ethnicity and culture can live together as one people. I will examine this issue in later chapters but I must first identify the theological foundations of the Caribbean diasporan church by attending to the relationship between theology and the Caribbean diaspora. This is the subject for exploration in the next chapter.

5 Theologizing Diaspora: The Theological Heritage of the Caribbean Diasporan Church

The foregoing chapter discussed the dialectical traditions of Caribbean theology but in order to demonstrate the Christian distinctiveness of this theology, consideration should be given to its Christological basis. Jesus Christ as Emancipator from sin and oppression is central to Christian identity. Expressing this perspective, Luke reports Jesus' self-claim:

> The Spirit of the Lord is on me, because he has anointed me to preach good news to the poor. He has sent me to proclaim freedom for the prisoners and recovery of sight for the blind, to release the oppressed, to proclaim the year of the Lord's favour (Lk. 4:18-19; NIV).

This reference to Jesus describes his identity and purpose in the world. Jesus is a prophet and his purpose is inclusive of the whole gamut of human existence. In this regard, New Testament scholar, Fred Craddock, points out that the person Jesus is the prophet God commissioned to realize God's kingdom on earth. This is not a spiritual or futuristic event but a present holistic reality. According to Craddock:

> by reading Isa. 61:1-2, Jesus not only announces fulfillment of prophecy (v. 21) but defines what his messianic role is. Isaiah 61 is a servant song, "anointed me" means "made me the Christ or Messiah." When understood literally, the passage says Christ is God's servant who will bring to reality the longing and hope of the poor, the oppressed, and the imprisoned. The Christ will also usher in amnesty, the liberation, and the restoration associated with the proclamation of the year of the Jubilee (v. 19; Lev. 25:8-12).[1]

In his commentary on this text, Robert C. Tannehill not only acknowledges the holistic nature of Jesus' purpose but observes that this was a "remarkable social legislation designed to give the poor a new start."[2] This new beginning commences in the here and now. This was a demanding and radical declaration that Jesus made. When Jesus said, "Today this scripture has been fulfilled in your hearing" (v. 21), he means, for Craddock, that:

> The age of God's reign is here; the eschatological time when God's promises are fulfilled and God's purpose comes to fruition has arrived; there will be changes in the conditions of those who have waited and hoped. Those changes for the poor and the wronged and the oppressed will occur today. This is the beginning

of Jubilee. The time of God is today, and the ministries of Jesus and of the church according to Luke-Acts demonstrate that "today" continued.[3]

In this chapter, therefore, I argue that the Caribbean diasporan church premises its existence on this faith in Jesus Christ as the emancipator who comes to fulfill God's promises on earth and in human lives, as evidenced primarily through the testimony of faith.

This testimony of faith as the basis of the church is expressed by the Reverend Samuel George Simpson, pastor of the Bronx Baptist Church in New York. He declares: "It is faith that builds a church."[4] Simpson's testimony is both an individual and collective symbolic expression of the faith of the Caribbean diasporan church. Simpson speaks both as a pastor and more importantly as one of the pioneering pastors of the Caribbean diasporan church. His role and work will be discussed later in this study but it is noteworthy that the building of Caribbean diasporan churches is an expression of faith.

Also, the music tradition of the church affirms the testimony of faith as a theological premise of the Caribbean diasporan church. This perspective is expressed by the classic song, "We've Come This Far By Faith."[5]

We've come this far by faith. Leaning on the Lord;
Trusting in his holy word, He's never failed me yet.
O can't turn around, We've come this far by faith.
Don't be discouraged when trouble's in your life,
He'll bear your burdens and removes all misery and strife.
That's why we've come this far by faith.

Just the other day I heard someone say
He didn't believe in God's word;
But I can truly say that God had made a way
That's why we've come this far by faith.[6]

This song communicates what the people believe about their pilgrimage and how they were able to reach where they have reached and become what they have become and are becoming. This is also an account of the source of their power to live as a diasporan people. The song further demonstrates that the people of the Caribbean diaspora did not enter the diaspora in search of a faith nor to discover faith during their sojourn. They brought their own faith, religion and theology with them.

Faith is expressed through testimony, the music tradition, as well as through church document as further indication of the Christocentric basis of the Caribbean diasporan church. The decision of the ecumenical meeting, The "Verdun Proclamation of 1992 of the Caribbean/African American Dialogue and the Caribbean Conference of Churches" supports this claim:

The one factor which allowed the peoples of the Caribbean to survive was their belief systems or religion. These religious beliefs and practices gave these people, especially the African population, the fortitude they needed to withstand the dehumanizing practices of the Europeans.[7]

The significance of faith in the life and society of Caribbean people cannot be overemphasized. Caribbean people have a heritage where faith is an integral element. This faith resides in the African heritage as expressed by African philosopher of religion, John Mbiti.

To be human is to belong to the whole community, and to do so involves participating in the beliefs, ceremonies, rituals and festivals of that community. A person cannot detach himself from the religion of his group, for to do so is be severed from his roots, his foundation, his context of security, his kinships and the entire group of those who made him aware of his own existence. To be without one of these corporate is to be out of the whole picture. Therefore, to be without religion amounts to a self-excommunication from the entire life of the society, and African peoples do not know how to exist without religion.[8]

The issue, however, is not about the contents of faith as an objective body of belief or the nature of faith as a subjective act, but a theological interpretation of the diasporan experience in light of the Christian faith. In examining this issue, I explore in this chapter how Caribbean diasporan Christians express their faith in Jesus Christ by focusing on the theological foundations of the Caribbean diasporan church. I propose two theological foundations,[9] namely: Caribbean emancipatory theology to which I give particular attention to the major classic texts,[10] and the theological doctrines of the Incarnation and the Event of Pentecost; however, attention should be given first to the significance of the theological foundations.

Theological Heritage

The theological foundations are significant because they ground the church's identity in the Christian faith and, as such, distinguish the church from other organizations. The classic texts on Caribbean emancipatory theology, for example, contain Caribbean theological history and tradition and provide the foundation for the development of a Caribbean diasporan theology. They also constitute an essential aspect of the faith that the Caribbean people brought with them to the diaspora. Writing of the significance of Caribbean theology, William Watty declares:

It is a re-orientation which has to do as much with methodology as with content. Essentially it is something which can be done only by Caribbean people, and therefore it cannot merely be a matter of exchanging an absolute theology for one which happens for the time being to be universally in vogue, but rather an inward odyssey into our peculiar heritage, predicament, and destiny.[11]

My arguing for the theological foundations of the Caribbean diasporan church is Caribbean-centered. It is, therefore, hermeneutically outside mainstream theology but, ideologically, it stands in the liberation theology tradition. With this understanding, the Caribbean experience is both at the beginning and at the center of this theology. As Noel Titus writes:

> Caribbean theology cannot be European theology, not even Third World theology. It needs to be a theology which responds to Caribbean reality. Such a theology should draw on Caribbean lore – its mythology, folk wisdom or proverbs – in order to explicate the experiences of Caribbean people in language that evokes deep responses from such people. This would mean a greater relationship between our theology and literature to enable us to discern how Caribbean people interpret their reality. And it is an aspect of our work that requires conscious and consistent effort.[12]

Caribbean theology then concurs with other liberation theologies of the importance of engaging experience in theological discourse. But Caribbean theology engages the Caribbean diaspora experience as it relates to the local and universal struggle for emancipation to constitute one of the theological foundations of the Caribbean diasporan church.

Further significance of the theological foundations of the Caribbean diasporan church resides in the dialectical nature of Caribbean Christianity. As previously discussed, diasporan life is complex and adverse. In order to survive, Caribbean people have to forge their own identities. Having explored these identities, I want to ground them theologically. In so doing, I want to demonstrate that the dialectical religious tradition is a resource for the survival of the people of the Caribbean diaspora. Caribamericans draw on this tradition as a combative and empowering resource in resisting opposition and pursuing the realization of our full humanity.

As I have discussed in the previous chapter, Caribbean Christianity is formed out of two different religions, namely African derived religions and European Christianity. The nature of Caribbean Christianity reflects the nuances in the people's life and making of their faith. Paying attention to this dialectical tradition departs from the normative practice and categories and thus provides a new paradigm for theological reflection. For this reason, I argue that the dialectical tradition in Caribbean Christianity constitutes a dimension of the theological heritage of the Caribbean diasporan church.

As to the theological foundation of the doctrines of the Incarnation and Pentecost, these serve as a theological paradigm for interpreting the Caribbean diasporan experience. These doctrines resonate with the diasporan experience, not to justify the experience but to give meaning to the diasporan experience. It is on this basis I argue that the Incarnation of Jesus Christ is a symbolic manifestation of God becoming a diasporan person and the Event of Pentecost is a contemporary expression of the Holy Spirit. Thus, these two doctrinal principles are hermeneutical tools used to interpret the Caribbean diasporan experience and identify and engage the structural and systemic issues that create diasporas. These principles also seek to not only establish communities and relationships but to eradicate and emancipate ourselves from those factors that engender division, differences and oppression. The doctrinal foundation further demonstrates how faith transcends race and culture and provides a creative response to migration which brings a new perspective to bear on the complex reality of diaspora. It is to these two theological foundations, therefore, that the discussion now turns.

Emancipatory Theology

The first theological foundation this chapter addresses is Caribbean emancipatory theology.[13] The term Caribbean emancipatory theology signifies a critical reflection on the Caribbean experience in light of the gospel of Jesus Christ. It takes very seriously the place of Caribbean people in the world as persons created in the image of God. As Ashley Smith suggests:

> Caribbean Theology is an attempt by Caribbean Christians to interpret the revelation of God within their peculiar historical, ethnic, political and cultural context.[14]

Smith's definition is especially helpful to my interpretation of Caribbean theology. I understand Caribbean theology to refer to the distinct body of theological thought that reflects our collective social and religious experiences. William Watty summarizes this perspective:

> Theology is reflection on praxis. It is the record of experience. It is an obituary of something which has already been lived out. Its concerns are not with abstractions but with concrete realities.[15]

While the above definitions signify the meaning of the term Caribbean theology, they do not describe the nature of Caribbean theology. In this regard, I shall examine three themes as essential features of Caribbean theology, namely freedom, protest, and community. This exploration probes the meaning of emancipation and attends to some of the distinctive features that are not exclusively of Caribbean origin or character but which are nonetheless the dominant features of Caribbean emancipatory theology.

Freedom

From its inception Caribbean emancipatory theology has been defined as a theology of freedom. One of the first and major texts on Caribbean emancipatory theology is Kortright Davis' *Emancipation Still Comin': Exploration in Caribbean Emancipatory Theology*. In this groundbreaking work, Davis argues that emancipation is a gift from God that we receive by faith in response to God's initiative in Jesus Christ. God calls human beings to freedom, and emancipation is the human response and acceptance of it. According to Davis:

> Emancipation as a divine activity is even more profound than psychological freedom, for it originates in the sovereign action of the God who not only creates but also recreates and sustains.[16]

Why, then, do Caribbean people understand faith as emancipatory? Emancipation is the common desire and pursuit of past and present generations of Caribbean people who are united through faith. With faith as uniting factor, there is an expression of commitment to emancipation and declaration of the end of oppression.[17] Davis persuasively states:

> Emancipation is the major thrust of Caribbean existence, however much the signs of its authenticity may be obscured. Emancipation is the common project of those whose lives have been constantly encountered by structures of poverty, dependence, alienation, and imitation. Emancipation has been the common bond that welded together Caribbean struggles for the better life – whether through education, emigration, or plain perspiration. Emancipation has been the vision of God in the context of Caribbean history; for every time the region has been written off with a sure and certain Gehenna, God seemed to answer with a greater certainty of survival and meaning for the region.[18]

The belief in freedom as the essence of Caribbean emancipatory theology is not just the assertion of a personal right or of a socio-political cause or movement as Davis would have us believe. Freedom is the tacit acceptance of emancipation as a gift and act of God for the total freedom of persons and society. In support of this perspective, Noel Erskine argues that "Black religion began the process of decolonizing theology when it insisted that God was the freeing one who was at work in history setting the victims free."[19] For Erskine, therefore, the freedom is expressed through the decolonization of theology which begins with reflection on experience in light of the gospel of Jesus Christ. He declares:

> The point of departure for reflection on a Caribbean experience will be my own background within the church in Jamaica. My theological education and life as a pastor in the church in Jamaica indicated that theology as it was practiced within the church did not address the identity problem that slavery created among Caribbean peoples. God as presented within the Caribbean church was not often the symbol of freedom but, rather the extension of the European and North

American church experience. I recall praying ..."Lord, wash me whiter than snow."... God, when understood through the medium of other people's experience, is in danger of losing identity for oppressed peoples.[20]

While Erskine's contention about the decolonization of theology is an important dimension of Caribbean emancipatory theology, he nevertheless has not adequately described the nature of Caribbean theology. His notion of decolonizing theology makes the task of decolonization reactionary and consequently puts Caribbean theology in a subordinate relationship to Euro-American theology. Since freedom is the essence of Caribbean theology, this theology therefore cannot merely react to the dominant theology because decolonization is only an aspect of Caribbean theology. Thus, I contend that Erskine's perspective of Caribbean theology attends only to the decolonization of Western theology but neither to the emancipation of the human person nor the social and systemic structures from injustice. He also gives scant attention to the contextualization of Caribbean theology.

The Caribbean theologian, Lewin Williams, describes contextualization in his book, *Caribbean Theology*. Williams seeks to decolonize theology but departs from Erskine's reactionary approach to Euro-American theology by constructing a Caribbean contextual theology.[21] The work proposes that the Caribbean experience is the basis for an authentic and relevant Caribbean theology. This, Williams demonstrates by discussing the factors and elements and offering a critical evaluation of a Caribbean theology. He writes: "The arguments range from the failure of missionary theology to address Caribbean self-development, to how theology ought to be shaped to address contextual problems."[22] He contends further:

Caribbean indigenization must find the will to re-interpret its faith so that it may rectify the lack of historicity in the reality of the reign of God and the problems of justice which arises from it.[23]

The importance of this study for the Caribbean diasporan church is to demonstrate that church comes out of a faith tradition that takes experience as a starting point for its existence. By focusing on the Caribbean context, however, Williams does not give any particular attention to either the African or Euro-American origins of the Caribbean faith. While focusing on the Caribbean is significant, his concern, however, is primarily the contemporary context. Consequently, he leaves unanswered questions about faith heritage of Caribbean people that help to define Caribbean theology. Williams' contextual theology, therefore, does not draw any theological insight from the liberative character of the Caribbean theological tradition. This then leads me to consider the issue of protest in Caribbean emancipatory theology.

Protest

Protest is an essential factor in Caribbean emancipatory theology. Providing some indications of this, Robert Stewart, in his work, *The Role of Religion in Post Emancipation Jamaica*, delineates an historical account of Caribbean emancipatory theology by examining the role of religion in the formation of identity and as an agent of protest. In doing so, he addresses the missionary work of the European church, the problems the missionaries faced and the response of the Black majority citizens.[24] According to Stewart:

> Through religion, social forms and activities were created that linked the blacks to each other, that welcomed new African arrivals, and that relegated encounters between Afro-Jamaica and Euro-Jamaica.[25]

These activities led to the creation of an alternative religion which functioned as the "basis of identity and resistance."[26]

Stewart's work is significant because he provides information about the formative years and foundation of Caribbean Christianity. For example, Stewart shows that the concern of European Christianity was for the spread of the gospel and advancement of the institutional church whose primary concern was the conversion of the non-Christian population. Expressing this perspective, Stewart suggests that:

> The main work of the missionaries was conversion, the Christianizing of slaves, and, if possible, the amelioration of master/slave relationship. But they were enjoined by their home committees from preaching abolitionism.[27]

The contents of their work were, therefore, preaching, teaching, and the observation of moral rules.[28] Stewart notes that this form of Christianity

> emphasized preaching, instruction, and observable response in word, moral behaviour, and church attendance... [They] preached the inherent depravity of humankind, a disease of heart and soul inherited from Adam's fall, which humanity could do nothing on its own to repair. To believe that any righteous act aside from the acceptance of God's forgiveness could undo that state of sin was itself the sin of pride.[29]

The response of the Caribbean Christians to this practice was not only the rejection of European Christianity but the formation of their own religion.[30] In support of this response, Stewart explains:

> The failure of white religious leadership both to penetrate and to be fully accepted in an Afro-creole world ensured that black religious culture would develop according to its own values, mores, and customs.[31]

Stewart's argument that Caribbean Christianity was formed in response to European Christianity does not mean it is a reactionary religion. Caribbean Christianity constituted an alternative to the then existing European religion and also served as a source of identity and protests against European domination.[32] Caribbean Christianity served this purpose because the Christianization of the African population in the Caribbean was not the original intent of European Christians. The intent was rather to eliminate the cosmology of the Africans which was regarded as heathen and contrary to European culture and religiosity.[33] As Brian L. Moore and Michele A. Johnson observe, the missionary response was to seek to eliminate the African derived world-view by replacing it with "new ideas about the nature of the spirit world and the nature of God."[34]

What European Christians did not realize was the incorporation of elements of African cosmology in Caribbean Christianity. As Philip Curtin observes:

> Since the whites were not anxious to force Europeanization further than was necessary for plantation work, the slaves were left to educate their own children. Consequently, there developed a new culture, compounded of the diverse African and European elements.[35]

It is this aspect of Caribbean Christianity that I maintain distinguishes European Christianity from Caribbean Christianity. This distinction is expressed through protest against oppression and injustice. The Jamaican Baptist pastor and theologian, Burchell Taylor, attempts to address this issue in his work on the life of Onesimus, "Voiceless Initiator of the Liberating Process."[36] Using Onesimus as a paradigm for emancipation, Taylor argues that his initiative as a slave to enact his emancipation is instructive and illustrative for all oppressed people. In defense of this view, Taylor states:

> He was simply not accepting slavery as something to which he must be subjected. He did not think that he was fated to be a slave by virtue of his class or any other feature of his humanity. His act of running away was protest action. It was an act of defiance and rebellion of the human spirit against oppression and indignity.[37]

In light of this emphasis, Taylor grounds a Caribbean theology in the emancipatory gospel. He gives not only a reading but a liberative account of the text. For example, Taylor's emancipatory point is premised on the life and work of Jesus Christ. On this basis, Taylor stands in the Caribbean theological heritage but he fails to acknowledge the factors that belie and warrant rebellion and protest. Taylor's interpretation, however, is an invitation to examine the factor of community formation as another aspect of Caribbean theology. In so doing, I provide another dimension to the nature of Caribbean theology as a theological foundation of the Caribbean diasporan church.

Community

Along with freedom and protest, community formation is another feature of Caribbean emancipatory theology. One expression of this feature is the formation of congregations. The work of Caribbean theologian William Watty helps us to understand this dimension of Caribbean theology.

Writing about the meaning of Caribbean emancipatory theology, Watty argues that the Exodus-event has been incorrectly used as a paradigm for liberation. It is his understanding that it has been used as a political act rather than as a communal one. It is here that I differ from Watty. He concludes that the life of Jesus and the Early Church demonstrate that liberation, as Watty uses the term, means community.[38] For Watty:

> Liberation consists in belonging to another community which both neutralizes oppressive power and refuses alliance with any worldly power by which people are oppressed… [Liberation] involves the creation of a new community, a counter-community, an anti-power, by which all forms of oppression are exposed and neutralized and from which all forms of oppression are exorcised.[39]

The church becomes this counter-cultural community through faith in Jesus Christ. Using the life of Jesus as the basis for a theology of faith, Watty asserts that through Jesus Christ the New Age or the Kingdom of God has been inaugurated. The old has passed and the new which the church represents has come.[40] For Kortright Davis, this is

> an attempt to interpret contextually the meaning of human freedom in light of a popular faith in God of Jesus Christ, whose Gospel of liberation and whose life of historical confrontation have constantly inspired and strengthened such faith.[41]

While I concur with Watty in his proposition of the church as the embodiment of the New Age that Jesus inaugurated, by de-centering the Exodus-Event he idealizes the church in that he offers no critical assessment of its practices or regard for the contextual realities. It is here I argue that the Exodus–event is a symbol of emancipation for Caribbean people. From the inception of the emancipatory movement, the oppressed have identified with the Exodus-event through their experience with the biblical Israel. The Exodus-event serves as the basis for resistance to oppression and paradigm for liberation.[42] An example of this is the emancipatory movement in Jamaica which includes the "Baptist War" of 1831 and the Morant Bay Rebellion of 1865 in Jamaica that enslaved people used both to secure their freedom and to establish a Caribbean emancipatory tradition.[43] According to Lawson:

> With this archetypal event firmly in their possession as prime motivation, they created meaning and sense out of the chaotic, brutal, corrupt and senseless experience of slavery in the Egypt of Jamaica.[44]

Thus, Watty's one-sided view of community is a partial representation of the meaning of emancipatory faith as community.

Burchell Taylor attempts to provide a more holistic perspective of community. In Taylor's discussion on the church as the community of the emancipated, he contends that the church is the framework for the realization of emancipation which includes "equality, solidarity and human dignity…"[45] He continues to argue in his essay, "The Liberated Community as Subversive and Liberating in an Unjust Society,"[46] that in the sending of Onesimus, back to his master, it was not a return to oppression but to the community of faith for acceptance as an equal which embodied the emancipatory gospel. This is an account of how the church is to live out the meaning of the gospel.[47] Taylor concludes:

> It is the community that would provide the framework for full effect of the new situation and condition. It would provide the necessary and immediate framework for the working out of the liberating practice prompted by the acceptance of Onesimus on the basis suggested.[48]

In Taylor's interpretation of the church as a community of faith, he portrays the church as an ideal society but leaves unanswered the issue of the church living in an oppressed society which would suggest that it was also an oppressed community. This perspective borders more on moralizing than presenting a critical and constructive analysis of the existential realities. The argument, however, can be made that the church represents what society ought to be and the account of Onesimus bears witness to the vision and movement towards the realization of a just society.

In this regard, Neville Callam, the Jamaica Baptist Union pastor and theologian, delineates the notion of faith as community in an article, "Ethnicity and the Church's Catholicity: Ministry to the Caribbean Diaspora in North America." Callam argues that the church is to have "a serious sense of self, space, community, mission and ecumenical commitment."[49] He proposes a theological definition of the church as community to be "an expression of the one Church which belongs to God, which is grounded in the Gospel and which expresses communion of those who live in a personal relationship with God."[50]

In Callam's perspective, the church as a community with an emancipatory faith and as a community of the emancipated is an expression of the "Triune God."[51] Therefore, he argues:

> If the church in via is to be the church, it must be a dynamic centre which affirms our creatureliness in the community of those who are made in the image of God and know that this community extends not only beyond the Church itself, but also beyond the merely human.[52]

Callam's analysis is an indispensable contribution to Caribbean diasporan ecclesiology. Yet, his perspective locates the identity of church in the doctrine of the Trinity and not in the context of the Caribbean diasporan people. Thus, his point of departure of faith is doctrinal and not the existential realities of the diasporan existence.

Katie Cannon's theological reflection on Black women in general and African American women's experience in particular, and especially Caribbean diasporan women, supports my critique of Callam's perspective of the church. Cannon writes:

> Black religion and the black church serve as a sustaining force, assuring boundless justice. During these stormy times, the Black church tradition renewed hope and strength, touching these women's lives in all their ramifications, enabling migrant women to carry on in spite of obstacles and opposition. It was the interpretive principle of the Black church that guided black women in facing life squarely, in acknowledging its raw coarseness. The White elitist attributes of passive gentleness and enervative delicacies, considered particularly appropriate to womanhood, proved nonfunctional in the pragmatic survival of Black migrant women. Cultivating conventional amenities was not a luxury afforded them. Instead, Black women were aware that their very lives depended on their being able to decipher the various sounds in the larger world, to hold in check the nightmare figures of terror, to fight for basic freedoms against the sadistic law enforcement agencies in their communities, to resist the temptation to capitulate to the demands of the status quo, to find meaning in the most despotic circumstances, and to create something where nothing existed before.[53]

Caribbean emancipatory theology is contextual and how it relates to the diasporan experience is the source for the identity of the church. This context includes the migration experience, the struggle for survival and the realties of diasporan existence. Robert Beckford describes the importance of context for Caribbean emancipatory theology in the diaspora.

> A spirituality of liberation for the Black Church must be one that is tied to its cultural context. Black expressive cultures are as diverse as they are dynamic – this is their strength. Consequently there is a rich reservoir of concepts, themes and ideas which are waiting to be used in the struggle for justice.[54]

This approach is characteristic of contemporary Black theology[55] in Black British society. If context is limited to one's own and the basis for understanding the world, then that engenders a false sense of superiority and ultimately leads to parochialism. James Cone warns Black theologians against committing this fatal error. According to Cone:

> When people can no longer listen to other people's stories, they become enclosed within their own social context, treating their own distorted visions of reality as the truth. And then they feel that they must destroy other stories, which bear witness that life can be lived in another way.[56]

Social context must be regarded as part of the reality of the Black diasporan family and which should be understood in relationship to the universal struggle for emancipation. Contextual faith and theology are connected to and are in the tradition of emancipation established by Marcus Garvey, Claude McKay, C. L. R. James and others who have constructed a philosophical framework that regards the Black diaspora as one.[57] Nevertheless, if this theology is limited to the Black struggle, it would still be parochial and provincial. It must be understood, even judged, in light of the history and tradition of the Christian faith.[58]

A critical contradiction emerges in that the interpretation of the Caribbean diasporan church, as an expression of this tradition, does not take the context of the people seriously enough to be a source for theological reflection. Nevertheless, this neglect provides an invitation to attend to the important aspect of the dialectical religious tradition of the Caribbean diasporan church.

The Doctrinal Foundation

In this chapter, so far, attention has been given to Caribbean emancipatory theology as a theological foundation of the Caribbean diasporan church. In continuing the discussion, I will now consider the doctrinal foundation of the Incarnation and the Event of Pentecost. The discussion considers these two doctrinal beliefs to be diasporan events and, as such, they serve as a theological framework for interpreting the Caribbean diasporan experience. From this perspective, the discussion begins with the doctrine of the Incarnation of Jesus Christ and is followed by a discussion of the Event of Pentecost.

The Incarnation of Jesus Christ

The general understanding of the Incarnation of Jesus Christ is a theological construct to demonstrate the humanity of God or God becoming human.[59] Black theology, in particular, affirms this classic theological interpretation but at the same time departs from this perspective by asserting that the work of the church is to continue the Incarnation of Jesus Christ. The leading proponent of this view is the African American theologian, J. Deotis Roberts, who delineates this understanding in his classic book, *The Prophethood of Black Believers: An African American Political Theology for Ministry*.[60] In this work, Roberts grounds the ministry of the church on the Incarnation by focusing on the priestly, prophetic and public aspects of Jesus' ministry.[61] For Roberts, Jesus is the model of the church's ministry and, as such, the purpose of the church is to continue the ministry of Jesus in the world. Roberts asserts:

> The church that Jesus founded is an extension of the incarnation. Jesus is viewed by Christians as God's supreme salvific revelation to humans through fleshly and historical embodiment. The church is the means by which that revelation is manifest in community and throughout history. This being so, the church becomes important as the context of ministry. It is through the church's mission and ministry that God's will is to be done on earth.[62]

While affirming the centrality of the Incarnation in theology in general and Black theology in particular, a Caribbean diasporan perspective maintains that the Incarnation is a diasporan event. This perspective signifies a departure from Roberts' perspective which limits the meaning of the Incarnation to the function of the church. Thus, the Incarnation is a basis of constructing diasporan theological self-understanding. The Christian Scripture states:

> In the Beginning was the Word, and the Word was with God and the Word was God. He was with God in the beginning… The Word became flesh and made his dwelling among us. We have seen his glory, the glory of the One and Only, who came from the Father, full of grace and truth (Jn 1:1-2, 14; NIV).

This declaration raises two issues for the study. One is that God acted on God's own accord. God took the initiative to enter human history. The biblical witness states: "But God demonstrates his own love for us in this: While we were still sinners he died for us" (Rom. 5:8; NIV).

The second is that Jesus was a particular human being. He was incarnated in a particular gender, nationality and ethnicity. Thus, he was male, Jewish and Black.[63] The issue is that the Incarnation expresses the particularity of faith and of human existence including the totality of social and existential situations that constitute the nature of life in a particular context. With this understanding, I contend that the Incarnation concerns the meaning of Jesus Christ for the Caribbean diaspora. Another way of stating this is to ask the questions, what does Jesus Christ mean for us and how does he reveal himself to us today in our social and historical situation?

As discussed earlier, the Incarnation of Jesus Christ is a symbolic expression of diasporan experience. It involves movement, exile, longing for home and formation of identity, as the term diaspora indicates. It is a movement, even dispersal, from eternal existence to earthly existence. Also, the Incarnation involves a change in identity from divine to human, as Paul argues, in what theologians define as the "kenosis."[64] In expressing this understanding of God becoming human in Jesus Christ, Paul writes:

> Who, being in very nature God, did not consider equality with God something to be grasped, but made himself nothing, taking the very nature of a human servant

being made in human likeness. And being found in appearance as a man, he
humbled himself and became obedient to death – even the death of the cross
(Phil. 2:6-8, NIV).

While theologians and New Testament scholars are still debating the
meaning of this idea of the Incarnation of Jesus Christ, the general
understanding is that God became human in Jesus of Nazareth and through
him humans can encounter God. The New Testament scholar Fred
Craddock offers a valuable perspective. After discussing the idea of the
pre-existence, existence and post-existence of Jesus Christ, Craddock
notes:

> Because in Jesus of Nazareth they experienced God, the Christians used pre-
> existence as one way of saying that in the very human, crucified Nazarene they
> had encountered a reality beyond all contingencies of time, place and history.[65]

Craddock's claim does not directly relate to the Caribbean diasporan
experience but it lends support to the Incarnation as a diasporan act. His
view indicates further how the Incarnation can be used as a symbol for
interpreting the contextual manifestation of God in human history.

The prophetic writings further attest to this assertion. These writings
acknowledge Jesus as the Emmanuel, which means God with us.
"Therefore the Lord himself shall give you a sign...," according to the
prophet Isaiah, "and will call him Immanuel" (Isa. 7:14; NIV). The Christian
Scripture identifies this person as Jesus. According to the "Birth Narratives":

> This was how the birth of Jesus Christ came about... All this took place to fulfill
> what the Lord had said through the prophet: "The virgin will be child and will
> give birth to a son, and they will call him Emmanuel – which means God with us"
> (Matt. 1:18-23; NIV).

The migration Jesus experienced is another way in which the Incarnation
of Jesus Christ can be perceived as a diasporan event. The Scriptural
testimony states that immediately after Jesus' birth, he migrated to Egypt.
In giving his account of this significant event, the Gospel writer states:
"When they had gone, the angel of the Lord appeared to Joseph in a
dream. 'Get up,' he said, 'take the child and his mother and escape to
Egypt...'" (Matt. 2:13). After a period of time, Jesus and his family
journeyed from Egypt back to their home country. The biblical record
declares: "After Herod died, an angel of the Lord appeared in a dream to
Joseph in Egypt and said, 'Get up, take the child and his mother and go to
the land of Israel'" (Matt. 3:19ff). In this respect, the Incarnation symbolizes
the diasporan experience. Through this experience, the Caribbean diaspora
can identify with Jesus Christ and use the Incarnation as a framework for
providing meaning for their lives.

In fact, I argue that Jesus identifies with the Caribbean diaspora in the particularities of their existence, which, in this case, is the Caribbean diasporan experience. Thus, the Caribbean diaspora, for example, can understand the diasporan experience as a revelation of God in history. Otherwise put, it is who God is that is being revealed through the particularities and specificities of the Caribbean diasporan experience. As such, the experience is not only a socio-political phenomenon but rather can be recognized as the context in which we discover how God becomes human. William Watty attests to this claim:

> In the Caribbean [diasporan] context we will discover Him when we take seriously those historical forces which have made us a unique people with a particular culture, when we explore the significance of our racial differences…our religious inheritance, our community consciousness, the value we place on our past and our place in the world… We must also try to understand the social and economic forces which have given rise to these characteristics, and ask which of them are for our good and must therefore be consolidated and enhanced and which caricature our human dignity and must therefore be exorcised and be renounced.[66]

The Event of Pentecost

The Event of the Day of Pentecost is the other doctrine of faith that constitutes the doctrinal foundation of the Caribbean diasporan theological foundation. This Event of Pentecost is significant not only because it is a diasporan act but it also provides a theological framework for interpreting the Caribbean diasporan experience. In this regard, the Event of Pentecost attempts to answer the question: who are the people of God today? It considers the faith, scattering, struggles, diversity and formation of churches among the Caribbean diaspora. Thus, I argue that the Caribbean diasporan church is a contemporary manifestation of the Event of Pentecost.

Pentecost was originally a Jewish harvest festival known as the Feast of Weeks. It took place at the end of their harvest where they brought their offerings of bread and animals as expressions of gratitude to God according to their religious laws (Exod. 25:16; Lev. 23:15-21; Num. 28:26; Deut. 16:9-12; NIV). Following the destruction of the first temple in 586 BCE, this festival eventually developed into a celebration for the giving of the Law. The people believed the Law reveals God's character and will, which ultimately lead into a covenantal relationship with God.[67] In the Christian tradition, this is a revelation of God through the Holy Spirit based on Jesus Christ and, though faith in him, leads to the formation of a new community as God's people.

This historical meaning of Pentecost is not how it is understood in Black theology. In Black theology, Pentecost is understood primarily both as a movement and as an experience with the Holy Spirit. As a movement, it is described as "Pentecostalism" and as an experience, the emphasis is on speaking in tongues or Baptism of the Holy Spirit. In defining Black theology's meaning of Pentecost, Black British theologian, Robert Beckford, asserts:

> Black Pentecostal churches are churches with distinctive Black Pentecostal roots (origins) and routes (developments)… Pentecostalism is a movement consisting of many denominations. The common experience of all Black Pentecostal churches…is the baptism of the Spirit.[68]

Beckford's interpretation of the Event of Pentecost is one view of the meaning of Pentecost, but it is a generalization of the identity of the church. His definition identifies the Black church with Black Pentecostalism and the experience of the Spirit. While these two events are essential to the identity of the church, a distinction must be made between them and the church. Put differently, Pentecostalism and the Baptism of the Holy Spirit are not the church. He furthermore follows in the pattern of J. Deotis Roberts concerning the Incarnation of Jesus Christ by limiting the interpretation of the Event of Pentecost to the function of the church. Beckford demonstrates this in his discussion on Black Pentecostalism. He argues that the function of Black Pentecostalism is that of a counter-cultural community, the bearer of identity and means of self-actualization.[69]

Beckford, however, departs from Roberts' pattern by expounding the emancipatory dimension of the Event of Pentecost which Roberts, in his treatment of the Incarnation, omits. Beckford attributes the emancipatory dimension of Black Pentecostalism to the notion "Dread."[70] He writes, "Naturally, dread within Black Pentecostalism is that which displays emancipatory fulfillment."[71]

In Beckford's interpretation of Pentecost, he identifies and roots the church in the Pentecostal experience but not in the Event of Pentecost as a diasporan act. This act, I argue, constitutes one of the doctrinal premises of the Caribbean diasporan church. In the first place, like the Incarnation, the Event of Pentecost is a gift from God. Luke, the gospel writer, asserts this understanding. In his response to the question of the meaning of Pentecost he states:

> …what shall we do? Peter replied, Repent and be baptized, every one of you, in the name of Jesus for the forgiveness of your sins. And you will receive the gift of the Holy Spirit. The promise is for you and your children and for all who are far off – for all whom the Lord will call (Acts 2:38–40; Joel 2:28-32; NIV).

Interestingly, there is a similar understanding of salvation. For St. Paul,

> Because of his great love for us, God, who is rich in mercy, made us alive in Christ even when we were dead in transgressions – it is by grace you are saved…through faith – and this is not from your selves, it is the gift of God… (Eph. 2:4-10; Gal. 4:26-29; NIV).

God gave this gift at the birth of the church on the Day of Pentecost, which is believed to be the historical birthday of the church made of people from diverse origins[72] similar to the nature of the Caribbean diasporan community.

In the second instance, like the Incarnation, the Event of Pentecost is a diasporan act. Pentecost was an annual celebrative gathering of the Jewish diaspora in Jerusalem who were dispersed throughout the Roman Empire. The Spirit of God that breathed life to create the universe was the same Spirit that was operative on the Day of Pentecost. Giving an account of this act, Luke reports:

> When the day of Pentecost came, they were all together in one place. Suddenly a sound like the blowing of a violent wind came from heaven and filled the whole house where they were sitting... All of them were filled with the Holy Spirit... Now there [sic] were staying in Jerusalem God fearing Jews from every nation under heaven... (Acts 2:1-42; NIV).

As this newly formed community of Christ followers grew and became a distinct community of faith, they got a new identity. They were described as a commonwealth (Eph. 2:12; NIV), race, nation and people (1 Pet. 2:9-10). The idea of a distinct identity finds ultimate expression in the eschatological vision of their nature and destiny. The writer of the Apocalypse of Revelation gives the following account.

> After this I looked and there before me was a great multitude that no one could count, from every nation, tribe, people and language, standing before the throne and in front of the Lamb (Rev. 7:9ff; NIV).

This account is a testimony of the diversity of biblical faith. It is a diversity not only according to the social locations but also according to ethnicities, nationalities, races and cultures.[73] As indicated through the Pentecost Event, the Spirit of God sets in motion an explosion of the creation of new and distinct communities of faith which I maintain the Caribbean diasporan church symbolizes.

As a contemporary manifestation of the Event of Pentecost, the Caribbean diasporan church grows and becomes a distinct community of faith made out of a diverse people. This distinct community is no less or more than what God has done in history through the Incarnation of Jesus Christ and the Event of Pentecost. Attesting to this is the maxim "All o' we is one,"[74] the Caribbeanization of Jamaica's motto, "Out of many, one people"[75] and the guiding philosophy of Marcus Garvey's United Negro Improvement Association, "One God! One Aim! One Destiny!"[76]

These expressions, in addition, underscore and inform the quest to forge communal existence out of the crucible of diasporan experience that the Caribbean diasporan church represents. Furthermore, the same Spirit that created the biblical community of faith is the same Spirit at work in the creation of the Caribbean diasporan church. The biblical testimony affirms this act.

> Brothers, you know that some time ago God made a choice among you that the Gentiles might hear from my lips the message of the gospel and believe. God who knows the heart showed that he accepted them by giving the Holy Spirit to them, just as he did to us. He made no distinction between us and them for he purified their hearts by faith... Now we believe it is through the grace of our Lord that we are saved, just as they are saved (Acts 15:7-9, 11; NIV).

This idea is advancing the belief that work of the Spirit is not limited to one person, people and place. Consider, for example, the case in Galatia. Paul informed the Galatians that the same Spirit that was working in the "super-apostles" was the same Spirit working in his ministry as well. He states; "For God who was at work in the ministry of Peter as an apostle to the Jews, was also at work in my ministry as an apostle to the Gentiles" (Gal. 2:8; NIV). It is this same understanding of faith, I argue, that applies to the Caribbean diasporan church. Thus, we can conclude that the doctrines of the Incarnation of Jesus Christ and Event of Pentecost constitutes one of the theological foundations of Caribbean diasporan ecclesiology.

Conclusion

In this chapter, I examine the theological foundations of the Caribbean diasporan church. The discussion demonstrates that the Caribbean diasporan church originates out of an emancipatory theological heritage. The central argument is that the Christian religion and faith which the Caribbean people brought with them into the diaspora affirm that they are a completely emancipated people. The Caribbean diasporan church premised their faith on this emancipatory theological heritage. This heritage consists of Caribbean emancipatory theology and the doctrines of the Incarnation of Jesus Christ and the Event of Pentecost.

What this discussion further demonstrates is that the Caribbean diasporan church has its own distinct tradition of faith. It is this tradition that the church must allow to define and to form its identity and not that which has been borrowed from sources alien and different from its own. If the Caribbean diasporan church is going to be a prophetic and emancipatory community of faith, then it must cultivate, nurture and utilize a theology born out of its own history and heritage as a resource to provide an authentic faith and to emerge as an autonomous emancipatory ecclesiastical community of faith. This task is what constitutes the theological development of the Caribbean diasporan church which forms the discussion for the next two chapters.

6 Pilgrims from the Sun: The Quest for Survival

As previously discussed, this study seeks to construct a theology for the Caribbean diasporan church. In moving forward, this chapter and the one that follows are attempts to provide an overview of the theological development of the Caribbean diasporan church. In this chapter, I trace the theological development of the Caribbean diasporan church by examining the theological self-understanding that undergirds the church's formation. For the purpose of clarity, I want it to be known that my primary concern is not the important issue of identity and mission of the church, but the theological meaning of the diasporan experience. As such, I give attention to the notion of the particular social context of the Caribbean diaspora, with specific consideration to the relationship between faith and social context so as to identify the theology that emerges out of such context.

In this regard, theologian James Cone, arguing about the relationship between faith and social context, in his classic work, *God of the Oppressed,* asserts that there is an inseparable relationship between social context and theology. "Whatever people think about God, Jesus Christ and the Church," according to Cone, "cannot be separated from their own social and political status in a given society."[1] This does not mean, however, that the faith and the context are one and the same thing. For Cone, they are two different realities but they operate in a dialectical relationship.[2]

Expressing a similar understanding of the meaning of being the church, Black British theologian, Robert Beckford, in his controversial text, *Dread and Pentecostal: A Political Theology for the Black Church in Britain,* insists that theology, and especially Black theology, must take very seriously its social context. "Interpretation in the Black Church," Beckford argues, "does not occur in a vacuum."[3] Beckford, however, departs from Cone regarding the nature of the relationship between theology and context. Whereas Cone regards this relationship as dialectical, Beckford regards it as intertextual. He explains:

> Although many testimonies and songs mention the guidance of the Holy Spirit or influence of Jesus today, a complex process of interpretation is going on. Such is the level of intertextuality that it is difficult to identify where the primary influence is found.[4]

There is, for Beckford, no single factor that shapes theological understanding, but a combination of existential realities that result directly from the diasporan experience such as displacement, alienation, marginalization, despair and other related issues.

The contention is that social context is essential to Black theology because context influences the forms that embody, symbolize and express theological ideas. Both in Cone's dialectical approach and Beckford's intertextual approach there is an oversight of the theological presuppositions that are brought to the context. The social context is the text and meaning created through the interaction between the text and these theological presuppositions. Implicit in this presupposition is a belief in and prior experience of God. The faith practitioner, in other words, comes to the context with a prior meaning of God as was discussed in the previous chapter.

The pre-existing meaning is the concept of God that the believer brought with him or her to a new situation. This meaning is as important as the social context. The interaction between faith and social context, whether this is dialectical or intertextual, occurs within a context. If this context is what defines the meaning of being the church, then being church would be relative and would bear no relationship to the larger community of faith. Since a prior belief is brought to the social context which interacts with this context to construct meaning, this indicates that the constructed meaning is larger than itself and belongs to a reality beyond itself. This leads to the conclusion that the relationship between faith and social context is meta-contextual indicating that the church belongs to something larger as well as beyond itself. Petrine theology expresses it well. "But you are a ...people belonging to God..." (1Pet. 2:9; NIV).

In like manner, the Caribbean diasporan church belongs to God – a Reality larger than and beyond the church itself. However, a particular social context shapes the identity of the church. At the same time, the church came to the diasporan context with a particular self-understanding. Caribbean diasporan Christians came to the new resident country, the particular social context, with the understanding of being pilgrims, which defines the beginning or the formative years of the diaspora. With this perspective, I use in this chapter the term "pilgrim" to define the earliest theological development of the Caribbean diasporan church. In so doing, I argue that Caribbean diasporan experience can be interpreted as a pilgrimage that the people expressed through religious relationships in communities of faith. Advancing this argument, I examine the context and suggest three possible interpretations of the pilgrim paradigm as constitutive elements of the theological beginnings of the Caribbean diaspora. Both the context and these three issues are considered in turn.

Context

The development of a Caribbean diasporan ecclesiology began in a hostile and changing environment. These hostilities and changes define the social context in which the church forms its identity. The factors of the social context are racism, the relationship between Caribbeaners[5] and African Americans (a family feud), travel and changing immigration laws.

Racism is one of the factors that shaped the social context of newly arrived Caribbean immigrants. Describing this context, historian Winston James calls it a "Mid-night."[6] In his *Holding Aloft the Banner of Ethiopia*, he contends that this new society was racist.[7] When Caribbean people started to migrate to the United States of America during the early twentieth century, racism was legalized by the American government. The ideology of racism was practiced through the doctrine of "separate but equal" as the legal policy of the land enacted in the infamous law, *Plessy vs. Ferguson*.[8] This treatment of fellow human beings was not only new but strange to the Caribbeaners. While they might have been aware of segregation prior to their migration to the new resident home, they were not expecting it as a national policy.

Caribbeaners encountered this experience not only in the general society but in the church, the one institution that they felt should offer and promote equality.[9] The reality of this policy and its effects on Black life are major factors that led to Caribbeaners, such as Hubert Harrison, Richard Moore, Marcus Garvey and others, who James calls radicals, to seek greater involvement in American public life. They immersed themselves in the quest for justice in order to transform the society. "Without doubt, then," James writes, "the midnight darkness of the moment in which these migrants from the islands entered the country contributed to the speed and depth of their radicalization in America."[10]

The tension between African Americans and Caribbeaners is a second factor that shaped the context of the development of Caribbean diasporan ecclesiology. Although this issue received considerable attention by other scholars and this study has addressed it in an earlier chapter, it is important, nevertheless, to mention that this sibling rivalry existed and it is a part of the Caribbean diaspora's existence and history.

Reflecting on this issue, Heather Hathaway, in her pioneering study on the Black diaspora in American society, *Caribbean Waves*, provides an examination of the historical context that shaped the theological development of the Caribbean diaspora church. She notes a number of factors that contributed to the strained relationship between both groups of people. These include competition for the same limited employment opportunities, differences in education, skills and experiences, social status and political ideology.[11] Hathaway writes:

The ethnic and national differences between African Americans and African Caribbeaners became vital issues for the black American community overall as inter-racial tensions led at times to the fragmentation of a united black effort toward obtaining equal rights for the race as a whole.[12]

This fragmented nature of the relationship between these two Black communities, however, indicates that they are different from each other and so this difference is an expression of the diversity of the Black community. It can also be said that the coming of the Caribbeaners to America, though met with hostilities and difficulties, was a meeting of the family, the beginning of a family reunion. For example, Caribbeaners and African Americans were probably meeting each other for the first time because neither had previously visited each other's country or had any previous contact or relationship.

Facilitating this reunion were the opportunity to travel and changing immigration laws. These constituted additional factors that shaped the context of Caribbean diasporan theological development. Although migration between the Caribbean and the United States was taking place from the late nineteenth century, the Caribbean population in America was too small and dispersed to form any organized community[13] and to create a diaspora. The premier Black newspaper, The *New York Amsterdam News*, reported that slaveholding United States citizens bought and brought to New York enslaved humans from the then British and Danish colonies of the Caribbean.[14] It was not until the 1890s with the beginning of the banana trade between the Caribbean and the United States that migration led to the beginning of the Caribbean diaspora in America.

In 1924, the United States enacted legislation that restricted migration. This new law and subsequent ones constitute the fourth factor that shaped the context of the theological development of the Caribbean diasporan church. Migration patterns occurred in three periods. The first period began in 1899 with the beginning of the migration to the United States and ended with the anti-immigration law of 1924.[15] During this time there was a steady and consistent movement of people between the Caribbean and the United States but it was radically curtailed by the new immigration policy. According to the immigration records, a total of 412 new people arrived in the United States and by 1924, there were approximately 12,500 of them.[16]

The second period took place between 1924 and 1965. This was a period of minimum migration to the United States. During this forty-year period approximately 2 million people migrated.[17] Taking place during this period were events such as the economic hardships caused by the Great Depression of the 1930s, the devastating aftermath of the First World War, the anti-immigration policy of the 1952 McCarren-Walter Act and the 1962 Commonwealth Act of Great Britain.

The McCarren-Walter Immigration Act, for example, was undoubtedly designed to limit and control the Caribbean migratory process. The law permitted 100 persons from each Caribbean country to migrate annually to the United States. During this period of hostility, the pattern of migration shifted from the United States to Great Britain but was practically terminated by the 1962 Commonwealth Act which restricted Commonwealth immigration.[18]

The Caribbean diaspora in the United States experienced very little growth during this second period of migration. Because the restrictions limited the number of people who could emigrate, this severely impacted the diaspora's numerical composition while also conversely influencing its structural development. The nature of the Caribbean diaspora, therefore, changed the perspective of their self-understanding. For example, it was incumbent on Caribbean people, finding themselves in a new environment, becoming increasingly involved and settled in society and starting to rear families, to consolidate themselves in the host country and defer the dream of returning home as planned.[19]

Writing of the diaspora in the British context, Joel Edwards defines this era (1924–65) as the period of consolidation. Edwards correctly observes that this was the time when the Caribbean diasporan church grew. Families were reunited and individuals secured their own accommodation. The original intent of these Caribbean migrants was to achieve their goal of earning enough money so that they could return to their home country. They, however, were soon to discover that such a goal was unrealistic. The realization that their residence both in Britain and America would be more permanent than they originally thought was one of the contributing factors for establishing communities of faith or churches.[20]

A third period began with the Hart-Cellar Act of 1965.[21] This law represented a shift in United States immigration policy. The Hart-Cellar Act rescinded the restrictions of the 1924 and 1952 Acts, replaced them with new provisions and increased the number of Caribbean people who could emigrate to the United States. An annual quota of approximately 20,000 persons from each Caribbean country was permitted to migrate. This immediately increased the numerical composition of the diaspora. It also changed the diaspora's self-understanding and engendered further development. Residents could sponsor their family members to live in the country, the government encouraged naturalization of these non-citizens and they also pursued civic involvement.[22]

The period from 1899 to 1965 was characterized by varying patterns of growth in the Caribbean diaspora's population. This population was too small and dispersed to make any significant impact on the society or function as a distinct community in relationship to the larger society. Thus, the Caribbean diaspora was not only an invisible community[23] but it lacked the numerical, economic and political power to influence public policies.

The emergence of the Caribbean diasporan ecclesiology took place in the context of racial adversity, changing migration policies and limited growth of the migrant population. This context of the Caribbean diaspora, I argue, marks the beginning of the theological development of the Caribbean diasporan church which I define as the pilgrim stage. It is to the meaning of this self-understanding, then, that we direct our attention.

A Pilgrim People: Interpreting the Caribbean Diasporan Church Beginnings

What does it mean to be a pilgrim as it relates to the Caribbean diasporan experience? The Caribbean diaspora is historically and generally understood as a migratory movement of pilgrim people.[24] I use the term pilgrim to define the first period of Caribbean migration based on the people's belief of living away from their homeland for a temporary duration. Caribbean people did not migrate to reside permanently in a foreign county. They migrated with the intention to achieve their goals of an education and enough money to purchase a home and care for their family and then return to their native home after a maximum time of five years.[25] Using the pilgrim paradigm as the framework for the theological interpretation of the Caribbean diasporan experience, I am proposing three primary theological interpretations of the experience; namely, a search for a better life, a search for respect and a search for community. These are considered accordingly.

The Search for a Better Life

The search for a better life is one of the theological interpretations of the Caribbean diasporan experience that the pilgrim paradigm symbolizes to constitute an aspect of the church's theological development. Ransford W. Palmer's interpretive study on Caribbean migration, *Pilgrims from the Sun: West Indian Migration to America*, provides insight into this phenomenon. Palmer argues that Caribbean migration is one of the results of slavery, but he suggests that the motivation for migration resides in the desire for a better quality of life. These Caribbean migrants wanted employment and opportunities to provide a better quality of life for themselves and their families. This better life included owning a house and obtaining an education.[26] Attesting to this assertion, Palmer writes, "Thus the willingness to sacrifice leisure for work and the present for the future has been a powerful force behind the advancement of West Indian as a group."[27]

The search for a better life did not begin with Caribbean migration to America. It began from the first act of rebellion against oppression. Palmer concurs: "...the history of Caribbean migration up to WW II was essentially a history of the flight from the legacy of slavery. Colonial capitalism was unprepared to provide the region's freed labor with a decent livelihood."[28] This search for a better life, therefore, is part of the Caribbean migration tradition. It is a continuous struggle for emancipation and one of the means of coping with the inherited dependency on colonial capitalism and United States imperialism.

Reflecting on this search reveals the nature of the struggle of the Caribbean diaspora and the need for the church to be identified with the cause of the victims of history and the exploited. Palmer, however, does not deal with the meaning of the diasporan experience beyond the scope of the social and material world. For him, the better life is limited to material prosperity expressed in Caribbeaners' goal of home ownership and obtaining an education.[29] These are specific manifestations of materialistic purpose which attest to Palmer's understanding of the church as merely a social institution. Palmer has very little to say on this topic, as indicated in the following statement.

> The church has played an important role in the life of the West Indian community. In the early days, many who were Catholics met and organized social events... It was from these meetings that the West Indian Social Club emerged.[30]

With particular reference to the meaning of the pilgrim metaphor as a search for a better life, Palmer's perspective is, therefore, limited to a materialistic interpretation of the diasporan experience and social function of the church. An alternative to this perspective is offered by Bonham C. Richardson. He agrees that the Caribbean diasporan experience is a search for a better life but he does not understand it as a wholly social and materialistic pursuit. He understands the search of a better life as an inherent act of protest or resistance against that which oppresses. Recognizing the origin of Caribbean migration in slavery, Richardson argues that "the need to resist, to escape, and generally to assert individual freedom – needs thwarted throughout slavery – could be expressed by going away."[31] Palmer's perspective, however, represents the historical and social realities that shape the meaning of the experience. It expresses, also, the social dimension of this pattern of theological thinking. While Richardson provides an ideological interpretation of migration, which, understood theologically, is an emancipatory act, Palmer articulates the social content of Caribbean diasporan ecclesiology which limits the church to a mere social institution.

The Search for Respect

The term pilgrim also represents a search for respect as a second theological interpretation of the Caribbean diasporan experience. While Palmer understands the Caribbean diasporan experience as a search for a better life, Kortright Davis, professor of theology at Howard University, understands this experience as a search for respect.[32] He states:

> The Caribbean spirit abroad is always in search of something more than it was often possible to realize at home. But that search is never to be understood in terms of an external exile, or burning of bridges left behind, or even of a rupture of roots and origins which give character and purpose to that searching spirit. The spirit is abroad in search of respect, respect for itself, respect for its stature, for its home and its origins, respect for its formative institutions and cultural values, respect for its way of life and its vision for the future, for the full recognition and acceptance by other spirits of what the Caribbean spirit abroad has to offer to the common good of the whole social order.[33]

The church is what sustains and nurtures the Caribbean diaspora as it is the means of maintaining a sense of purpose and accountability. As such, the church is the primary means through which this purpose is fulfilled. This is what Davis means by stating:

> When we therefore attempt to make an analysis of what it is that keeps the Caribbean spirit alive in North America, we dare not ignore the fact that it is much more than the bright light, fast cars, and the little pots of gold just barely within our grasp or barely within our reach. It is a fertile and integrative force of spiritual, cultural, and socio-economic geography, which not only gives us a sacred sense of challenge and opportunity, but also keeps us focused on why we are here, and what we are expected to accomplish.[34]

The church lives out this self-understanding in three ways. Davis describes these ways as syndromes or responses to the diasporan experience. He locates this in the biblical tradition using the biblical figures of Abraham, Nehemiah and Jeremiah. The Abrahamic tradition (Gen. 12-25:11; NIV) is that of preserving human life after leaving one's home and place of origin. The Nehemiahic tradition (Neh. 1-13; NIV) is about prospering in the host country, while there is an active interest and involvement in the welfare of the homeland. The Jeremiahic tradition (Jer. 29:4-7; NIV) is that of establishing roots and becoming involved in the affairs of the host country. It is a matter of making the host country home.[35] These three syndromes, according to Davis, operate simultaneously in the Caribbean diasporan church "as a centrifugal force and makes the quest for respect become more urgent."[36]

The above mentioned biblical figures were pilgrims although they became so under different circumstances but they were not seeking respect[37] as Davis argues. In the biblical tradition, pilgrims are people of faith responding to God's call. Regarding the Caribbean people, if respect is what Caribbean diasporan Christians seek, then it means they are seeking to be validated by others and have not fully accepted themselves and would therefore not be pilgrims in the biblical tradition. Caribbean Christians, however, ground their lives as pilgrims in the emancipatory gospel of Jesus Christ. Jesus is the great emancipator who liberates from all that oppresses and has fully restored our full humanity so that we can be our authentic selves. This emancipation is about God's acceptance (Eph. 1:6; NIV) and justification of all persons through faith (Rom. 5:1ff; NIV).

The Caribbean diasporan church affirms that God entered human history through Jesus Christ not only to emancipate from sin and oppression but also to destroy and defeat the powers that oppress. The power of lack of self-respect has been broken and Caribbean Christians must believe that this liberation is taking place in their present situation. In a world where the Black self is devalued, the good news is that oppression has been defeated and the Black self is to be accepted and affirmed.[38] What God has done historically though Jesus Christ is being realized in the daily experience of Caribbean Christians who accept their emancipation as God's new people (2 Cor. 5:17; NIV) who are called into freedom. According to the New Testament, "It is for freedom that Christ has set us free. Stand firm then, and do not let yourself be burdened again by a yoke of bondage" (Gal. 5:1; NIV). Using the pilgrim paradigm, the Christians of the Caribbean diaspora express their freedom through their affiliation with other communities of faith.

The Search for Community

The search for community is the third theological interpretation of the Caribbean diasporan experience as a pilgrimage. This was the practice of seeking a community of faith to which they could belong as members. This membership was realized in two ways, namely, through individual and congregational affiliation. The former refers to the membership of an individual in a local church and the latter refers to the membership of a local church in a denominational church.

Individual Affiliation

I noted earlier that Caribbean Christians migrated with the intention of obtaining a better life and then returning to their homeland. Those who regarded themselves as Christians joined existing churches and, as a people without social organization or a social home, they viewed becoming affiliated with existing churches, especially those with whom they had prior relationship, as their most natural option. The practice of becoming members in these churches was done as a temporary measure and as an expression of their faith since these Caribbean Christians did not plan to remain permanently in the resident country. In one of the earliest works on Caribbean immigrants, the sociologist Ira Reid observes in his *Negro Immigrant* that Caribbean immigrants became members of the churches in their community[39] particularly the historic denominational churches such as the Anglican, Baptist, Methodist, Moravian and Presbyterian.[40] This resulted from a pre-existing relationship with the church in their homeland. It was not uncommon, therefore, for individuals, upon on entering the country to attend and become members of one of their affiliated churches. For example, during the 1930s, some Caribbean Christians became members of the Brooklyn Heights Holy Trinity Episcopalian Church, in Brooklyn, New York. The relationship, however, was brief because the leadership of the church consigned them to the section designated for Blacks. This was a rude awakening for Caribbean Christians to racism and segregation in God's house. Caribbean diasporan Christians, therefore, rejected this form of Christian practice by seeking membership of a Black church,[41] although the experience was similar in some African American churches.[42]

Additionally, affiliation was practiced through leadership. Caribbean diasporan clergy pastored African American congregations. Watkins-Owens gives the following account of Caribbean clergy who were members of and worked in African American congregations:

> In September 1900, the Bishop of New England Conference of A. M. E. Church was a West Indian, the presiding elder was a West Indian, the secretary was a West Indian, the pastor of Ford Chapel, Newport, Rhode, Island was a West Indian, the pastor of the second largest A. M. E. Church was a West Indian, and the pastor of the much sought after Church in Greenwich, Connecticut was a West Indian...[43]

Watkins-Owens is seeking to demonstrate that Caribbean diasporan pastors were in many positions of leadership in the church and probably wielded influence. It further reflects the importance of church membership to the Caribbean diasporan people.

Individual affiliation was the best available option for acclimatization to the new society. The church served as the major agent of socialization to new society. Writing of this process, and of the pivotal role of the church, Ira Reid states: "Religion and the church are the last bulwark of the Negro immigrant traditional systems."[44] These Caribbean immigrants went through a process of organization of their status in order to adjust to the new environment. In most cases, the immigrant comes from a society where one is a member of the majority population and is now a member of the minority.[45] Winston James, writing on the role of Caribbean diaspora in the American context, concurs with Reid on this issue. James regards this as one of the strengths of the Caribbean immigrants that distinguishes this community from the Black diaspora in general. He states:

> The black migrants from the Caribbean entered the United States with what we may describe as a majority consciousness; that is, they were accustomed, for the most part, to negotiating a world in which they constituted the overwhelming majority of the population.[46]

In this remark, James is seeking to point out that Caribbeaners came from a society where they were not only members of the majority culture, but where the civic, social, religious and political leadership constituted of people who looked like them. This was unlike the situation in the resident country. The majority consciousness of Caribbeaners gave them a sense of identity and pride that enabled them to deal with oppressive and dehumanizing forces such as racial inferiority. Lennox Raphael, reflecting on Caribbeaners' consciousness, attests to my claim. He notes that Caribbeaners are constituted "with a sense of identity and pride, real at times, and a pride in himself, along with the ability to ignore the white man while accepting him as a fellow competitor, but not as an ethnically superior human being."[47]

This focus on accommodation, however, does not take into account the faith of the people and their nationality. Both faith and nationality are significant to Caribbeaners' identity and existence in a new land. Reid's accommodationist approach deals with how the Caribbeaners adapted to the new society and became part of it despite their original intent. The significance, nevertheless, of Reid's work demonstrates that becoming affiliated with other churches was an attempt to secure the survival of the Caribbean diaspora.

Along this pattern of reasoning, Irma Watkins–Owens observes that the Caribbean diasporan church was the agent for the preservation of the faith and culture of the Caribbean diaspora through the observation of cultural events, national observances such as Emancipation Day and the involvement of pastors in the socio-political affairs of their communities.[48] She notes that "Caribbean immigrant churches perpetuated island traditions such as those that related to weddings and funerals."[49]

This leads us now to consider the implications of the practice of membership through individual affiliation with mainstream American churches, particularly those with whom the Caribbeaners had a pre-existing denominational relationship in the Caribbean. As I have argued throughout this study, the church is central to the Caribbean diasporan community. These pilgrim people grounded their relationship in faith. Omar McRoberts, writing about the membership of Caribbean Christians in both African American and the white denominational churches, observes that while African Americans found Caribbeaners "clannish," Caribbeaners found

African Americans "elitist."[50] Consequently Caribbean Christians established their own churches as soon as they were able to do so within the particular denomination.[51] McRoberts explains, with respect to the establishing of a new church:

> As soon as West Indians had formed a critical mass...they established the St. Cyprian's Episcopal Church. In 1913, the congregation held its first services in the lower Roxbury home of Miss Ida Cross. Members of the congregation previously were disappointed to learn that the only "colored" church in Boston was "high Episcopal" meaning they adhered to strict, staid Anglican ritual standards.[52]

The move to establish a denominational church is an important development in Caribbean diasporan ecclesiology. It demonstrates that ecclesiastical identity is an expression of faith and that individual membership in a church is an embodiment of faith. This kind of membership, however, is not an adequate portrayal of living the faith.

Congregational Affiliation

A fuller and more adequate embodiment of the search for community is realized through congregational membership in a denominational church. For example, whereas individual membership refers to an individual affiliation with a local church, congregational membership refers to a local church's affiliation with a denominational church. The Jamaican Methodist clergyperson, who later became a Unitarian clergy, the Reverend Egbert Ethelred Brown (1875–1956) is a representative of this practice of the pilgrim theological self-understanding. He organized one of the first Caribbean diasporan churches on March 7, 1920, the Harlem Community Church. Brown was born in Falmouth, Trelawny, Jamaica, on July 11, 1875. Fully convinced of his call to be a minister of the gospel, he studied for the ministry at the Unitarian seminary, the Meadville Theological School in Youngstown, Pennsylvania, from September 1910 to June 1912. Following his graduation, he returned to Jamaica for eight years and worked to establish a Unitarian church which never succeeded. He later returned to the United States determined to establish a Unitarian church among the Black community.[53]

Mark D. Morrison-Reed, in his study on Brown, *Black Pioneers in a White Denomination,* argues that the life and ministry of Egbert Ethelred Brown "represents only one story of a struggle to overcome the separation between blacks and followers of a liberal faith"[54] and he embodied the ideals of the Christian faith by acting out its values and beliefs.[55]

In contrast to the works of Reid and Watkins-Owens which demonstrate affiliation through individual membership with a local congregation, Morrison-Reed illustrates congregational membership within the white denominational church. In addition to being a resource for Black theological scholarship, Morrison-Reed provides an insider account of the Black experience in a white organization. He writes:

> A vast cultural and economic chasm exists between blacks and liberal religionists, preventing them from communicating easily. But have the Afro-American, the descendant of bondage, and the liberal religionist, the inheritor of freedom, anything to say to one another? Indeed they have concern, freedom being the foremost among these, yet they live with this rift.[56]

Morrison-Reed's concern, however, is using the life of Brown to "bridge the gulf between the black and the Unitarian communities..."[57] Despite this noble endeavor, Morrison-Reed is misguided when he uses Brown as a theological resource for addressing the social ill in the Unitarian church, which for Morrison-Reed, was class. He argues:

> Black religion is a religion of the disinherited, and Unitarianism is a religion of the middle class... Both divisions within the liberal religious traditions, the Unitarians and the Universalists, had a tenuous relationship with the black community. The life of Egbert Ethelred Brown represents only one story of a struggle to overcome the separation between blacks and followers of the liberal faith.[58]

I will not deny that the work of Ethelred Brown can be used as a resource for racial reconciliation but that was not Brown's purpose in establishing and affiliating with a white denominational church. Brown understood his diasporan journey as a pilgrimage. It is not clear if he began with that understanding but this was the perspective he expressed in his later evaluation of his life and ministry when he described his journey from Jamaica to the United States as a "voyage of faith,"[59] a "pilgrimage from Montego Bay to Harlem,"[60] a "pilgrimage of faith."[61]

The establishment of the St. Martin's Moravian Church in Harlem, New York, is another example of how Caribbean diasporan churches practiced their pilgrim theology through affiliation with denominational churches. The St. Martin Church was organized and established by the Kittian, the Reverend Dr. Charles D. Martin in 1908. Both the pastor and Caribbean membership were original adherents of this denominational church in their homeland. The St. Martin Church, however, was probably not known in the community as the Harlem Community Church was known. Notwithstanding this difference between the two churches, both are representatives of the nascent Caribbean diasporan ecclesiology.

Conclusion

In concluding this discussion on the beginning of the theological development of Caribbean ecclesiology, it is significant to reflect on this pattern of theological discourse so as to keep salient the central issues that characterized this era of the church. I attended to the social context in which the Caribbean diasporan church emerged, arguing that this early beginning of the Caribbean diaspora was regarded as a pilgrimage that is defined by a search for a better life, a search for respect and a search for community.

In the inception of the Caribbean diaspora, the church provided the means for survival and acclimatization to the new society. The society was hostile towards people of African descent. As such, Caribbeaners had to contend with racism, endure rejection, and cope with changing immigration laws. In response to such adversities Caribbeaners sought membership in local and denominational churches.

This was primarily an institutional relationship where they functioned either as individual Christians or as a congregation. In the former case, the relationship was personal and temporary because these immigrants did not plan to reside permanently in the United States of America. For the latter, the relationship was corporate and permanent where the church functioned as an internal prophetic witness by offering primarily a theological critique of racism and established a Caribbean diasporan Christian intellectual tradition. These two issues, however, I will discuss in greater detail in Chapter 8. But for now, put differently, the church served as an internal critic of ecclesiastical praxis and affirmed Black intellectual ability and learning as essential Christian activity and vital to human liberation. Marcus Garvey, in recognition of this tradition, states:

> Never forget that intelligence rules the world and carries the burden. Therefore remove yourself as far as possible from ignorance and seek as far as possible to be intelligent.[62]

Inasmuch as the pilgrim paradigm provides a historical understanding of the theological development of the Caribbean diasporan church, the development is limited to affiliation with white religious institutions. How this ecclesiology developed from faith though religious institutions to become organic and distinct communities of faith is the subject of the next chapter.

7 Missionaries in the Caribbean Diaspora: Doing God's Work in a New Land

This chapter continues the discussion on the theological development of the Caribbean diasporan church by exploring the practice of mission through the formation of churches. The exploration defines mission, examines Caribbean diasporan missionary tradition so as to determine the historical context, and identifies the definitive practices of the missionary engagement of the church.

In the previous chapter, I employed the theological motif of pilgrim as both the framework and paradigm to define the church. But with the change in the numerical composition of the diasporan community, the theological understanding of the diaspora changed from the pilgrim's quest for survival to the missionary's journey towards peoplehood.

Contributing to this change of theological understanding is the increase in the Caribbean diasporan population that resulted from the Hart-Cellar Immigration Act of 1965 which rescinded the previous policies and replaced them with pro-immigration ones. This made it possible not only for more people to travel but made provisions for categories of people who had not been allowed to travel to do so now.[1] For example, parents could now sponsor unmarried children and their next of kin to live in the country. The 1990 United States Census attests to this increase of diasporan growth. The Census reports that during the period between 1965 and 1990, over 600,000 new Caribbean immigrants were admitted into the country.[2]

In addition to having more people to form a distinct community, as indicated above in the 1990 United States Census Report, Caribbeaners became integrated into the society and had the need to organize themselves as members and people of a common ethnic identity.[3] Constance Sutton notes that "Caribbean peoples...are not readily induced to shed their cultural heritages or separate Caribbean-based identities...[4] Rather, they endeavor to preserve their Caribbean identity through family and social and civic organizations, as Ransford Palmer observes. He states: "The central institution around which this is accomplished is the family. Around the immigrant family is a network of associations woven into the ethnic fabric of community."[5]

These changes in migration patterns suggest that Caribbean people were not migrating for a limited period, which contributed to their becoming constitutive elements of American society.[6] Thus, a new phase in the formation of the Caribbean diaspora was created that changed the theological understanding of the disapora from a pilgrimage to a mission field.

Although organizations were established to sustain Caribbean identity, the growing Caribbean diasporan population was in need of their own churches. The need for churches became an opportunity for missionary work through the preaching of the gospel and the establishing of new congregations. Caribbean people came from a society where religion is an essential institution. Frances Henry observes that "there is a wide range of Christian and non-Christian religions in the region"[7] and that Caribbean Christians maintain their religious practice in migrating to a new country.

Caribbean Christians also believed that it is a personal and corporate responsibility to fulfill the mandate of Jesus to evangelize the world. The Jamaican Church of God pastor, Guy Notice, affirms this perspective. He declares:

> The proclamation of the Gospel of Jesus Christ to unconverted everywhere is called for, and to establish churches for those whom have come to know Christ as Savior and Lord, training them for Christian service that ultimately indigenous churches may be established to carry on the work of the Lord.[8]

Given that Notice's assertion may not fully reflect the perspective of the Caribbean diasporan church, it nevertheless indicates that this missionary mandate is premised on what is commonly called the "Great Commission."

> All authority in heaven and earth has been given to me. Therefore go and make disciples of all nations, baptizing them in the name of the Father, Son and Holy Spirit, and teaching them to obey everything I have commanded you. And surely I am with you always, to the very end of the age (Matt. 28:18-20; NIV).

Although Notice's perspective is only one interpretation of this text,[9] it is employed by Caribbean diasporan Christians as the basis to engage in missionary activities to establish churches. This chapter, however, is not a theology of mission but an exploration of the practice of mission as a factor in the development of a Caribbean diasporan ecclesiology.

Mission: A Perspective from the Caribbean Diaspora

The Caribbean theological tradition understands mission as an inclusive and contextual engagement of the church in society that addresses all aspects of human life.[10] The inclusive and contextual nature of mission are the undergirding factors, and as such deserve careful attention.

Inclusive[11]

A landmark study in defining Caribbean mission is the proceedings of a mission conference conducted by the Caribbean church in 1975. In the early 1970s, Caribbean pastors and theologians began to do theological refection on the Caribbean missionary tradition in light of Caribbean history and experience. This resulted in the publication of the book, *Out of the Depths*, edited by Idris Hamid, consisting of a collection of essays on the theme of mission. These Caribbean pastors and theologians explored the historical and spiritual experiences of the Caribbean people in seeking to establish the theological basis, framework and content of a Caribbean missiology. As Hamid states:

> The new mission-thinking that emerges here takes very seriously the total life of man [humanity]: his living and working conditions; his social and political organizations; the issues of justice and human rights. It will engage in battle with the Western world concerning a proper definition of man [humanity].[12]

He continues to express the nature of this missiology as involving questioning and articulating the faith in light of Caribbean history, experience and life.

> This exercise in mission, will force us, as it has been doing, to go back to the scriptures, to the rich and varied traditions of the Christian Faith and to our own religious experience to inquire with urgent freshness what is the substance and meaning of our faith.[13]

Hamid broadens the meaning of mission to include the socio-political dimensions of life. Unfortunately, he does not include the spiritual dimension of life. For example, Hamid argues that:

> The new mission-thinking that emerges here takes very seriously the total life of man: his living and working condition; his social and political organization; the issues of justice and human rights. It will engage in battle with the Western world concerning a proper definition of man. It rejects outright the prevailing definition of man as a producer or consumer. It rejects the working proposition that to have is to be, or to consume is to be, or to produce is to be.[14]

When Hamid speaks of mission to include the total life of the person, he specified only one aspect of the dimension of human life which is the socio-political. While this is consistent with the meaning of mission, inclusivity is more than the socio-political. An authentic inclusivity embraces all persons, cultures, social contexts and aspects of the human existence.

Writing of the inclusive nature of Caribbean mission which is a feature of Caribbean theology, Philip Potter and Barbel Wartenberg-Potter note:

> The whole purpose of the grace of God revealed in Christ has been liberated from the "present evil world, from the curse (doom) of the law and from the elemental spirit of the world…" God has enabled us through the Spirit to draw near to God as Father/Mother and to each other as sisters and brothers.[15]

In view of this claim, Hamid's perspective on the meaning of Caribbean mission is not absolute and final but an initial step to begin further exploration of the issue.

Contextual

The social context of time, place, culture and circumstances is the second factor that constitutes the meaning of Caribbean mission. William Watty embraces Caribbean mission as inclusive but goes further to argue that it is contextual. Watty argues that mission is to be understood in light of the context of those whom God called and that the Bible does not offer a monolithic but a progressive perspective of mission. As such, it is not sufficient to regurgitate what the Bible says but to state the context out of which the confession or belief emerged and to examine the relationship between faith and context.[16] Watty insists that mission is the "faithful response to the Lord who has called it into being, it is ipso facto a 'God–send' to the world."[17] In his continuing articulation of this perspective, Watty observes:

> Different people, according to their situation, have different ways of hearing the gospel, different ways of accepting and rejecting Christ, different forms of putting him to death and different ways of experiencing him alive. The common unifying factor is simply that He secures for every man his freedom and dignity as a child of God in which freedom alone he can truly live as a responsible being in God's world.[18]

This definition of mission symbolizes one of the most significant theological initiatives of the Caribbean church. The definition signifies a point of departure from Euro-American theology of mission which, according to Carlos F. Cardoza Orlando, was primarily for "evangelizing those 'pagans' which had come from African to the Island of the Caribbean."[19] The event is also problematic. The representatives at the conference were from the historic denominational churches. The representatives from the non-historic churches such as the Pentecostals and the Evangelical churches were not represented. This work, therefore, does not accurately reflect the churches of the Caribbean but reflects the missiology of one aspect of Caribbean Christianity. The work, however, is of great value in that it marks the beginning of the decolonization of Caribbean theology but, more importantly, the decolonization of missiology.

In a significant essay on mission and colonization, Ashley Smith underscores this perspective by arguing that the Caribbean church's interpretation of mission is an act of decolonization. It is a form of rebirth and heralds a new era for the entire church where these organic churches redefine the meaning of mission. Smith observes:

> Just as by freeing themselves from their apprehensions former colonies have helped liberate their colonisers, so by insisting on assuming full responsibility in the Apostolate, the younger Churches have forced their "Mother Churches" to look again at the meaning and implications of missions with special reference to the Apostolate of the laity, the liberating and reconciling Gospel, and the global nature of the "One Holy 'Catholic' Church."[20]

From this perspective of mission as an inclusive and contextual decolonizing engagement of proclaiming and practicing the emancipatory gospel of Jesus Christ, the Caribbean church initiated and promoted an active missionary movement. On a superficial level, this initiative of de-colonizing mission contradicts the meaning of mission as argued in this discussion and opens the Caribbean church to the accusation of both promoting and being an agent of neo-colonialism. The basis for this perception is the assumption that the Caribbean church's missionary engagement is similar to the Eurocentric practiced from which the Caribbean church departs. The charge would be correct if it were not to help others to become aware of God who is already present with them. Equally important, God commissioned the church to go into the world to proclaim the gospel, serve and liberate humanity from sin and oppression. In this regard, mission could be conceived as a response to God's mandate of making Christ's emancipatory purpose known and available to all persons within their cultural, social and religious traditions and contexts.[21]

The Missionary Tradition

Three practices emerge from the Caribbean diasporan ecclesiastical experience that define the Caribbean missionary tradition. These are the sending of missionaries to foreign countries, the appointment of missionaries to serve the diasporan community and the experience of the call to mission.

The Sending of Missionaries

The Caribbean diasporan church came out of a missionary tradition of sending Christians to evangelize foreign countries with the gospel. This practice began in 1842 when Caribbeaners were trained and sent as missionaries to Africa by both the London and the Scottish Missionary Societies.[22] Keith Hunte notes that "the promoters of these missionary efforts considered it important to recruit local blacks, though not exclusively"[23] for this endeavor. This missionary work, however, was not administered by the Caribbean church because no autonomous Caribbean church existed. In this regard, it was a European missionary endeavor using Caribbean Christians as missionaries. This initiative at the same time could be interpreted as the precursor to an autonomous Caribbean missionary tradition. Writing of the Caribbean missionary tradition as modeled by Philip A. Potter, the Caribbean missionary and former General Secretary of the World Council of Churches, Michael Jagessar, makes the honest observation:

> While Potter agrees that the word "mission" conjures up negative images for many, he recognizes and affirms that it is as a result of the mission of the church that slavery was opposed, education became a reality, a necessary "middle class" was nurtured to lead the struggle for independence, and the socio-economic and political state of the people in the Caribbean was addressed.[24]

Emancipation is an essential element in Caribbean missionary tradition but it does not accomplish this emancipatory purpose as Jagessar argues. While attributing the move to abolish slavery to the church, he overlooks that the church sanctioned and practiced slavery. Additionally, speaking of a "necessary middle class" in Caribbean society, Jagessar unwittingly articulates an elitist ideology that contradicts the emancipatory praxis advocated by the Caribbean missionary tradition. This implicit classism does not clarify but rather problematizes the nature of the Caribbean missionary tradition.

Although the term "mission" evokes negative thoughts and has negative connotations of imposition of European cultural expectations and mental enslavement, mission is not inherently negative. The term mission expresses the practice of the Caribbean church in carrying out the mandate of taking the gospel of Jesus Christ to all humanity. It is the carrying out of the mission of Jesus who is the Christ, and through his life God offers salvation to all persons. The Caribbean missionary theologian, Philip Potter, explains:

> Through the incarnation, death and resurrection of Jesus Christ, God has made us responsible for his purpose in the world to work for radical change, conversion, salvation, in the face of the principalities and power of nature and of man so that he may be released to become God's poema, "created in Jesus Christ for good works which God prepared beforehand, that we should walk in them."[25]

The Caribbean missionary tradition affirms the belief that Christian mission is grounded in the nature of the Triune God and the Incarnation of God in Jesus Christ. Mission proceeds from God the Creator, the sending of the Son, Jesus Christ, and the Creator and Son sending the Holy Spirit, and together their sending the church into the world. The witness of Scripture is clear on this issue. It states, "As the Father sent me, so send I you" (Jn 17:18; NIV). This testimony of Scripture indicates that the church is sent under the same conditions as Jesus. The response of Christians, therefore, to the missionary command of Jesus is both responding to and participating in God's mission in the world.[26]

A Case of Responding to the Call to Mission

An example of this endeavor is Horace Russell's The *Missionary Outreach of the West Indian Church: Jamaica Baptist Missions to West Africa in the Nineteenth Century.*[27] This study explores the nature of the relationship between the Caribbean and West Africa church. It examines the work of the Baptist church in Jamaica, the relationship between the Jamaica Baptist and the colonial missionary agencies, and the development from a "mission to a church."[28]

The importance of Russell's study for Caribbean theological scholarship cannot be overstated. It does not only demonstrate the Christian witness of the Caribbean church in West Africa but it provides insights into the relationship between faith and liberation and makes known the contribution of the Caribbean church to world Christianity and society. The missionary work of the Caribbean church, according to Russell,

> was undertaken by a people, who interpreted their freedom in the widest social and political terms but always within the framework of their faith...which transcended the physical and spiritual limits which the slave society and its theological assumptions imposed upon them. In so doing...developed a model of missionary endeavor and left as a legacy to the missionary enterprise a unique and dynamic structure of Christian witness, which was to be emulated not only in their time but also in subsequent years.[29]

Although Russell acknowledges the holistic and contextual nature of Caribbean mission, his perspective is limited in two ways. First, his perspective represents a strictly denominational interpretation as he examines the missionary work of a single denomination. He contends that the work concerns the "ecclesiastical aspects of the relationship between the West Indies and West Africa in the Nineteenth Century."[30] The study, however, focuses on the work of the Jamaica Baptist Union which is certainly not an ecumenical but a denominational church. Here I argue that the Baptist work is only one representation of the work of the church but, at the same time, it must be understood that the Baptist never professed to be acting on behalf of the whole church. Furthermore, Caribbean Baptists, particularly the Jamaican Baptists, is a foremost missionary organization. This therefore explains the prominence of the Baptist church in this study and, more importantly, in the missionary endeavor.[31]

The second limitation of this study is Russell's decentralization of Africa. Russell dismisses the centrality of Africa in the motivation for the missionary endeavor by arguing that it is due to a combination of factors including the doctrine of universalism, thanksgiving for freedom and ecclesiastical pluralism.[32] Russell locates this in the theology that the European Baptist brought to the Caribbean. He states: "There was first the B.M.S. missionaries who had come to Jamaica endowed with universalism"[33] as derived from the influences of the Baptist leader, Andrew Fuller and the Methodist, Thomas Coke.[34] In attributing such significance to the influence of European Baptist theological thought on the Caribbean Baptist missionary tradition, Russell has overlooked that the European Christians, especially those in the Baptist tradition, who went to the Caribbean, went to a cultivated and developed mission field. The British historian, Brian Stanley, supports this claim.

> The West Indies mission occupies a unique place in the nineteenth-century history of the Society. Alone among the early BMS fields, the West Indies were not wholly unevangelised territory. BMS missionaries came, not primarily as evangelists to the heathens but as pastors and teachers of an existing Christian negro community. In no other Baptist field during the nineteenth century was church growth so spectacular, and nowhere else was progress towards the autonomy of the indigenous church so rapid, not so firmly insisted on by the society.[35]

By decentralizing Africa, Russell overlooks the African origin of Caribbean Christianity. In the first instance, it was not the Europeans who brought pluralism to the Caribbean. Those who came to the Caribbean brought with them their own culture[36] as noted in the previous chapter. Russell also seems to have overlooked that Blacks were actively engaged in missionary work, at least a decade prior to the Europeans. Clement Gayle, in his seminal work on George Liele, the African American who established in 1784 the Baptist ecclesiastical tradition in Jamaica, was the first person to conduct any successful mass evangelism among the African Caribbean population. In this regard Liele was the first Black missionary to the Black population in Jamaica.[37] Gayle observes that:

> The denominations and ministers who came before Liele either did very little work among the slaves or that what they did was very ineffective. In the early days the Roman Catholics showed much interest in the Indians, but similar interest was not shown among the negro slaves.[38]

Gayle is convinced that Liele was first and foremost a missionary to his own people. Gayle contends that:

> …George Liele completed nearly ten years of missionary work in Jamaica before Carey reached India… Liele was a man full of missionary zeal and that, in coming to Jamaica, preaching the gospel was uppermost in his mind.[39]

Furthermore, while Russell's study concerns the Caribbean missionary tradition, it is of course not a work about the Caribbean diasporan church. The study is about the missionary work of the Caribbean church in their ancestral homeland. What Russell's work indicates, however, is that the Caribbean church has been involved in missionary endeavors before there was a Caribbean diaspora. Since the missionary endeavor preceded the emergence of a Caribbean diaspora, the question this raises for this study is what motivated the Caribbean church to advance a missionary cause if it is not race as Russell argues?

The Motivation for Mission

In response to this question of the motivation for mission, I consider two issues. The first is that the Caribbean church did not pursue missionary endeavors among people of other nationalities. As indicated earlier, the missionary pursuit was to the African continent but also within the Caribbean. In the Caribbean, for example, emancipation from slavery, the immigration of Indians and the need for social services were regarded as missionary opportunities. Keith Hunte makes the observation that "while the attention of churches in the West Indies was steadily drawn to the mission field in Africa, certain churches sought to do something about missionary opportunities at home."[40] The scope of this work was beyond the ability of one denomination. As a result, the Anglicans restructured a single diocese into three and then shared the missionary work among themselves, the Presbyterian and the Methodist churches.[41]

Regarding the missionary work of the Caribbean church to Africa, historian Arthur Dayfoot notes:

> West Indian Christians of European race could assume that the culture and religion of their homeland was Christian. But what of Africans and East Indians who had become Christian in the Caribbean as a result of missionary work there? They retained a consciousness of their origins even as they accepted the Christian faith.[42]

Dayfoot buttresses this idea by correctly alluding to George Liele, the pioneering Black missionary of the Caribbean who identified Caribbean Christians as "Ethiopian Christians."[43] Thus, Liele demonstrated a contextual usage of the Bible and how the Caribbean church understood and identified itself with particular biblical characters.

In the second instance, the evangelization of the Caribbean diaspora was undertaken by the Caribbean diasporan church. Again, the endeavor was not directed to any other diasporan community. Arthur Dayfoot, in his useful and informative book, *The Shaping of the West Indian Church 1492–1962*, observes that race is a central factor that leads to missionary outreach and the establishing of Caribbean diasporan churches; however, the response was not favorable. They were met with hostility and rejection, as Dayfoot states:

> At first it was assumed by the older churches that the members of the British-based churches would integrate with the churches of the same denominations. But because of…race…this proved disappointing in practice.[44]

The Jamaican Presbyterian theologian, Ashley Smith, offers a stinging commentary on this issue. He writes:

> The hostility of some native Christians in North America and Great Britain to the presence of immigrant Christians in their churches exposes not just the ignorance of the Christianisers of the meaning of Christ's missionary command but also the superficiality of the nominal or cultured Christianity of Europe and Europeans across the globe and the need for a complete new approach to the evangelization of man whatever the color of his skin or characteristic of his culture.[45]

Both Dayfoot's and Smith's observation describe the hostile context in which Caribbean diasporan church carried out its mission. What is not clear, however, is how did they were able to fulfill the missionary mandate. This is the question the discussion seeks to answer.

The Practice of Mission

Having demonstrated the existence of a Caribbean missionary tradition, I will now discuss two practices of executing the missionary mandate, namely, the appointment of missionaries and the call to mission. The above mentioned experience of hostility did not quell the missionary zeal of the Caribbean diasporan Christians. Caribbean Christians interpret the migration experience as an opportunity to evangelize and transform the world because they see God as being actively involved in human history and willing human emancipation.

Appointment to the Caribbean Migrants

The appointment of missionaries was one response to this challenge. The term appointment of missionaries in this study refers to the practice of sending missionaries as pastors, teachers and other professionals to work with Caribbean nationals in their locations of dispersion including countries such as Africa, Canada, England and throughout the Caribbean. The practice had its precedence in the Society for the Propagation of the Gospel, the Jamaica Baptist Missionary Society, the Salvation Army and the Methodist Church.[46] These missionary organizations and churches were among the earliest to recruit and appoint missionaries to the migratory destinations where Caribbean people were moving.[47] Consequently, as Arthur Dayfoot observes, these migratory destinations became "the nucleus for church activity."[48]

Inez Knibb Sibley gives an historical survey of the missionary work of the Baptist church of Jamaica (1793–1965). She observes that up to that time, the Baptists as one of the pioneering missionary organizations were actively involved in West Africa, Haiti, Cuba, Central America, Grand Cayman and the Turks and Caicos Islands.[49] In the 1960s the Jamaica Baptist Union commissioned pastoral workers to serve as missionaries in the United Kingdom and Canada in the 1980s.[50] The United Church of Jamaica and Grand Cayman continued the same practice into the 1990s.[51]

Appointment in the United Kingdom

Both the Jamaican and British churches became concerned that the growing Caribbean diasporan population in Britain was not integrating into the national churches. Instead, they were establishing their own churches. To combat this development, the Baptist Union of Great Britain solicited the support of the Jamaica Baptist Union in cooperation with the Baptist Missionary Society to provide qualified clergy to work as advisors to the British church on integrating Caribbean nationals into its ecclesiastical life. In its deliberations on this matter, the Baptist Missionary Society clearly opposed the development of Caribbean churches, which, from their perspective, constituted religious segregation. It was decided that integration should be the operative principle but segregated gatherings should be regarded as a temporary expedient with integration in mind.[52]

The British Baptists did not want Caribbeaners to establish their own churches on British soil. According to Horace Russell, this was out of fear of practicing religious apartheid. Consequently, British and Jamaican Baptist churches appointed missionary pastors from Jamaica, to work with Caribbeaners in the United Kingdom. But as Horace Russell observes, these appointees were more religious consultants than pastors. He writes: "They did not live where the people lived nor share in full the experiences, frustrations and limitations of their daily lives."[53]

The British Baptist residence resistance to establishing Caribbean diasporan churches in the United Kingdom is expressed further in the nature of the work of the proposed missionaries. Their appointment was temporary, the role was advisory and the assignment was confined to specific communities where Caribbean nationals resided. According to the records:

> Integration of the West Indians into the church life of this country was to be encouraged rather than the setting up of separate Churches; that a Jamaican Baptist minister of good standing should be brought to England in order to advise Baptist ministers and churches on integration rather than setting up separate churches; and that such visits be for twelve months.[54]

These missionaries were placed during the time in office in four different locations for three months. There was one exception to this decision. C. S. Reid served a two-year appointment as pastor of the Moss Side Baptist Church, Manchester.[55] This integrationalist thrust was not very effective and did not last very long. The failure of this is one of the factors leading to the rise and development of the Black British Pentecostal Church tradition.[56] Those who followed the integrative approach are usually members of the historic churches because at the beginning of the migration to Britain, the historic churches were the dominant religion in the Caribbean and they were also a part of British social, political and religious establishment.[57] In contrast, the Pentecostal movement was a recent development in the Caribbean. This movement originated from America and was established in the Caribbean by the Church of God, Cleveland, Tennessee, in 1918.[58]

Appointment in the United States

Missionaries were also appointed to serve the Caribbean diasporan church in American society. The Reverend David Morgan was appointed by the then Home Mission Board of the Southern Baptist Convention in the early 1960s. Reverend David Morgan is one of the pioneering missionaries of the Caribbean diaspora. Prior to migrating to the United States in 1961, Morgan worked as pastor in his native country, Panama and in his adoptive homeland, Jamaica. He came to America as an educated and experienced pastor and with a pre-established relationship with the Southern Baptist Convention. Morgan was able to secure their support without much difficulty in his effort to evangelize the diasporan population.[59]

Writing about the origin and development of the Caribbean diasporan church and the role of the Southern Baptist Convention, Morgan gives the following account:

> "How shall we sing the Lord's song in a strange land?" This question was taken to Dr. Paul James, pastor of the first Southern Baptist Church established in New York, the Manhattan Baptist Church. Dr. James prayerfully considered the matter for a Jamaican work [sic] in New York. Upon the advice of Dr. Lloyd Corder, the Reverend and Mrs. David Morgan, missionaries of the Home Mission Board serving on the Canal Zone, were invited to come to accept the challenge.[60]

Morgan established churches in New York and Florida that are today some of the leading ones in the diaspora. The first church he established was the Evergreen, formerly, First Baptist Church, in Brooklyn New York and the last was the Metropolitan Baptist Church in Florida.[61] Samuel Simpson, one of David Morgan's mentees, has made it known that it was Morgan's vision to establish churches in America for Caribbean people. In Simpson's words:

The idea of starting a Southern Baptist Church in the Bronx was the first of Dr. Morgan's church planting dreams… Dr. Morgan shared with me and Lola, my wife, his desire to start a work in the Bronx with me as mission pastor, and asked us to seek the Lord's will.[62]

One Mission but a Different Method

Considering that this pattern of mission is a continuation of a missionary tradition, it is following the practice of the colonial missionary enterprise. As in the case of Morgan, the missionaries depended on the agencies for support which meant their loyalty was first to the agency and not to the people whom they served.[63] Taking this further, the appointees were not free, for instance, to address issues of justice and social concerns because their mission was to save souls.[64] In the words of Bosch, "The fact that missionaries were sent not to educate and guide others but to be in their midst in a spirit of true self-surrender tended to take the back seat."[65] In relationship to the Caribbean diaspora, it could be argued that the missionary agenda was not to address and promote issues that concern diasporan existence such as immigrant rights, the impact of migration on individuals and families and matters concerning the process and experience of living in a new country.

In contrast to colonial missionary practice, Caribbean theologian, Harold Sitahal, describes the nature and meaning of the Caribbean missionary practice as incarnational. Mission is a "responsibility to respond to a need or a moral imperative, a theological imperative, meaning the responsibility to pronounce the word of God, in the prophetic sense"[66] to the people of God in their particular context. He notes further:

God humanized himself in order to work for the deliverance of mankind. Being humanized, "nothing human was alien to him." He therefore had a first hand experience of human social, political and economic problems. To do its missionary activity the Church must also adopt the same incarnational strategy.[67]

Michael Jagessar concurs with this perspective of mission as incarnational in his work on the missionary theologian Philip Potter. According to Jagessar:

Potter maintains that mission is God's activity and not the possession of human beings. When it becomes human mission "it is fashioned in their image, not the purpose of God as he acts in history."[68]

Incarnational mission enters into solidarity with the people by being present and participating in their lives. Since the mission of the church is also the mission of God, incarnational mission is participating and partnering with God in the fulfillment of his purpose in the world. It reveals God's character and embodies God's kingdom, which is not limited to personal salvation and to public life with its social and systemic structures and policies. The church, as Potter notes,

> needs not only an eschatological approach to the understanding of mission, but an eschatological style *of life,* parousia, *presence to and with people whom* God loves, for whom Christ died, and for whom the Spirit waits to fill with the multiform grace of life, as sign of the kingdom present to come.[69]

The Call to Mission

The call of God is the other hallmark of the missionary tradition of the Caribbean diasporan church. I base this hallmark on the view held by Caribbean diasporan pastors that it was the call of God that caused them to be living and working in the Caribbean diaspora. The idea of the call to mission is not limited to Caribbean diasporan pastors but is rather a common belief held by the church.[70] For this study, the call refers to the moral and theological pastoral authority that legitimizes and authorizes the establishment of Caribbean diasporan churches and distinguishes them from other organizations. It also provides the reason given for emigrating from the Caribbean.

A Personal Call

The Jamaican pastor, Samuel Hines, the second pastor of the Third Street Church of God in Washington DC, gives his reason for migrating to the United States in 1969 to that of the call of God.

> As you know by now, I am a native son of Jamaica. Seven years after being ordained to the Christian ministry, having served as senior pastor for five churches in Jamaica (four of these churches comprised one circuit of churches on the Island), and having traveled extensively in the British Isles and the United States, I was called to pastor a small church in Washington D.C. In 1969 after much intense prayer, for the Holy Spirit's leading, I answered the call to come to the capital city of the United States.[71]

The significance of the role of the call of God in Hines' life is measured partly by the commentary on his work in Washington DC, the capital of the United States, by the former President of the country, George W. Bush. Bush commended Hines for leading a congregation that is contributing to the spiritual and moral life of the country. George W. Bush writes: "Indeed, because the faith and values nurtured within its walls are the foundation of strong families and communities, your Church has been a source of strength for our entire country."[72]

Though there were other tributes paid to Hines, including that of Richard C. Halverson, Chaplain to the United States Senate[73] and for his work of reconciliation,[74] the most significant that affirms his call to work as a pastor in the Caribbean diaspora is his own acknowledgment that God made him leader of the church. In a letter to his congregation, December 1990, Hines writes: "To the Flock (over which God has made me overseer)."[75]

Samuel Simpson, pastor of the Bronx Baptist Church, New York, expresses a similar understanding regarding his work as a pastor in the Caribbean diaspora. The Home Mission Board of the Southern Baptist Convention appointed Simpson and his wife, Lola, as missionaries to work with and establish Caribbean diaspora churches in Bronx, New York.[76]

Simpson roots his call to the pastoral ministry in the biblical prophetic tradition. He makes the observation that "There is a divine call to which you must personally respond, positively or negatively."[77] Writing about his call to the ministry, Simpson personalized the call of Jeremiah. "Before I formed you in the womb I knew you, and before you were born I consecrated you; appointed you a prophet to the nations" (Jer. 1:5; NIV).[78]

It is noteworthy that the call is the demand of God and a deep sense of conviction to do the work of ministry. In the case of Simpson, he took steps to fulfill this demand of God and conviction which he expresses in the nature of ministry he performed. While we will discuss aspects of Simpson's work in Chapter 8, the importance of the call should be noted. The significance of the call is determined by the contributions Simpson made to American society. He is not only a pioneering pastor but he commenced his ministry during one of the most difficult times in American history. In 1966, when Simpson started the Bronx Baptist Church, the Bronx was likened to Berlin at the end of the Second World War in 1945.[79] Karen L. Willoughby reports that:

> Little did Simpson know that within a year of his arrival, the community would begin deteriorating until in the early 1970s it was described in local newspapers as looking like Berlin after World War II. Nearly 70,000 fires were started…in the south Bronx during Simpson's first seven years.[80]

Beyond the social context in which Simpson lived out his call to ministry, the significance of his call can also be detected in his role as a civic leader and community builder but, above all, in the holistic ministry he practiced, as the following statement states:

> Today he continues a pastor of Bronx Baptist Church, where about 250 attend Sunday morning worship, and Wake Eden Community Baptist Church, where about 200 attend. The churches have started day care centers, after-school centers, nursing home ministries and more.[81]

More recently, Wesley Green, the Caribbean pastor of the Christway Church, Florida, emphasized the centrality of the call mission. His call to work in the Caribbean diaspora did not come from a congregation but was born out of his experience and the opportunity and need to establish Caribbean diasporan churches. Green was a successful Baptist pastor in Western Jamaica and traveled frequently between Jamaica and the United States as a missionary. In these travels, he discovered two problems which Caribbean people faced in the American diaspora. These were the cultural gaps between the Caribbean community and African Americans and the racial division between the Caribbean community and white America.

In his observation of the religious, social and cultural context, it became apparent to Green that Caribbean people were not comfortable in either the white or African American churches and that there were various groups of Caribbean people throughout the state of Florida. Green saw this as an opportunity to establish a church for Caribbean people as a means of not only bridging the gap between both the black and white American community and the Caribbean community but also organizing a church where Caribbean people would be at home. In Green's words:

> There was more of an urge to establish a church where Caribbean people would be comfortable and having certain ingredients that would bring familiarity and ease in worship. I was determined to exploit that situation to help both sides because there was ignorance on both sides of the coin.[82]

The Communal Call

The call is integral and central to understanding the Caribbean diasporan missionary tradition. It shows both a biblical and theological understanding encompassing a call to a relationship with God, a vocation and commitment to a task. This interpretation of the call, however, reflects one of the two aspects that constitute the call to mission, namely, the individual and the communal. In the case of Hines, Simpson and Green, their personalization of the call in their characteristic individualistic manner misconstrues the biblical meaning of call to ministry. Their understanding engenders a practice of faith at the expense of the common heritage and history of Caribbean Christianity as a Black religion.

The African American ethicist, Peter Paris, writes about the communal nature of the call as reflected in his book, *The Spirituality of African Peoples: The Search for a Common Moral Discourse*. Although Paris' work may be representative of the African diaspora as a whole, which the title suggests, its focus is on the African American community. Excluding an implicit form of ethnic imperialism, Paris argues for the importance of the communal in Black society. He states: "All African peoples agree that the tribal or ethnic community is the paramount social reality apart from which humanity cannot exist."[83] Paris agrees that the sense of and belief in community are woven into the fabric of peoples of African descent. Paris continues:

> As social cohesion and social order increased among freed African American peoples, their leaders exemplified the moral norms and traditions of the community that had been preserved through slavery and modified in form. In continuity with the native Africa, the well-being of the community was the foremost moral value among the slaves.[84]

For the Caribbean diasporan church, therefore, the call to mission has to be grounded in and informed by the communal character of its heritage if it is to be authentically Caribbean and emancipatory.

The one-sided emphasis of the call, exemplified by these Caribbean diasporan pastors, contradicts also the biblical notion of the call as a communal event. In the Bible, God calls individuals to various ministries but the individuals always come from within the community. The communal character of the call to the missionary endeavor is exemplified in the Acts of the Apostles. Those called to this work came out of the community, were sent out by the community and were accountable to the community as in the case of Paul and Barnabas.

> 'In the church at Antioch there were prophets and teachers… While they were worshipping the Lord and fasting, the Holy Spirit said, 'Set apart Barnabas and Saul for the work to which I have called them.' So after they had fasted and prayed they placed their hands on them and sent them off" (Acts 13:1-3; NIV).

The case of Saul and Barnabas symbolizes the precedence that those who are called to the mission of God should be sent out by the community and not appoint themselves as missionaries of the church or undertake mission as a personal and private enterprise. Their ministry emerged out of the community, which commissioned them in response to the command of the Spirit. The communal character of call to mission is further expressed in the Petrine writings which understand the whole church as being called to mission.

> You also, like living stones, are being built into a spiritual house to be a holy priesthood, offering spiritual sacrifices acceptable to God through Jesus Christ… But you are a chosen people, a royal priesthood, a holy nation, a people belonging to God that you may declare the praises of him who called you out of darkness into light (1 Peter 2:4, 9; NIV).

This means God calls the whole people of God to carry out the mission of God in the world. In his *The Church in the Power of the Spirit*, theologian Jürgen Moltmann offers an apt description of the nature of the call to mission. Those called by God, "come from God's people, stand up in front of God's people and act in God's name."[85]

In the case of the Caribbean diasporan church, it is the call to minister to a broken, fragmented and marginalized community. The migration process disrupts personal, family and communal living. In this context, the mission of the church includes the restoration and rebuilding of lives and communities. The community, therefore, becomes the context for experiencing and living out the call to mission.

Conclusion

What has emerged from the discussion in this chapter is that although the Caribbean diasporan church is a contributory factor in the changing character of American society and religion, its primary concern was geared towards personal aspects of religion including personal salvation, social services and church planting. This emphasis is noticeable in the church's lack of involvement in social justice. For example, while the Caribbean diasporan church was actively engaged in establishing churches, they did not relate their faith to the African American struggle for liberation from racial oppression. This was the era of the Civil Rights Movement and the birth of Black theology as an intellectual discipline and no mention was made or evidence extant to indicate any involvement in these events. This lack of involvement in social justice reflects both a dichotomy between faith and justice and a spiritualized perspective of the missionary task.

I will not contest the fact that Caribbean diasporan churches were offering a variety of social services to the community but these were acts of caring rather than addressing the causes of injustices. The church was not engaged in the work of preventing that which caused the need for care. It is not adequate to feed the hungry without seeking to prevent that which caused the hunger, to work with the victims of crime without seeking to address the cause of the crime, or to liberate the oppressed without seeking to address the cause of such oppression. The Civil Rights Movement of the sixties and the emergence of Black theology provided opportunities to address the root causes of injustice; however, the Caribbean diasporan church was unable to respond appropriately.

This shortcoming of the Caribbean diasporan church implies that the church has not completely fulfilled the call to bear witness to the emancipatory purpose of Jesus Christ. It does not mean, however, that the church was ineffective in the work that it did. Indeed, the church attempted to be an emancipatory community of faith but we have not yet examined how it seeks to fulfill the missionary mandate. It is, then, to this task of discovering how the Caribbean diasporan church carried out its mission in the resident homeland which becomes the subject for discussion in the next chapter.

8 A Voice in the Diaspora: Seeking the Welfare of the "City" Resident Homeland

In the previous two chapters, I explored the contours of the church's theological development using the pilgrim and missionary paradigms. Building on these two theological notions, I shall call attention to the particular contribution and role of the Caribbean diasporan church in the resident homeland. I shall contend, therefore, using the ministry of Egbert Ethelred Brown and the missionary practice of establishing congregational and denominational churches, that the Caribbean diasporan church is the Christian theological voice and symbolic expression of diasporan peoplehood. As such, the church functioned as a moral agent, a source of learning and a symbol of Caribbean diasporan autonomy.

In ordering this discussion, I will consider three dominant ways in which the church fulfilled the function as a voice of the Caribbean diaspora in the resident country; namely, by providing a theological critique of racism, the initiation of a Caribbean diasporan Christian intellectual tradition and the establishing of an autonomous Caribbean diasporan church tradition. Before proceeding, however, it is essential to discuss the theological guide the church uses to define its role in the resident society.

A Theological Framework

The role of the Caribbean diasporan church in the resident country is grounded firmly in the Christian faith. For this reason, the development of this church tradition cannot be understood without reference to the theological factor that informs the Caribbean diasporan religious experience. In this respect, it can be argued that the message of the letter of Jeremiah to the exilic people of God (Jer. 29:4) provides a theological framework for interpreting the role of the Caribbean diasporan church in the resident country. Although the recipients of this letter did not accept unanimously the instruction of the prophet Jeremiah,[1] I still maintain that the message of the letter can be used as a theological lens regarding the role of the Caribbean diasporan church for three primary reasons.

One reason is that, like the recipients of the letter, the Caribbean diasporan church, as a community of faith, is under the same Divine mandate to work for the common good of the resident homeland and not just for its own interest which is so common among diasporan life as I have discussed in Chapter 6, where I pointed out that when Caribbean people first emigrated, their first call to duty was survival. Put differently, during the beginning years of the Caribbean diasporan community, they were not concerned about involvement in the society or about the development of their community but how to live on a daily basis. Notwithstanding this reality, the theological meaning of Caribbean diasporan life is more than individual survival. The Divine mandate states: "Seek the welfare [well-being] of the city [resident homeland]...for in its welfare [well-being] you will find your welfare [well-being]" (Jer. 29:7; NIV).

A second reason for using the message of this letter as a theological framework for interpreting the role of the Caribbean diasporan church in the resident country is that the experience of these biblical people resonates with that of the Caribbean diaspora. This includes displacement, despair, fragmentation, marginalization and other factors that constitute diasporan existence which in one sense can be regarded as exilic. While the Caribbean diasporan people were not exiled in the same sense as these biblical people, the diasporan experience, nevertheless, resonates with the exilic experience.

The people of the Caribbean diaspora are not victims of socio-political circumstances who should spend their lives moping over the past or on the periphery of the society. Instead, the Caribbean diaspora must accept its resident home as the place where it must live and practice its faith.[2] Accordingly, the people of the Caribbean diaspora must structure life according to God's emancipatory purpose, which is to pursue the life of wholeness for all humanity. This common good Jeremiah describes as *Shalom* (27:7), which is a calling to seek justice, do good and practice righteousness in the world.

In this respect, the Caribbean diasporan church has a sacred responsibility to the resident homeland. The Caribbean diasporan church must face the reality of diasporan existence and accept the responsibility of being totally involved in it. Old Testament scholar, Walter Brueggemann, describes this role as prophetic and missional. He writes:

> Prophetic faith is hard-nosed realism that is resistant to romantic, ideological escapism. No pretense based on religious fantasy can extricate God's people from their actual place in history. Those who permit religion to abrogate historical-political reality speak a lie.[3]

The third reason the message of this letter can be used as a theological framework for defining the role of the Caribbean diasporan church in the resident homeland is the wisdom that the letter provides for diasporan living. The letter is clear about the relationship between a diasporan people and its resident homeland. A diasporan people and its resident homeland have an interwoven destiny. In this case, there is an interwoven destiny between the Caribbean diaspora and its resident homeland. The task involves working for both the well-being of the diaspora and the resident homeland.

The diaspora must be committed to serious acts of emancipatory practices because it does not exist for its own sake. It is a member of and constitutive element of the larger and wider society. This awareness protects the Caribbean diasporan "community from withdrawing into its own safe, sectarian existence, and gives it work to do and responsibility for the larger community"[4] where its role in the resident homeland includes an active involvement and engagement in public life and passionate pursuit of wholeness of life for all humanity.

Confronting "Sin in the Camp": A Theological Critique of White Supremacy

One of the first functions of the Caribbean diasporan church in the resident society is that of a prophetic voice offering a theological critique of white supremacy. This is exemplified in the ministry of Egbert Ethelred Brown. The mission of Egbert Ethelred Brown, as noted in Chapter 6, was to achieve racial integration in his denomination and to establish a Unitarian congregation in order to fulfill such a purpose. In pursuit of this goal, he provided a theological critique of systemic racism both in the church and society. With particular reference to this issue, theologian James Cone, in his theological inquiry, concludes that "racism is particularly alive and well in America [the world]. It is [Euro-America's] America's original sin and it is institutionalized at all levels of society."[5]

In an open, direct and courageous response to this problem, Brown declared his mission to be fulfilling his two dreams of achieving "genuine interracial churches in America and a Unitarian church in Harlem."[6] Brown began his diasporan journey at a time when Blacks were not regarded as human beings and racial segregation was legal from May 18, 1896 when the United States Supreme Court decided to legitimize the principle of "separate but equal" until July 2, 1964 with the passing of the Civil Rights Act. For Brown, segregation was a sin. He was determined to dismantle such an evil system and destroy this inhumane practice. Writing of his intent, Brown states:

> Unswerving loyalty to a great ideal and to a well-defined purpose has, I hope, marked my twenty-seven years of unbroken service in Harlem.... the reason is

that your writer personally found himself in the forefront of the fight against such iniquities as segregation and racial discrimination, police brutality, lynchings, and cannot separate his own experiences from the general trends of events.[7]

Here Brown is not only describing his experience of American racism but expressing the purpose for his life in the United States. He is also expressing the inseparability of personal oppression from universal oppression. The personal is a part of the universal. Thus, the struggle for individual liberation is not a mere personal struggle but a global struggle. For this reason, I contend, Brown did not establish an independent congregation. He remained a member of this predominantly white denominational church and worked within it to transform its racist theology.

Brown challenged the church that if it wished to be consistent in its faith of seeking freedom, equality and justice in society, then it must first embody these ideals. Brown recognized the hypocrisy of the American church with pastoral sorrow and prophetic critique:

> The disturbing fact is that the churches in America approved segregation in the continuing existence of separate churches for whites and Negroes. Our Unitarian churches are a current partner in this sorry business. My first dream is that one day in the not too distant future our Unitarian churches will be genuinely inter-racial – and I mean in their pulpits as well as their pews.[8]

Brown continued his prophetic critique by offering the challenge to consistency in the living out of the Christian faith. "If we are fighting for social justice in the world around us, then we must be consistent and remove the barrier which keeps colored people from our churches."[9] He based his unsparing critique of societal injustice on the life of Jesus and the gospel he preached. In a sermon, "If Jesus Came to Harlem Whom Would He Denounce?"[10] the sentence is one example of the nature of Brown's preaching. Brown was very forthright in his criticism and insightful in his observation that the preachers of the gospel were not living lives consistent with the demands of the gospel. Those attracted to the ministry were unlearned, and those who knew better were silent. Using the life of Jesus and the gospel account of his cleansing the temple, Brown argued that Jesus was not a weak, docile and compromising prophet but rather a courageous, angry and outspoken one. According to Brown, Jesus was:

> uncompromising in his denunciation of the hypocrisy of the unworthy leaders of his people, of those who prostituted the temple to a business exchange and he was capable of showing forth his wrath in dramatic fashion.[11]

This assertion by Brown suggests that God wills justice for all persons. In this sense, Brown is an outspoken advocate or prophet for justice. Morrison-Reed attests to this claim. He observed that, along with other Caribbean clergy like the Guyanese, the Reverend Wesley Holder, pastor of the Harlem Community Church, Brown was actively involved in civic and community affairs through civic organizations such as the National Equal Rights League and the West Indian Trading and Development Company.[12] As members of the Harlem Job Committee and the Harlem Tenants League, they worked for the employment of Blacks and promoted the cause of churches to establish business enterprises.[13] In one of many letters to the editor of the premier Black newspaper, the *Amsterdam News*, Brown writes:

> The Negro...has too much of the wrong kind of religion... The kind which encourages him to transfer his interest from here and now to some existence in some otherworld, [which embraces] servile contentment instead of provoking rebellious discontentment...which destroys his personal responsibility by leading him to believe in the possibility of escaping punishment for his wrong doing. [What is needed is] a religion of the present and the practical profoundly concerned with this world... The virtue of discontentment is a necessary preliminary to making this earth a place wherein dwell justice and peace and love... [Every man must] shoulder his own responsibility [and] every man must work out his own salvation. Our colored ministers must...cleanse their religious meetings from the over-emotionalism which dangerously borders on fanaticism.[14]

In opposition to injustice and unrighteousness, Brown advocated that followers of Jesus are to model their lives on Jesus:

> Brethren who hear me I charge you that are also ambassadors of Christ, servants of Righteousness and of Truth and I call upon you to go forth from this place filled with rage and anger at these despoilers of the temple and raise your voice in the name of your Master and denounce them.[15]

In light of this claim, Brown is calling for Christians to use the power of the mind so as to bring the Christian faith to bear on the issues of society. And moreover, God has not only liberated the mind to think but thinking is also a theological act.

Initiating a Caribbean Diasporan Christian Intellectual Tradition

The forging of a Caribbean diasporan Christian intellectual tradition is another role of the Caribbean diasporan church in the resident society. In examining this role, the discussion defines and addresses the issue of Black intellectual emancipation in the development of a Caribbean diasporan Christian intellectual tradition. While there is no developed Caribbean diasporan systematic ideology, this study considers the polemical responses of Egbert Ethelred Brown to the ideology of anti-intellectualism

and white supremacy as formative and constitutive factors of Caribbean
diasporan Christian intellectual tradition.

What is the Caribbean Diasporan Christian Intellectual Tradition?

The Caribbean diasporan intellectual tradition is the belief and practice of
using reason as a guide for the liberation of oppressed peoples and whose
development began with the migration of Caribbean intellectuals to
America[16] and Great Britain[17] in the late nineteenth century. Prominent
among them were Robert Love,[18] T. E. S. Scholes,[19] Edward Wilmot
Blyden,[20] Marcus Garvey,[21] Claude McKay,[22] C. L. R. James,[23] Richard B.
Moore[24] and others[25] who have established and represent different
Caribbean diasporan intellectual traditions. The intellectual tradition that
this study advocates, however, is a Christ-centered intellectual tradition
that is informed by Caribbean history, culture and diasporan religious
experience for the emancipation and empowerment of persons and the
transformation of society. This intellectual tradition understands that
knowledge of the gospel is understood through faith and therefore takes
into account the faith and ideas that Caribbean people brought with them
to the diaspora to create not only their own world-view, identity and
culture but to transform their resident homeland. More fundamentally,
this model of intellectual tradition is the discipline of loving God with the
mind using ideas to influence both personal and public lives to fulfill
God's emancipatory purpose for humanity. It is a tradition that goes beyond
the cultivation of the mind, loving ideas and creating academic
specialization, to the interpretation of the mystery of the Christian faith
and relating such to the social existential reality of the people. As such,
the tradition affirms the Christian gospel as God offering hope to humanity
and empowerment to the oppressed to resist oppression and fight for
freedom. Concurring with this claim, James Cone declares:

> If the Black church is going to deal creatively with the relevant issues of the time,
> develop transformative paradigms, implement effective strategies, then we have
> a responsibility to develop a creative theology [intellectual tradition] that will
> hold us accountable to the gospel of Jesus Christ. The Black church needs
> prophetic and professional theologians [an intellectual tradition] that will help
> the preachers [people] to understand the gospel and how to make it relevant in
> the twenty-first century.[26]

Put more succinctly, the Caribbean diasporan Christian intellectual
tradition is the use of the mind as a guide from the perspective of faith
for living and the conducting of human affairs. Ultimately, without this
intellectual tradition, the Caribbean diasporan church risks becoming
enslaved to a foreign knowledge and theology, false ideology and a

misguided faith. This tradition helps to clarify the meaning of the Christian faith for the diaspora and to face the issues that constitute diasporan life. For this reason, if we are going to be true to ourselves and faith, we need this Christian intellectual tradition that thinkers such as Egbert Ethelred Brown have helped to establish. For as James Cone claims:

> The Black Church needs all of the intellectual and spiritual resources we can muster to cope with the complex and dangerous world we live in. Do not underestimate evil's power to confuse and corrupt the mind and spirit. We are struggling not just against flesh and blood, not just against an individual instance of oppression, but against structural evil.[27]

Cone's insightful analysis of the need for learned leadership in the Black church is instructive for the Caribbean diasporan Christian intellectual tradition. It is at this point that it becomes obligatory to identify the response of the Caribbean diasporan church to this challenge.

Liberating the Mind

It is obvious that the perspective of Cone is consistent with that of Egbert Ethelred Brown, who demonstrated that in order for the Caribbean diasporan church to face these challenges, the leadership will have to do more than maintain the important discipline of Bible reading and cultivating the essential virtue of sincerity. Cone says it best:

> Ministers need to do more than just read the Bible to answer these problems. Ministers need to study. Sincerity is not enough. If sincerity is not buffered with intelligence, it can become a very destructive force in society.[28]

In this respect, Egbert Ethelred Brown, while he did not develop a systematic body of theological thought, can be regarded as initiating a Caribbean diasporan Christian intellectual tradition premised on his polemical responses to the practice of anti-intellectualism in Black religion and the notion of intellectual inferiority of Black people in Euro-American intellectual tradition.

Correcting Anti-intellectualism

Brown, as noted earlier, was committed to the development and use of the mind as the norm for human living. One reason for this commitment was the liberation of Black people from anti-intellectualism. Anti-intellectualism is the opposition to the use of the mind to love God. For Brown, faith and reason were compatible. He vehemently dismissed the anti-intellectualism that was characteristic of Black religious practice of the time. In a sermon, "A Challenging Question," Brown avers, "Christianity is the religion of the whole man [person] which calls on us to worship God with the heart and soul but also with the mind..."[29] Brown was convinced that the mind is both a gift from God and the highest expression of human distinctiveness. He maintains:

> ...by keeping our intelligence intact, by honoring the sacred gift of reason which is humanity's unique gift, the gift which differentiates us from all other animals makes a man [human being] a man [human being].[30]

Thus, this statement acknowledges that anti-intellectualism is detrimental to the welfare of the people of God. The learned prophetic biblical tradition acknowledges anti-intellectualism as one of the major causes of the destruction of God's people. The prophet Hosea states it as follows. "My people are destroyed because of lack of knowledge" (Hos. 4:6; NIV).

Ethelred Brown detested anti-intellectualism which he thought was not only a disgrace but a sin. He likened the unlearned clergy, for example, to the act of desecration of the temple during the time of Jesus as the people used it for other purposes other than the cause of righteousness. For Brown, ignorance is a poor commentary and reflection on the whole Christian ministry. He reflected:

> Is it not, I asked these brother ministers of mine, a sad reflection on the whole ministry that of the phenomenon of an illiterate man claiming thousands of followers?[31]

Brown's contention is that anti-intellectualism in the ministry is a scandal that warranted the wrath of God in keeping with Jesus' clearing of the temple.[32] The echo of this claim can be heard in the assertion of James Cone in his advocacy for Black Christianity to take seriously the life of the mind. Cone urges:

> Unfortunately, the Black church is not known for promoting the intellectual side of the Christian ministry. We love God with our hearts and souls, but we often forget that we were also called to love God with our minds... Too few Black people have developed the intellectual interest and passion to become first-rate scholars and theologians.[33]

Listening to this challenge to love God with the mind demonstrates that God has not only liberated the mind but there is also the liberation of the mind, as the writer of the epistle to the Romans states: "...be transformed by the renewing of the mind..." (Rom. 12:1-2; NIV).

Affirming the Black Mind

In addition to liberation from enslavement to anti-intellectualism in Black religion, Brown also addressed the heretical belief of Black intellectual inferiority in Euro-American theology. Brown is convinced, and correctly so, that the mind of Black people is equally their guide for living as it is for other human beings, including white people. He addressed this issue during the establishment of a church in the professed enlightened and liberated denomination, the Unitarian Church of America.

The notion of Black intellectual inferiority is a legacy of Enlightenment thinking, as Voltaire, the French philosopher, one of its most celebrated proponents, states:

> The Negro is a species of [human] as different from ours as the breed of spaniels is from that of greyhounds. The mucous membrane, or network, which nature has spread between the muscles and the skin, is white in us and black or copper-colored in them...
>
> If their understanding is not of different nature from ours, it is at least greatly inferior. They are not capable of any great application or association of ideals, and seemed formed neither for the advantages nor the abuses of philosophy.[34]

This racist view is expressed further by the infamous Scottish philosopher, David Hume, who writes in his essay "Of National Characteristics":

> I am apt to suspect the negroes, and in general all the other species of men (for there are four or five different kinds) to be naturally inferior to the whites. There was never a civilized nation of any other complexion than white, nor even any individual eminent either in action or speculation. No ingenious manufacturers amongst them, no arts, no science...
>
> In Jamaica indeed they talk of one Negro as a man of parts and learning; but 'tis likely he is admired for very slender accomplishments, like a parrot, who speaks a few words plainly.[35]

This is the prevailing ideology to which Brown was responding when he established a church that embraced faith and reason. It was Brown's purpose to emigrate from Jamaica to the United States to establish one such church for Blacks. "As far as I am concerned," he wrote in *The History of Harlem Unitarian Church*, "I sailed from the Island of Jamaica determined to establish a Unitarian Church in Harlem, and all that mattered to me in March 1920 was that the venture should be launched without delay."[36] This was a different kind of church. It existed as an inclusive religious community to serve humanity and to seek the "Truth."[37] The church's records also described it as follows:

> The Harlem Community Church, a thorough-going liberal church, deliberately seeking to minister to men and women who have intellectually outgrown the fundamental doctrine of orthodox Christianity.[38]

Yet, a pervasive belief among some Unitarians, at that time, was that Black people did not have the intellectual capability to understand the tenets of Unitarianism. Ironically, it was the Unitarian's commitment to the life of the mind that appealed to Brown to become a member of the organization[39] which could become the home of the thinking Black person. He said: "I believed in and still believe in Unitarianism as the religion of the future – the religion with an emancipatory message which all peoples of every race may understand and accept."[40] Brown understood Unitarianism to uphold the ideals of holistic emancipation and the equality of all persons. These ideals were the reasons he was attracted to this religious tradition. Brown expressed these ideals as follows:

> At the beginning of my ministry it was my task to keep the flag of Unitarianism flying in a segregated city within a city – to prove not to the world, but to Unitarians, that Negroes are becoming Unitarians, and that therefore Unitarianism is a universal religion.[41]

Although Brown established and maintained relationship within a predominantly white denominational church, his critique of racism identifies this issue as a theological problem which was not only an anomaly from but a critique of Western theological tradition. In recent times, the father of Black theology, James Cone, has acknowledged this inherent error and weakness in this tradition and offers a penetrating critique when he writes:

> Though racism inflicts massive suffering, few American theologians have even bothered to address White supremacy as a moral evil and as a radical contradiction of our humanity and religious identities.[42]

From this theological critique of white supremacy, we can learn that to be engaged in the struggle against oppression is not an option but a mandate to confront and unmask all attempts to evade and avoid it. For Cone, this task is not to excuse the oppressors from the consequences of their actions but to expose their hypocrisies and falsify their claims. Consider the following stinging indictment of Cone.

> White theologians and philosophers write numerous articles and books on theodicy, asking why God permits massive suffering, but they hardly ever mention the horrendous crimes Whites have committed against people of color in the modern world.[43]

It is noteworthy that Black theology has made a connection with this prophetic stance in its attack on white religion. Just as Brown was unsparing in his critique of racism so were Black theologians. Thus, Black theology undertakes the task to detect and expose the sin of white supremacy in Euro-American theology, claiming that "Black theologians could not remain silent of the ever increasing manifestations of racism in the white church and its theology...and thus uncover its demonic and sinister nature."[44] In light of this endeavor, it is not fortuitous that there is a developing Caribbean diasporan Christian intellectual tradition. In support of the need for this intellectual tradition, Cone asked rhetorically:

> What is the prophetic word of ministry to the African American community [Caribbean diasporan community] and America and the world today? What are

we going to do about this terrible human predicament – about all of the hurt, the pain, and the suffering that people endure today?[45]

Undoubtedly, Cone's astute questions are applicable to the Caribbean diasporan church. The most seminal relevance of his questions relates to the embryonic theological development of a Caribbean diasporan Christian intellectual tradition. Brown, as the founding father of this tradition, did not explore nor engage the tradition's own resources for theological reflection. Brown correctly argued for the dismantling of racism but he was not prepared to establish an independent Caribbean diasporan church. His intent was to reform his denomination rather than to revolutionize it, which the establishment of a Black independent Unitarian church would have represented. It meant, therefore, that his church was under the control of an organization he regarded as sinful. His approach was one of working within a system for change rather than working from outside the system. Brown's reformist approach, nevertheless, reflects the nature of a nascent Caribbean diasporan ecclesiology.

What is more problematic is that this emerging intellectual tradition patterned the Euro-American theological tradition, holding this tradition as its ideal, norm and model for learning and truth. This tendency is evident in Brown's writings where he puts forth this tradition as ideal through his constant references to white writers and thinkers without any mention of similar Black persons or sources. In a sermon "The Search for Truth," his four sources of authority, Francis Bacon, John Ruskin, Abraham Lincoln and Marcus Aurelius were all white males.[46] This indicates that although Brown believed in the intellectual equality of his fellow Black sisters and brothers to all others, he never considered their thoughts as being an equal source of authority to whites'.

Brown's practice of appealing to Euro-American authorities without any reference to Black authorities suggests further that he never regarded Blacks as equals to whites and that he subconsciously acknowledged the Euro-American intellectual tradition as normative. One could, of course, argue that he was only reflecting the mode of thinking of his time as this perspective would be inconsistent with his quest for racial justice. The lack of self-awareness and use of Black culture and thought in this emerging Caribbean diasporan intellectual tradition, therefore, demonstrates that it was not fully liberative. Nevertheless, the life of the mind, as Brown demonstrates, is essential to the affirmation of Black humanity against the denigration of the Black intellect which is endemic to Euro-American thought. For this reason, it will be necessary for the Caribbean diasporan church to seek to develop its own intellectual tradition capable of challenging Euro-American intellectual and theological hegemony and which should also seek to engender dialogue and relationship on the basis of mutual respect and equality.

Indeed, in large measure, meeting this challenge calls for the church to pay careful attention to the claim of the premier Black theologian, James Cone.

> The black church, therefore, needs to find ways to bring charismatic preachers under the control of critical theological reason and the prophetic judgment of God. The black church needs seminary-trained, university-educated prophetic theologians, who are as committed to their intellectual vocation as pastors are to their call to preach.
>
> The preacher proclaims the gospel and the theologian explains it so the preacher will not get carried away with his or her eschatological rhetoric. The preacher inspires people to make a commitment to the gospel and the theologian analyzes the preached word and subjects it to the justice and mercy of God revealed in Jesus Christ.
>
> To be a profound preacher, therefore, one must be a critical and prophetic theological thinker. As preacher, one proclaims God's love for the poor, and as theologian, one reflects on the meaning of divine love for the poor when their poverty seems to deny that claim.[47]

Given the charge of Cone, the work of Egbert Ethelred Brown can be considered an example of the Caribbean diasporan church as an agent of emancipatory change in the resident country. In this regard, Brown's belief in and commitment to the use of the mind as guide for human living is not only grounded in the Christian faith but is a direct challenge, radical reconstruction and a prophetic critique of Western intellectual tradition which promotes white supremacy that the Greek and Enlightenment philosophy legitimized and Euro-American theology reflects.[48]

An Autonomous Church

In addition to the role as a moral and intellectual voice of the Caribbean diaspora, the Caribbean diasporan church functioned as an agent of self-determination in the resident homeland. Self-determination takes different forms, but in this study I argue that it is expressed through the emergence of autonomous Caribbean diasporan congregations. This being the case, I turn attention to the issue of autonomy by proving a definition and a description of the term as it is understood within the Caribbean diasporan theological discourse.

Defining Autonomy

While Caribbean Christians are deeply conscious of the universality of the Christian faith and embrace the ecumenical spirit of the faith, they are self-consciously independent.[49] Writing in recognition of this belief of autonomy, in regard to political independence, C. L. R. James has this to say:

> For a community such as ours, where, although there is race prejudice, there is no race antagonism, where the people have reached their present level in wealth, education, and general culture, the Crown Colony system of government has no place. It was useful in its day but that day is now over. It is a fraud, because it is based on assumptions of superiority which have no foundation. Admirable as are their gifts in this direction, yet administrative capacity is not the monopoly of the English; and even if it were, charity begins at home, especially in these difficult times.[50]

It is against the Caribbean spirit to practice the Christian faith in isolation from the general Christian body, but that does not mean dependence on others in order to do what they believe they are called to do. The neo-colonial mentality and practice which are usually characteristic of denominational missionary agencies that are actually and potentially imperialistic, are fiercely resisted by the Caribbean diasporan church. Working with denominational agencies was more an expression of Christian kinship and the sharing of the one common faith. The Christian faith teaches "there is one body and one Spirit – just as you were called to one hope when you were called – one Lord, one faith, one baptism, one God and [parent] of all, who is over all and through and in all" (Eph. 4:4-6; NIV).

The Caribbean spirit of autonomy is grounded in the Christian faith but expressed through the formation of independent Caribbean organizations. The establishing of independent organizations was one of the first major contributions of the Caribbean diaspora to American society and the Black struggle against oppression. Winston James, for instance, observes that the establishing of the United Negro Improvement Association, which was the largest, most powerful and influential Black organization in the history of the world, was an expression of Caribbean diasporan autonomy. The United Negro Improvement Association had a membership of approximately four million including people from America, Africa, Australia, the Caribbean and Europe.[51] Also, the Caribbean intelligentsia such as Claude McKay, W. A. Domingo, Cyril Briggs, Richard Moore and others who were leading members of Black organizations and who have played a significant role in the Harlem Renaissance is another manifestation of Caribbean diasporan autonomy.[52]

What makes this tradition of autonomy outstanding is its inclusive nature. Not only were women part of the membership of these organizations but they played a collective role in building them. While James is careful to observe the role of women, he considered their role only within the United Negro Improvement Association rather than in the Caribbean diasporan community as a whole. Caribbean women came from a tradition where they participated as a matter of course in the struggle against injustice. In their homeland, they were actively involved in the anti-colonial struggle. Fordham University's historian and immigration scholar, Irma Watkins-Owens, in a study on Caribbean women of the early twentieth century, recognizes the autonomous tradition from which these women came and uncovers the significant role they played in the formation of the Caribbean diaspora. "African Caribbean women's participation in various voluntary associations, especially homeland and fraternal, was widespread in New York."[53]

Additionally, the involvement and leadership of women in social organizations is more significant than has been recognized.[54] Women formed their own organizations that promoted their own cause for self-reliance and emancipation and raised finances to support some causes back in the homeland. They established organizations such as the American West Indian Ladies Aid Society and the radical Harlem Tenants League. Women's organizations were involved in political activities both in host and home countries.[55] These events reflected self-determination and resistance to oppression. The defying of the segregation laws, for example, to procure employment in the Needle Trade industry by Caribbean women, is a further demonstration of their militant and autonomous character.

Although unacknowledged, Caribbean women were instrumental in starting the desegregation movement in America and certainly in the Northeast. The women were in need of employment but were not allowed to work because of the color of their skin. As they went in search of employment, they saw the signs posted in the stores: "colored people were not wanted. We took them down and marched right in to apply. You bet, we got the jobs."[56] W. A. Domingo brilliantly describes the powerful influence of Caribbean women in the Black struggle for justice.

> This freedom from spiritual inertia characterizes the women no less than the men, for it is largely through them that the occupational field has been broadened for colored women in New York. By their determination, sometimes reinforced by dexterous use of their hatpins, these women have made it possible for members of their race to enter the needle trades freely.[57]

Caribbean people's desire for autonomy expressed itself in self-dependence and inclusivity. This practice of the people helped to shape the theological development of the Caribbean diasporan church as an autonomous Christian organization. The church embodies this autonomy in the formation of public and self-governed congregations. These two practices are now considered in turn.

The Nature of Autonomy

Now that I have defined autonomy, the discussion continues with an examination on the nature of this autonomy. I examine autonomy by focusing on how the church practices it as a public organization with particular attention to the two definitive components, the congregational and the denominational church and also on the issue of self-governing institutions.

A Public Organization

The Bronx Baptist Church serves to illustrate the congregational component of the public nature of the Caribbean diasporan church's practice of autonomy. This church began as a small prayer group in 1964 and grew into a premier religious institution. It began with seven people and within two years grew to sixty-four when it was constituted as a legal organization on November 6, 1966.[58]

In the beginning of the missionary work of organizing and establishing churches, these churches were first transplanted congregations and not necessarily organic ones. Organic congregations are the product of the diasporan community but the membership and constituency consist largely of the second generation of migrants. The transplanted congregations are not only organized by the first generation of the diasporan Christians but they constitute the membership and define the constituency. In the case of the Bronx Baptist Church, recently arrived people constituted its membership. In their home country, they were members of the local and denominational church. Including the pastor, Samuel Simpson, but excluding his wife, Lola, the core group of Voris MountRose Walker, Hervin and Patricia Rattray, Hyacinth Francis and Cecilia Robinson[59] were members of the Jones Town Baptist Church, St. Andrew, Jamaica.

These people, who formed the nucleus for the development of a church in a new country, were mature Christians and leaders in their church prior to migrating to America. This pattern was replicated in the establishment of diasporan churches in the United States. Along with the Bronx Baptist Church, examples include the Bronx Bethany Church of the Nazarene (that was previously discussed) and others like the Flatbush Church of God in Brooklyn, the Gateway Church in Florida and many other Caribbean diasporan churches.[60]

The Bronx Baptist Church began with the usual religious meetings including worship service on Sundays and weekly prayer meetings during the week and as they grew numerically, they organized regular auxiliaries such as Sunday School, and women's, men's and youth fellowship as a means of communicating the gospel and seeking numerical growth. Describing this form of mission, Simpson remarked:

From the very beginning we placed great emphasis on Sunday School, visitation, witnessing, discovering community needs, Bible Study, vibrant worship, along with organized, specific prayer.[61]

The vision of the church, however, was larger than this traditional style of ministry; the vision was to be more than a spiritual organization. The plans for growth were an integral aspect of the formation. It is not clear if this was the vision of the church or the pastor but it seems clear that this vision did exist. In Simpson's account:

From day one we were planning for expansion; it would not be long before we would be planning for multiplication. Although only a few were meeting, we experienced a spirit of unity, togetherness, and excitement.[62]

With this kind of numerical and organizational growth, the Bronx Baptist Church realized that mission was more than individual salvation and personal experience. Although these have their merits, they only cater to the individual whereas the purpose of mission includes the total lives of persons and society. In this regard, the church offered a variety of social ministries and a series of community development initiatives including a Day Care Centre, Early Childhood Education and low-income renovation programs. The church was one of the organizing members of the Twins Parks Association – a consortium of religious and community organizations that provided housing for low-income individuals and families as a form of community and economic development.[63] Samuel Simpson, in a reflective account of this development, states:

With more time on hand, seeing the desperate needs existing in the community, I led the church to gear its programs and ministries to all of the people living under the severe tensions of inner city life... Besides proclaiming the gospel and having the usual training ministries for members, Bronx Baptist Church actively involved itself in the socio-political life of the community of the never-ending struggle to obtain such amenities as better housing, schools, sanitation, medical care, and justice for the helpless and inarticulate.[64]

The second component of the Caribbean diasporan church as a public institution is the denominational church represented by the formation of the Associated Gospel Assembly USA in 2005. The Associated Gospel Assembly, USA consists of a group of independent congregations that came from a single-parent body, the Associated Gospel Assembly, Jamaica. While the members did not migrate as a church, the individual members established local congregations in various places in America, including New York, New Jersey and Florida, where these individual congregations are being organized into a denominational church. Their document of corporate identity, "Policy and Procedure – AGA-USA,"[65] states as their purpose:

> To bear witness to the Christian truth, to evangelize the unsaved, oversee the establishment of new churches; to erect and assist in erecting such buildings as may be necessary for such purposes and to engage in preaching and establishing and maintaining houses for religious worship…foster growth between member churches…to assist in the teaching of religion missionary training…[66]

This is a very radical initiative. Among the Caribbean diasporan churches, although some are independent congregations and others affiliated with a denominational church, there is no Caribbean diasporan denominational church. The Associated Gospel Assembly symbolizes a movement from local church to denominational church indicating the development of a Caribbean diasporan autonomous church tradition. It is distinct from both the African American and the white American church traditions. This raises two issues pertinent to our discussion.

The first issue is that a collective pan-Caribbean identity appears central to an autonomous existence. The Associated Gospel Assembly exercises general oversight and centralizes authority of all the member churches. While they do not represent the entire Caribbean diaspora, they demonstrate a collective identity unlike any other Caribbean diasporan organization. Inherent in this collective identity is a latent pan-Caribbean consciousness and identity. The membership of the organization is made up of people from across the Caribbean. The pan-Caribbean consciousness, however, is not a foremost factor in their identity. Its collective identity centers on their faith in Jesus Christ as Christians as noted in their above mentioned purpose.

The practice of grounding identity in a non-contextualized faith is both a reflection of Euro-American Christianity and a disregard for ethnic identity. Euro-American Christianity bears no reference to a Caribbean heritage, nationality or ethnicity. Furthermore, it promotes a de-racialized Christian identity implying a non-racial Christian identity which is not only uncharacteristic of Black Christianity but an anomaly in the practice of Christianity in American society.

The second issue in question is the Associated Gospel Assembly's insular understanding of mission. Reflecting on their purpose, no mention is made of any engagement of the church beyond personal salvation. The only allusion to any social engagement is the supervision in the construction of houses of worship. This, however, is not done as a social act but as a form of personal spirituality. The Associated Gospel Assembly is committed to mission but only as personal salvation for the empowerment and training of its members and the evangelization of non-Christians. This purpose is limited, provides survival strategies and promotes a survivalist mentality that does not address social and systemic issues nor engage prophetically with the oppressive systems and structures that define the society in which the church is called to live and serve. Undoubtedly, the intent is to provide a spiritual center for the Christians of the Caribbean diaspora, but there is also the need to address the principalities and powers that mitigate against human dignity and well-being.

Ecclesiastical Self-government

The practice of self-determination through ecclesiastical self-government is another feature of the autonomous character of the Caribbean diasporan church. The Caribbean diasporan church has not only its own organizations but pursues its own agenda, elects its own leadership and governs its own membership. At their inception, most churches were established without having any formally trained leaders but were informal prayer and fellowship groups that grew to become churches. The Bronx Bethany Church of the Nazarene serves as such an example. This church began in 1959 with like-minded Jamaican Christians meeting for prayer and fellowship. They met in solidarity with each other and to discern the meaning of their existence in the host country which at that time was their "strange land" (Ps. 137:4). Describing this experience, the organizing pastor, V. Seymour Cole, writes:

> In this motley and vibrant city, with its skyscrapers, stock exchange and leading television and news media outlets came a group of people who also were trying to make their way in the system. Bound together by race, culture and faith, they sought out for themselves a place for prayer and fellowship. That place was the living room of Mr. and Mrs. Manchand at Fulton Avenue in the Bronx. Soon the prayer meeting would evolve in a Sunday evening service, which would meet in the Lutheran schoolroom across the street.[67]

In 1962, three years after the inception of the prayer group, they called their own pastor, V. Seymour Cole, a recent graduate of the Church of the Nazarene theological institution, Kansas City Bible College. After assuming the leadership, Cole took the initiative, two years later, of establishing formal denominational relationship with the Church of the Nazarene.[68] "On May 10, 1964," according to the church's record, "Reverend V. Seymour Cole led a group of 21 charter members into the Church of the Nazarene."[69] On this occasion, the church changed its name from the Bronx Bethany Gospel Assembly to Bronx Bethany Church of the Nazarene.[70]

The appointing of Cole as the pastor of the church is a significant initiative in becoming a self-governed institution. This raises two concerns. One concern is that the church is a movement of, by and for the people and not a clergy-oriented movement. This serves as a corrective and a reminder that personality-oriented churches are not the model for Caribbean disaporan churches. It goes further to express the belief in the apostleship of the laity. This is the belief that God also calls and sends the laity into the world as proclaimers of the gospel. Apostleship of the laity means the whole church is the agent and community of God's emancipatory gospel in the world.[71]

The second concern is an emerging pattern of Caribbean diasporan churches seeking denominational affiliation with Euro-American church tradition rather than or in addition to African American church tradition. In the formation and celebrations of the Bronx Bethany Church of the Nazarene, great effort was made to emphasize the acknowledgment and acceptance of their denomination. The records state:

> ...the union was sealed and the Rev. V. Seymour Cole...and people were warmly welcomed into the denomination by... Superintendent of the New York District...a dedication service was held in October 1968 with the General Superintendent...and District Superintendent participating.[72]

These were major historical moments in American church history as well as significant events in the society. Yet, the African American church was neither present nor involved. The conclusion that could be drawn from this practice is that the policy of some Caribbean diasporan churches was to be in relationship with a theological tradition alien to the experience and ethnicity of the Caribbean people. In giving an account for working with the Southern Baptist Convention, Samuel Simpson expresses this understanding:

> When a few I knew heard we were establishing a Southern Baptist Church in the Bronx they questioned our presence because of traditional Southern Baptist racist attitude[s] towards black people in the South where most of their churches were located... I knew time would give the answers if we were truly following God's leadership as best as we knew how. We found Christianity is not limited to culture, class, race or creed. Its uniqueness embraces them all – "Out of many people, one people" – the people of God.[73]

Of course, one could argue correctly that Christianity is inclusive and that the Euro-American churches were the ones with whom the Caribbean diasporan church had pre-existing relationships prior to their migrating to the United States.[74] This may be the case, but how do we account for the relationship that was forged between the first generation of Caribbean diasporan intellectuals and African Americans during the early twentieth century?

The influence of Caribbean thinkers on African Americans is considered a very important factor in the liberation of Black people and the transformation of American society. Harold Cruse discusses, though he fails to grasp, for example, the impact of Garveyism on the rise and development of the Black Power movement and may even be prejudicial in his analysis of what he called "West Indian" self-understanding. Cruse, however, agrees that the Caribbean experience plays a central role in the Black liberation struggle.[75]

Vincent Franklin advances this discussion by acknowledging the forging of the relationship between African Americans and Caribbeaners in the struggle for Black liberation. Franklin calls attention to movements like the Haitian Revolution and personalities like James Theodore Holly, an ordained Episcopalian deacon; Robert Campbell, an educator; Edward Blyden, a Presbyterian clergyman – Caribbean immigrants who have made a significant impact upon African Americans. The relationship continues especially through the writings of C. L. R. James as expressed by the African American historian, Manning Marable of Columbia University.[76]

The question still remains unanswered, however. How is it that progressively oriented Caribbean thinkers identified with the struggle for racial justice of our African American counterparts whilst the Christians of the Caribbean diaspora did not?[77] Furthermore, even after learning of the racist character of churches and experiencing racism within them, why does the Caribbean diasporan church still maintain relationships with these kind of churches and why has it not made any intentional move to establish relationships with any of the major Black denominations?

This issue is worthy of an answer because Black life is a history of struggle. In the case of the Caribbean, the people have always been involved in the quest for justice. In his study on Caribbean immigrants, Winston James correctly observes that

> Caribbean migrants came to America with a long and distinguished tradition of resistance with few parallels in the new world. They consequently entered the United States with a sense of self-confidence and pride that would have predisposed at least some of them to radical activity, as the harsh racism battered their self-esteem.[78]

The Jamaican W. A. Domingo, one of the organizing members of the nationalist organization, Jamaica Progressive League, writing about the Caribbean contribution to American society and particularly the Black struggle for liberation concurred with James. "It is they who largely compose the few political and economic radicals in Harlem; without them the genuinely radical movement among New York Negroes would be unworthy of attention."[79]

The nature of the heritage of the Caribbean diaspora in terms of its emancipatory tradition and diversity of ideological responses also influenced the question of the relationship between the Caribbean diasporan church and the white denominational churches. Dennis Forsythe identifies four traditions governing the relationship and the quest for emancipation.

There is the civic radicalism that embraces nationalism as the main objective of Black liberation accomplished through integration into the dominant society as represented by W. A. Domingo. The second is the communistic tradition, addressing the cause of oppression, as a class problem and not as a problem of racialism that C. L. R. James represents. A third response is the Black radicalism that interprets race as the cause of oppression and proposes that Blacks are to focus on their own history and heritage as the means of liberation which Marcus Garvey represents. This response, nevertheless, assumes an uncritical acceptance of capitalism and even promoted Black capitalism.

The final response is progressive nationalism that believes race to be the cause of Black oppression but proposes that liberation be achieved through the amalgamation of Black culture, power and socialism.[80] Claude McKay represents this response. He states, "I see no other way of upward struggle for colored people, but through the working class movement."[81]

Forsythe's interpretation of the Caribbean diaspora's responses to Black oppression demonstrates that Caribbean people have been involved in the Black struggle for emancipation. He further shows that for the first generation of migrants, and subsequently during the first and second stages in the formation of the Caribbean diaspora, the struggle for liberation was a foremost engagement. What Forsythe has overlooked, however, is the role of the Caribbean diasporan church in the desacralization of racism and the de-Euro-Americanization of God as represented by the work of Ethelred Brown and the Harlem Community Church, discussed previously.

Conclusion

This chapter considers the role of the Caribbean diasporan church in the resident homeland by examining the implications of the pilgrim and missionary self-understandings of the church's theological development. In the case of the pilgrim self-understanding, the church functioned as an internal prophetic witness by offering primarily a theological critique of racism and established a Caribbean diasporan Christian intellectual tradition. Put differently, the church served as the conscience or, more precisely, an internal critic of ecclesiastical praxis and affirmed critical thinking as an essential Christian activity and vital to human liberation. Marcus Garvey, in recognition of this tradition, states:

> Never forget that intelligence rules the world and carries the burden. Therefore remove yourself as far as possible from ignorance and seek as far as possible to be intelligent.[82]

Regarding the missionary self-understanding, the discussion addresses the issue of autonomous religious organizations that functioned as public and independent communities of faith. The emergence of this new and developing church tradition signifies a new era in American religious life in general and Black religion in particular. Caribbean diasporan churches as autonomous organizations changed the character of the religious and theological landscape of American society. These churches have become integral entities of the socio-religious structure and constitutive entities of their societies.

Inasmuch as we have considered the role of the Caribbean diasporan church in the resident society, still to be examined is the issue of the distinguishing features of the Caribbean diasporan church. This is the subject of the succeeding chapter.

9 The Distinctives of the Caribbean Diasporan Church

As I have stated throughout this book, this study is an attempt to construct a theology for the Caribbean diasporan church. We are now at the stage where it becomes necessary to articulate the defining characteristics of this church. What distinguishes the Caribbean diasporan church from other churches? What are the essential marks that separate this church from other organizations? What are the visible hallmarks of this church? The theological doctrine of the church that I seek to construct acknowledges that a theological doctrine of the church requires that we identify its distinguishing features.

The issue of the marks of the church is not anything new to theological discourse. This practice has its precedence in the earliest development of Christian theology as delineated in the Apostles' and Nicene Creeds.[1] The former acknowledges three marks – "one, holy, catholic church" and the latter acknowledges four marks of the church – "one, holy, catholic and apostolic" church.[2] Writing of the meaning of these marks from a European Protestant perspective, Jürgen Moltmann notes that they are "statements of faith, hope and action."[3] Discussing the merits of these claims is beyond the scope of this book. I call attention, however, to the claim that these marks of the church are creedal statements of faith that reflect the development of the church in the Roman Empire.[4] In this regard, it can be argued that these marks of the church reflect political concerns rather than the theological character of the church.

African American theology also addresses this issue of the marks of the church. Whereas in Euro-American theology, these marks are creedal statements of faith, in African American theology they are functional statements of faith. Theologian James Evans, Jr. in his important text on Black theology expresses this perspective. He identifies the marks of the church as preaching, fellowship, service, teaching, ministry and the ordinances of the Lord's Supper and Baptism.[5] Without disregarding the Euro-American perspective of the marks of the church which expresses the church's theological identity, for Evans, in African American theology, these marks of the church express the church's mission.[6]

Indeed, the marks of the church, as Moltmann notes, "are not merely important internal activities of the church; they are an even more important witness of the church's form in the world."[7] Moreover, concurring with Evans, the marks of the church "derive their meaning in the concrete historical solidarity of the Christian and Christ with the community of faith in the Spirit of freedom."⁸ Building on these two claims – the creedal and the functional – the Caribbean diasporan perspective that I am proposing, asserts that the marks of the church are organic.

By organic I mean the particular marks of the church that emerge out of the dynamic engagement of the church with the reality of diasporan existence. These distinctives are not definitive but are evolving, revealing not only a new dimension but a peculiar character of the theological understanding of the church. With this understanding, I will discuss three distinctives that have emerged in this study so far: namely, the church as a community of learning, alternative community of faith and as home. Now, I shall examine these distinctives in greater detail.

Community of Learning

In this study it has become clear to me that the Caribbean diasporan church is a community of learning. As we have seen in Chapter 2, learning is a definitive mark of Caribbean diasporan religious practice. This is based on the perspective and work of Egbert Ethelred Brown, the founding pastor of the Harlem Community Church in the beginning of the twentieth century. Although Brown's work represents a particular period in Caribbean diasporan ecclesiastical history, I maintain that his work can be regarded as a paradigm of the perspective I am advancing. As such, I consider the Hubert Harrison Memorial Church that Egbert Ethelred Brown organized as a paradigmatic illustration.

Brown portrayed the church as a community of learning by linking faith and learning. He demonstrated this by the name chosen for his church. Brown named the church he pastored in honor of Hubert Harrison, one of the leading public intellectuals of his time. According to A. Philip Randolph, Harrison is "the father of Harlem Radicalism,"⁹ and was regarded as "One of the fullest scholars and most effective teachers of history and literature that this country has provided."¹⁰ Harrison was devoted to learning and was an authority in literature, the social sciences, the history of Africa and the Black diaspora as well as current affairs. Historian Winston James claims that he was a "polymath with unbounded intellectual interest."¹¹ Harrison's great love for learning and his mighty intellect are observed in his crusade for knowledge. He declared:

> Read, Read, Read! It is not with our teeth that we will tear the white man out of the ancestral land. It isn't with our jaws that we can wring from his hard hands consideration and respect. It must be done by the upper and not the lower parts of our heads. Therefore, I have insisted ever since my entry into the arena of

racial discussion that we Negroes must take to reading, study and the development of intelligence as we have done before.[12]

The church was named The Hubert Harrison Memorial Church in honor of Harrison to attract the educated members of the Black community, or what Brown called the "students of his 'Outdoor University,'"[13] and to be an intellectual center.[14] This is explicated further in the following resolution:

> Whereas the late Dr. Hubert Harrison unstintingly devoted the major portion of his life to the great task of sharing with his fellows the wide and profound knowledge by much hard study he had accumulated, and thus in great measure contributed to the emancipation of many from superstition and fanaticism which are the children of ignorance; and
>
> Whereas this church has always been in full sympathy with this much needed work of education; and
>
> Whereas Dr. Harrison has often expressed his unqualified approval of the modern and liberal interpretation and presentation of religion for which this Church has uncompromisingly stood:
>
> BE IT RESOLVED that as a means of commemorating this invaluable work of enlightenment, emancipation and inspiration, and as a sincere tribute to its great worth and estimable benefit, this Church shall hereafter be named "THE HUBERT HARRISON MEMORIAL CHURCH."[15]

Writing of the significance of naming the church in honor of Hubert Harrison, John Howland Lathrop, pastor of the First Unitarian Congregation of Brooklyn, New York, wrote:

> The religious movements among the colored that play upon ignorance and crudity, and get for themselves headlines in the papers, belie the intelligence and quality of the race. And it is when such company as the Hubert Harrison Memorial Church stands forth in the spirit of liberalism and upon the soundest intellectual principles that this false impression is best counteracted.[16]

The naming of the church in honor of Harrison was not only about linking faith and learning but relating faith to public issues. Brown demonstrated this relationship through the innovative liturgy of his church.

Brown departed from the normative order of worship by instituting a forum, lecture, discussion pattern of worship. However significant, Brown's innovative liturgical experiment did not accomplish the goal he wanted. He said:

> At first the meetings of the church were distinctively religious. In fact, as far as the form of the meetings was concerned they were not different from the services of other churches – hymns, prayers, Scripture readings and a sermon… We became what was called a Forum Church – more poetically, a Temple and a Forum – that

is everything continued as it was formerly, except that every sermon was followed
by a free and full discussion from the floor.[17]

The pattern of worship did not engender the numerical growth in
membership or the increase in attendance that Brown desired. He
remained true, however, to his original intent to attract those who believed
they had outgrown the traditional Christian teachings, although Brown
did not specify what these were. He explained:

A definite attempt was made…to reach religious liberals, that is, those who have
outgrown the teachings of orthodox churches but who are nevertheless religious.[18]

Brown's promotion of the church as a community of learning is noticeable
in the church's promotional literature.

The Church is now a well-established institution and is indeed, what it claims to
be, namely, a Temple and a Forum: a temple wherein we worship the true and
good and beautiful, and receive inspiration for the life of service; A Forum
wherein mind sharpens mind as we strive to plumb the depths and span the
breath and scale the heights of knowledge.[19]

Advancing this perspective of the church, Brown declared: "Ours is
the pressing task to bring about the accordance of mind and soul by
which, and by which only, the vaster music may be made."[20] These
remarks indicate that learning is for Christian formation and to bear witness
to the Christian faith. More importantly, it is a rediscovery and restoration
of a neglected dimension of faith. The Christian tradition states:

The mouth of the prophets is to speak knowledge. For the lips of a priest ought
to preserve knowledge, and from his mouth human beings should seek instruction
because the priest is the messenger of the Lord Almighty (Mal. 2:7; NIV).

In fact, the church as a community of learning is one of the marks of a
true prophetic people of God. The prophet Jeremiah made this clear
when he said: "I will give you shepherds after my own heart, who will
give you knowledge and understanding" (Jer. 3:15; NIV).

Brown's linking of faith and learning was an attempt to relate theology
to the socio-political realities of his time. This is an expression of an organic
emancipatory theological praxis. Practitioners of this theological
engagement are defined as organic intellectuals who, according to Cornel
West, represent the ideal Christian intellectual.[21] In West's words, "This
ideal Christian intellectual is an organic intellectual, simultaneously
immersed in the tortuous realities of the day and enticed by the felicities
of the mind."[22]

Acknowledging the need for an organic relationship between the faith
of individuals and their social context, West's model of the organic
intellectual has to go beyond merely relating ideas to social context. It

must take into account the disparities that exist between the organic intellectual and the realities of the people it seeks to serve. Such a person would not come to the people as a depositor of truth but as a participator in the truth. The intellectual tradition that Brown advocated, does, however, go a stage further to embody ideas. Brown advocated living out ideas by practicing them.[23]

This is what Brown was attempting to achieve through his forum-style worship practice. A major limitation, however, of this practice was that it was more of a lecture/discussion and classroom oriented experience than a worship event. It was issue-centered rather than a worshipful Christian event where the faithful gathered for praise and adoration of God leading to empowerment and transformation of their lives. Understanding this forum-style practice of worship, nevertheless, within its social, intellectual and religious context, demonstrates the extent of Brown's commitment to the relationship between faith and the life of the mind. In this regard, it could be interpreted as an expression of loving God with the mind (Mk 12:30; NIV).

Advancing the notion of the church as a community of learning, the Caribbean Anglican pastor and theologian, Kortright Davis, declares:

> The Caribbean diasporan church must continue to be a corporate engine for the pursuit of knowledge, the dissemination of education, and the active support of those who would better themselves through the development of their intellects. No Caribbean Church should be without a vibrant and friendly scholarship assistance program, especially for young people.[24]

Thus, Davis indicates that learning is not a parochial congregational issue but rather an expression of Christian discipleship. It could also be argued that this claim of Davis may be reflecting an awareness of the prophetic declaration against ignorance, "My people are destroyed from lack of knowledge" (Hos. 4:6; NIV), the example of the first Christians, "They devoted themselves to the apostles' teaching" (Acts 2:42; NIV) and the admonition "grow in grace and in the knowledge of the Lord and Savior Jesus Christ" (2 Pet. 3:18). The function of the church as a community of learning is not entirely for acquiring religious information but to search for truth resulting in spiritual formation, practical training for effective service and emancipatory engagement in the society. In this regard, learning must be grounded in Caribbean culture, heritage and history, linked to the global struggle for emancipation and the realities of diasporan existence. Kortight Davis concurs:

> The Caribbean diasporan church must offer itself as a marketplace for the exploration and development of ideas, the testing of imaginative innovations, and the cultivation of human talents towards full human development.[25]

He further insists that the church is to find courage and inspiration from its rich pioneering intellectual tradition.

> We must never forget that Howard University, the great capstone of black scholars anywhere in the world, emerged out of the ideas generated at an ordinary prayer meeting in Washington, D.C., right on the verge of Emancipation.[26]

Davis identifies the African American intellectual tradition as evidence of a Black Christian learning tradition. While not disputing the importance of Davis' proposition, Black British theologian Anthony Reddie provides an alternative approach. He argues for using the experience of Caribbean diasporan fore-parents as a resource for learning. As such, Reddie recognizes the Caribbean diasporan church as a community of learning. For this reason, "the experience, memory and notions of faith"[27] of our Black fore-parents should be employed as a resource to nurture the learning tradition of the Caribbean diasporan church. According to Reddie:

> The importance of Black elders [fore-parents] lies in their unique position as people who represent the pivotal link between a world that was and the "world as it is today." These elder Black people have…their formative influences shaped by the religio-cultural world of the Caribbean.[28]

While it is important, however, to utilize the experience of Black elders as a resource for learning, by not specifying whether the Black elders are inclusive of social class and gender, Reddie's perspective risks being insular and exclusionary. Taking this limitation into account, the rich heritage of Caribbean diasporan fore-parents could serve as a means of emancipation. Reddie affirms this claim:

> In a world of globalization, White and structural inequality, Black Christian education possesses the critical force to conquer the worse excesses of racism and economic exploitation. Black Christian education [the Black Elders' experience] at its best is a radically prophetic enterprise that challenges the status quo.[29]

The establishment of a relationship between learning and justice is a further indication of the Caribbean diasporan church as a community of learning.

Alternative Community of Faith

Along with the church as a community of learning, I also discovered in this study that the Caribbean diasporan church is an alternative community of faith. We observed in Chapter 5 that the Caribbean diasporan church functioned as a public institution. I premise this perspective on the active process of practicing the Christian faith through the formation of autonomous congregations. The evidence for this assertion lies in the Caribbean diasporan church functioning as an agent of transformation and through this engagement, the church represents an alternative community of faith to the mainstream society.

The concept of an alternative community of faith has been used to describe the Church as an alternative to the dominant society, especially in Euro-American theological thought. Representing this school of thought in his writing on the prophetic ministry of the Church, the American biblical theologian, Walter Brueggemann, offers an apt definition of the Church as an alternative society:

> The task of a prophetic ministry is to nurture, nourish, and evoke a consciousness and perception alternative to the consciousness and perception of the dominant culture around us.[30]

As an alternative society, the church derives its identity from its calling and purpose, and therefore, it does not depend on the dominant society for validation. Brueggemann's contention of the church as an alternative society, however, resides in one's consciousness and perception and, as such, his perspective reflects an ideological interpretation of the alternative society rather than as a concrete historical happening. The alternative society goes beyond consciousness and perception to being an embodiment of the demands of the gospel – emancipation, reconciliation – in the historical context that God has been revealed through Jesus Christ.

In the African American theological tradition, the alternative society is understood in this regard as an invisible institution, as Albert Raboteau describes in his classic work, *Slave Religion*.[31] According to E. Franklin Frazier, it is a surrogate world[32] and Dale Andrews considers it to be a community of refuge as explained in his helpful work, *Practical Theology for Black Churches*.[33]

The understanding I propose is that of the church as an alternative society to dominant culture. It does not withdraw from the society nor assume a separatist attitude towards the society by being divorced from the society. It represents a Christian alternative to the dominant society in which it bears witness to God's emancipatory purpose. As an alternative society, the Caribbean diasporan church operates out of a collective identity with a common purpose in a diacritical relationship with the dominant society. To explain this, I examine the significant practice of the church as an agent of transformation.

Agent of Transformation

The Caribbean diasporan church as an alternative society forms alliances with African American socio-political organizations, provides physical, social and spiritual space for the diasporan community to participate in the public sphere and forge a new sense of collective self-consciousness. This is not a new phenomenon. From the beginning of their life in American society, the people of the Caribbean diaspora established organizations for mutual support, socialization and charitable promotion.

Alliances

There is, in fact, a tradition of Caribbean diaspora embodying an alternative society. This takes two forms. One is that Caribbeaners worked with the African American organizations in the formation of alliances[34] (discussed in Chapters 2 and 4). The second is that Caribbeaners established independent social and civic organizations such as the Bermuda Benevolent Association (1897), Montserrat Progressive Association (1914), Grenada Mutual Aid Association (1926),[35] and the Jamaica Progressive League (1936).[36] By the mid 1980s a series of these organizations had emerged. For example, in 1985, the Caribbean magazine, *Everybody*, published a guide to 158 Caribbean organizations though this did not represent a comprehensive account of these organizations.[37] The publication, nevertheless, is a recorded account of the existence of these socio-civic organizations but, at the same time, they were not representative of the entire Caribbean diasporan community. What is known as "The island Mentality," a form of particularism that is based primarily on social and political differentiation, is the result of colonialism and mistrust that continues to exist among Caribbean nations today. Elizabeth Thomas-Hope, writing on Caribbean identity, has made the observation that:

> West Indian parochialism is based on entrenched suspicion, even fear, of neighbors as competitors, rivals or agents of sedition… This fear triggered the collapse of the federation; Jamaica in particular, but also Trinidad, thought the smaller Island had too much power, too many benefits, too few responsibilities.[38]

While this practice still exists, there is a pan-Caribbean consciousness as illustrated by the existence of organizations such as the Caribbean American Chamber of Commerce, Caribbean Immigration Services and *The Carib News*. These organizations, however, are not defined as pan-Caribbean organizations.

Furthermore, these civic organizations addressed the needs of their respective home country. In the case of Jamaica, for example, the Jamaica Progressive League was organized to promote the independence movement in Jamaica and the nationalistic agenda of the political party, the People's National Party.[39]

These organizations fulfilled the purpose for which they were organized, but unless they redefined their purpose, they became irrelevant and, over time, defunct. This does not mean, however, that they were no longer needed but rather that they gave way to the emergence of newer organizations that sought to address different needs and serve a new generation.

New Self-awareness

With the growing diasporan population and the changing socio-cultural and religious context both at home and in the host country, the collective consciousness of the Caribbean diaspora also changed, which means that organizations with the scope to facilitate this collective consciousness were required. In recognition of this pan-Caribbean consciousness, Dennis Conway comments:

> Migration is more than ever a livelihood strategy in Caribbean societies, at home and abroad. Such transnational life brings multiplicities of identities to the fore, and there appears to be a growing pan-Caribbean consciousness in the cosmopolitan enclave communities of certain North American gateway metropoles – New York City, Miami, Toronto, and Montreal, in particular. Pan-Caribbeanism is being fostered by cross-cultural marriages, a widening and interwining of Caribbean family networks and the growing maturity of Caribbean societies. Moreover, the further incorporation of these micro-states into a globalizing new world order, where North American and European values and cultures themselves compete, change, or resist, has also contributed to the emergence of this consciousness.[40]

Although social and civic organizations served a valuable purpose in their time and continue to do so, they are not dynamic or inclusive. The Caribbean diasporan church is the largest and single most diverse, enduring and representative pan-Caribbean organization.[41] Unlike the social and civic organizations, the membership of congregations consists of a mixture of the nationals of the majority of the Caribbean countries.[42]

Kasinitz observes, as indicated earlier, that socio-civic organizations became irrelevant and were pursuing parochial issues which led to their demise. The identity of the people changed from what he calls immigrant to ethnic. For him, ethnic means a minority people group.[43] The term is, however, misleading because all people are ethnic. It would be more accurate to say that the identity of the Caribbean people changed, not necessarily according to Kasinitz's understanding but from immigrants to citizens. The immigrant identity has the connotation of one as an outsider and as a stranger but the identity of a citizen reflects the sense of belonging and one as an integral entity of the society. For the church, this is an opportunity for transformative actions.

Where the Caribbean diasporan church acted as an agent of transformation, it expressed the practice through the securing and erecting of places of worship. This signifies the end primarily of a private understanding and the beginning of a public understanding of the faith which marked the entrance of the church into the public sphere as an agent of transformation.

Changing Landscape

One of the most radical changes and transformation took place through building houses of worship. Grace Baptist Chapel is an apt illustration of this phenomenon. Grace Baptist Chapel was organized in 1987 and within three years of operating, they purchased property in a developing area of the community. However, the area was being used for a variety of illegal and immoral activities, from garbage dumping to prostitution. The neighborhood was known as "Prostitute City."[44] Ten years after they completed the construction of the building (1997), these illegal activities were no longer taking place in the community. The physical presence of the place of worship transformed the moral, social and spiritual life of the community. Writing of the transformation that diaspora churches engender in their communities, sociologist Omar M. McRoberts has made the observation that through their physical presence and activities, diasporan churches transform the social structure of their communities. McRoberts summarizes this perspective this way:

> The migrant [diasporan] churches used ritual interaction to equip members to function in and perhaps transform social worlds beyond church walls... The immigrant [diasporan] churches...render some practical social services to recent arrivals – services that prepared them for survival in the host country. Like parents who attempt to make a mark on the world by raising their children, these churches tried to change the world by injecting well-adjusted individuals into it.[45]

Grounding Transformation

The basis for this transformation is the belief that the church, as the people of the Truth of the gospel, has the moral responsibility to transform the community by the power to the gospel.[46] But if being a steward of the gospel is the basis for being an agent of transformation, then on what ground is the Caribbean diasporan church an alternative to the dominant society? Theologian, Jurgen Moltmann, offers an answer. "The Christian faith lives from the raising of the crucified Christ and strains after the promises of the universal future of Christ."[47] The church, therefore, does not need to be legitimized by the society. Christians understand that Christ legitimizes the church through his life and believe that God confirms it through the resurrection.

Focusing on the resurrection is not sectarianism, separatism, other-worldliness or idealism. It recognizes the reality of the purpose and will of God for humanity as grounded in the resurrection of Jesus Christ. The alternative society is about the realization of the Christian hope that Jesus inaugurated as the kingdom of God. The central motif in Jesus' life and ministry in the gospels is the ushering in of God's kingdom. Speaking in this regard, the gospel writer, Mark, states: "the time has come... *The kingdom is near. Repent and believe the good news*" (Mk 1:14-15; NIV).

An alternative society points to the belief of God's kingdom in human history. On the basis of this belief, the church does not accept the present situation as it is but undertakes the task of making it what it ought to be. It is a source of disturbance, an agent of subversion and the impetus for an alternative reality. In the process of doing so, it is at the same time helping to build God's eschatological community. Hence, the church as an alternative society does not only point to the reality but it becomes an embodiment of the reality. Expressing this understanding, Moltmann states:

> It is to point beyond itself, and paradoxically away from itself, to the doing of God's will, in which "knowing Jesus" as Lord really becomes whole and entire.[48]

This eschatological grounding of the alternative society raises questions about being otherworldly. There is the danger of emphasizing the otherworldly nature of the faith but this is not the absolute and definitive meaning of the eschatological hope in Black theology.[49] Dale Andrews notes that there is a distinction but not a separation between "otherworldly" and "this worldly" in Black theology. According to Andrews:

> Black eschatology does not separate "otherworldly" and "this worldly" hope. The greatest possible distinction is at the same time the greatest parallel; otherworldly promise translates into this-world hope and ways and being.[50]

As an alternative society, therefore, the Caribbean diasporan church is not an internally oriented, exclusive community but a future-oriented community in relationship with the whole world and all human beings. The purpose of the church is to serve humanity and as such it is to be involved in the world.[51] Central to the church fulfilling this purpose is the eschatological vision that nurtures the quest for emancipation, empowers human beings for living in the present and sustains hope for the future.

Home

The church as home may be seen as the third distinctive of the Caribbean diasporan church. I employ the term "home" to provide a more precise theological understanding of the Caribbean diasporan experience. Inherent in a diasporan experience is the convergence of issues such as transience, displacement, marginalization, fragmentation, acceptance, involvement and so forth. The church has become the home, the sacred place that provides the arena where these conflicting realities are addressed. In Chapter 2, on the Caribbean diasporan identities, I indicated that, as the foremost representative expression of the Caribbean diaspora, the church is the community and center where identity is formed and lived. It is the central place in the life of the diasporan community where the people meet God, maintain and nurture identity and find a sense of belonging and meaning for their lives in a hostile and oppressive society.[52] The church is also the source and framework for moral authority as well as the place where the deepest longings of the heart reside and where people encounter the God who emancipates and empowers for authentic living and restores the devalued self.[53]

In this regard, I contend that the Caribbean diasporan experience is a journey towards home. Home, however, has three primary meanings.[54] The first is the return to the ancestral home as advanced by Marcus Garvey through the United Negro Improvement Association in the "Back to Africa" ideology.[55] The second is the return to one's native country.[56] On emigrating from the Caribbean, the people left with the intent to return as soon as they achieved their goals and even if they did not return, they continued to live with that hope. The third understanding of home, which this chapter discusses, is the search for and formation of a community that emerges out of the collective experience of memory, history and culture.

Integral to diasporan experience is the radical reconfiguration of memory and history and culture. This radical transformation produces new hope and a new beginning facilitated through the creation of sacred space that nurtures acceptance, identity and security in resisting and facing the onslaught of diasporan existence. The advice the prophet Jeremiah gave to his people is instructive for the Caribbean diasporan church.

> Build houses and settle down; plant gardens and eat what they produce… Also seek the peace and prosperity of the city to which I have carried you into exile. Pray to the Lord for it, because if it prospers, you too will prosper (Jer. 29:4-7; NIV).

Home is not a short-term journey like a vacation, but a journey to a place of permanence; settling down and putting down roots. Also, home expresses the need for community and the deeply held belief that the church is the family of God as the Deutero-Pauline tradition states:

> …you are no longer foreigners and aliens, but fellow citizens with God's people and members of God's household, built on the foundations of the apostles and prophets, with Christ Jesus as the chief corner stone (Eph. 2:19-20; NIV).

The meaning of home as a search for community is also expressed in the Caribbean diasporan literary tradition. This tradition helps to interpret the diasporan experience depicting the nature of the experience including marginality, alienation, unsettledness and precariousness. The Jamaican writer, Claude McKay (1889–1948) represents this tradition. In a very important study on Claude McKay, Heather Hathaway traces the search for home in his writings. Hathaway writes:

> Described at various points in his life as a nationalist, a Communist, a radical, a proletariat, a rebel, a Catholic, an atheist, a humanist and even a fascist, few have considered McKay in terms of the characteristic that consistently and most profoundly affected all other aspects of his identity – his status as a migrant.[57]

Hathaway locates this identity in McKay's writings by exploring his earliest life. She traces the roots of McKay's migratory identity in his autobiography, *My Green Hills of Jamaica* and his poetic writings, such as *"Outcast,"* noting how McKay was both separated and felt different from others.[58] "I purposely distinguish McKay as a migrant (one who moves from place to place)." According to Hathaway,

> from an immigrant (one who moves to another region to settle) because his very need to settle to "keep going" – as he would like to title his autobiography – provides the key to understanding how this complex man could embody any or all of the above sobriquets during his lifetime.[59]

In McKay's classic novel, *Home to Harlem*, the protagonist, Jake, is the pilgrim person, who is on a journey and always encountering the harsh realities of diasporan existence. He is seeking a better life, yet encounters difficulties and has no place to call home. He had to deal with the issues of racism, sexism, morality, dislocation, poverty, violence and exclusion. In his conversation with Jake, Felice, his companion, confronted him with the issue of his life as a pilgrim.

> What you want to go knocking around them foreign countries for like swallow come and swallow go from year to year and never settling down no place? This is your country daddy. What you gwine [going] away from it for?[60]

Although Jake never professed to be a Christian, McKay uses him to depict the nature of the diasporan life. Clearly absent from his life was the centrality of religion. Religion, the church and faith in God were only considered as significant during times of crisis such as sickness and the uncertainty of life. In speaking of the illness of Jake, McKay writes:

> All you younger generation in Harlem don't know God. All you know is cabarets and movies and the gals them exposing them legs a theirs [sic] in them jumper frocks.

McKay continues,

> "You all ought to know, though, and think of God Almighty before the trumpet sound and it's too late for black sinners."[61]

McKay's account of Jake demonstrates the importance of the Christian religion in the lives of the people of the Caribbean diaspora as they seek a home. McKay shows that the people are never settled but are constantly migrating. There is no sense of place and belonging, no place to call home. This sense of alienation, displacement and desire for home is the dominant theme in McKay's writings, as expressed in the titles of some of his major works such as *A Long Way from Home*[62] and the classic poem, "I Shall Return."

> I shall return again. I shall return
> To laugh and love and watch with wonder–eyes
> At golden noon the forest fires burn,
> Wafting their blue-black smoke to sapphire skies.
> I shall return to loiter by the streams
> That bathe the brown blades of bending grasses,
> And realize once more my thousand dreams
> Of waters rushing down the mountain passes.
>
> I shall return to hear the fiddle and fife
> Of village dances, dear delicious tunes
> That stir the hidden depths of native life,
> Stray melodies of dim-remembered runes.
> I shall return. I shall return again
> To ease my mind of long, long years of pain.[63]

This poem describes the longing for home and depicts the nature of the diasporan life as one of homelessness, alienation, exile, uncertainties, restlessness and rootlessness. Writing of this experience, the Trinidadian novelist, Samuel Selvon, describes the experience of the Caribbean diaspora in the British context, in his classic novel, *The Lonely Londoners*. He illustrates the nature of the Caribbean diasporan life in his assessment of the protagonist, Tolroy.

> Every year he vowing to go back to Trinidad, but after the winter gone and birds sing and all the trees begin to put on leaves, and flowers come and now and then the old sun shining, is as if life start all over again, as if it still have time, as if it still have another chance. I will wait until after the summer, the summer does really be hearts [sic].[64]

In the end, however, Selvon concluded that Tolroy got so accustomed to his diasporan pattern of life that he became helpless. For example, all he could do was to long for home and reflect on family, friends and what life was like in the homeland.[65] What is uncertain is whether or not finding a home fulfills these Caribbean diaporan people's purpose in life. In searching for answers, they recognize the role of faith in human life which they express through the establishment of communities of faith. In this respect, the Caribbean diasporan experience resonates with the biblical tradition.

> By faith Abraham, when called to go to a place he would later receive as an inheritance obeyed and went, even though he did not know where he was going. By faith he made his home in the promised land like a stranger in a foreign country... For he was looking forward to a city with foundations, whose architect and builder is God (Heb. 11:8, 10; NIV).

The experience of leaving and uprooting from the homeland to reside in a new land creates its own turmoil, sense of disorientation and instability. As a way of survival and making sense out of life, Caribbeaners used their faith to interpret their existential conditions. With the understanding that they did not migrate to reside permanently in their new resident land, they became members of the existing churches in view of ethnic and theological commonalities. The intent was to ensure that they had a church home, a place to nurture their faith but, more importantly, a way of living out their faith. Thus, I argue, Caribbeaners' faith is not a private act but a communal event which the Caribbean diasporan church as home embodies.

Home does not represent an idealized life. Home also involves the whole range of the human experience but it is also a place of contradictions and conflicts. Taking place at home are mixed experiences encompassing the tensions, struggles, sufferings, joys and all that goes on in life. In other words, the convergence between public and private takes place at home. Home is created because the excluded cannot enter into the space of the oppressors or of those who are not members of the majority culture but have secured their own sacred space. And still, while home is imperfect and transient, it is created to resist the onslaughts of diasporan existence and, ultimately, it represents security, identity and belonging.[66] As Anthony Reddie observes:

> Home will be more than just a physical space. It has to be a place that affords me the opportunity to dream of other places, to think of mythical spaces where a part of my spirit will always belong... There is the importance of creating "safe" and "inclusive" spaces where people can reveal their authentic selves.[67]

Conclusion

In bringing this chapter to a close, I wish to reiterate that the distinctives of the Caribbean diasporan church is a work in progress. I am particularly mindful that I am doing theology both within the context and in relation to the context in which the people of the Caribbean diaspora live. In so doing, the marks of the church that I identify, define the organic character of the church rather than merely the church's identity that creeds express or the church's mission that its functions communicate. The organic character of the church is inclusive of both the church's identity and mission. This perspective, therefore, suggests that these marks of the church are contextually derived and, as such, are signs of the mystery of the faith that the church attempts to approximate in history.

The perspectives of the marks of the church are not to be understood as replacing one for the other or as putting one over against the other. Rather, the intent is to provide an additional alternative understanding of the dynamic interaction of a variety of theological perspectives. These varieties, described as creedal, functional and organic, exist together simultaneously and separately as signs of a faith seeking understanding and of a people seeking meaning, and provide a rich mosaic of faith as a source of strength for human living. Ultimately, however, they are insignificant if they are not in the service of God's emancipatory purpose in Jesus Christ. As the Caribbean diasporan church believes, emancipation is central to its theological self-understanding, mission in the world and contextual existence.

In light of this claim, the marks of the church with its creedal statements, functional acts and organic engagements, as well as the hope of emancipation it pursues, is of renewed relevance due to the distinctive identity and liberative possibilities the church represents in the world.

Conclusion

This study is an initial attempt to construct a Caribbean diasporan ecclesiology using the Caribbean diasporan experience as a source for theological discourse. While the study may not provide adequate answers to all concerned persons, the intent is to understand the theological meaning of the Caribbean diasporan experience. Thus, the study has sought to answer the question: How do Caribbean people understand themselves as the people of God?

From Whence Have We Come?

Using the Caribbean diasporan experience as a source of theological discourse, I attempted to answer the question in the following manner: After delineating the structure of the study, including my personal formative experiences, a constructive meaning of the term diaspora and the approach of undertaking this study, I explored the significance of engaging the Caribbean diasporan experience as a source for theological discourse. Chapter 1 addressed the omission of this experience from African American theology and the status of and need for the development of a Caribbean diaspora theological scholarship.

The study further unearthed three forms of Caribbean diasporan identity, namely, the cultural, cosmopolitan and Caribamerican. These are not mutually exclusive but rather interrelated identities. I argued, however, for an identity that encompasses the Caribbean diaspora in North America, noting at the same time that identity is not fixed but evolutionary.[1]

The study also explored the theological foundations of the Caribbean diasporan church. This established the theological basis of the church and argued that the Caribbean diasporan experience is a theological response to the quest for a better life premised on the theological principles of a dialectical theological tradition and the doctrines of the Incarnation and the Event of Pentecost.

I examined further the theological development of the Caribbean diasporan church by focusing on its social and historical context. I noted the theological beliefs that undergirded the formation and shaped the ecclesiastical self-understanding of the Caribbean diasporan church. Initially, the people of the Caribbean diaspora understood themselves as pilgrims and, as such, they practiced their faith through affiliation with existing churches rather than establishing new churches for themselves.

Continuing the discussion on the theological development of the Caribbean diasporan church, I attended to the change of the diaspora's identity from the pilgrim perspective to a missionary perspective of the Caribbean diasporan experience. The increase in the diaspora's population and acclimatization to the society changed the numerical composition and social nature of the diaspora. Consequently, the need arose to establish congregations that served the growing community of people living in a new and strange country. In this regard, the Caribbean diaspora was interpreted as a mission field. The discussion, then, considered the two practices, appointment of missionaries and organizing of congregations, that defined and established a Caribbean diasporan missionary tradition.

The book discussed the role the Caribbean diasporan church plays in the resident homeland. Of particular significance is the manner in which the church functions as a critique of personal and systemic racism and laid the foundation for a Caribbean diasporan Christian intellectual tradition and emerges as an independent church tradition although it falls within the Black Church Tradition. The role of the church in the resident homeland raises questions about the changing character of American religion generally and Black religion in particular. They reflect both the de-centering and centering of race by grounding faith in culture, heritage, history and experience. The result is the emergence of a distinct Caribbean diasporan church tradition setting in motion the development of a Caribbean diasporan ecclesiology.

Where Do We Go From Here?

In view of this discussion, where does Caribbean diasporan theology/ecclesiology go from here? What path should it take? This study is not a definitive and exhaustive study on the Caribbean diasporan church, but a beginning. Consequently, left unanswered are many more questions beyond the scope of this study or any single study. Theological attention needs to be given, for example, to the causes of migration,[2] immigration legislation, the relationship between the diaspora and homeland and the religious, moral, theological and existential challenges that confront Caribbean people in the diaspora. The development of the diaspora, nevertheless, warrants that future scholarship goes beyond the immediate ecclesiastical concerns to include issues such as the relationship between the Caribbean diaspora and the homeland and the development of the necessary and relevant infrastructures that will not only facilitate such relationship but advance the diaspora. This is an important issue especially since we are living in a post-national and global era. Indeed, the reality of a diaspora indicates that nation transcends geographical borders. As such, national homeland and its diaspora have not only an interwoven destiny but a mutual responsibility for the well-being of its citizens.

Before concluding this study, it is important to delineate a more precise direction for a Caribbean diasporan theology. The emergence of the Caribbean diasporan church tradition includes the development of an emancipatory diasporan theology that is both pastoral and prophetic, where the fundamental issues of gender,[3] religious pluralism and a prophetic critique of globalism are at the center of the church's priorities.

Including Women

Women have played a central role in the development of the Caribbean diaspora and church. Yet, Caribbean diasporan women have not been given the recognition they deserve for the central and definitive role they play and the contribution they have made in the development of the diaspora.[4] As the African American biblical theologian Demetrius K. Williams notes,

> Women have been the foundation of the black churches, culture, and society, yet their contributions have been generally ignored or relegated historically to second-class status where women have not been a major concern of the male dominated leadership of the church.[5]

Affirming this claim, Williams urges:

> The effects of black sexism in black churches in America will end only when men begin to seriously challenge and uproot the patriarchal assumptions and institutions that still dominate black religious, civil and political society.[6]

Without mimicking African American theology, the Caribbean diasporan church will do well to learn from their African American counterparts, especially what it teaches about Black women and their role in the church and society. The claim of the African American theologian, Cheryl Townsend Gilkes, concerning the Black church is also instructive for the Caribbean diasporan church and community. She asserts:

> If it wasn't for the women, the black community would not have had the churches and other organizations that fostered the psychic and material survival of individuals and that have mobilized the constituencies that have produced change and progress.[7]

If the Caribbean diasporan church will embrace the centrality of women in the church, then it will be more effective in offering a prophetic critique of human oppression, an agent of social emancipation and an approximation of divine justice.

One among Many

The Caribbean diasporan church has a unique opportunity to provide theological leadership within the interfaith dialogue or in the context of religious pluralism. Two factors facilitate this opportunity. The first is the religious heritage of the church. The Caribbean diasporan church originated out of a pluralistic religious culture. Kortright Davis carefully points out that Caribbean people have a complex religious system, are incurably religious and employ religion as a means of transmitting their culture. Davis argues:

> Religion in the Caribbean is a complex system of beliefs, values, rituals and behavior. It encompasses the shared experience of common relationships, common responses, common resistance and common resilience or survival toward the goal of social, spiritual, material fulfillment.[8]

This religious diversity is evident in the presence of a wide variety of religions such as Voodoo, Shango, Santeria, Revivalism, Rastafarianism and numerous Christian denominations.[9] This religious diversity is one reason the Caribbean is described as a meeting place for religions or a religious crossroad.[10] As George Mulrain explains, "The mottos from the region reflect attempts to come to terms with this plurality of peoples, races, cultures and religions and the need to create unity crossroad [sic]."[11]

The second reason derives from the first. This high concentration of religious heterogeneity and diversity is a distinctive of Caribbean religion. Davis summarizes this perspective in the following manner:

> I think it is safe to say that the high level of religious tolerance, the constant search for religious meaning and human vitality, the capacity to be conservative and heterodox at the same time, the integration of believers from different ethnic backgrounds, the confident assurance with which ultimate factors of life are encountered, all combine to mark out the Caribbean personality as being unconditionally religious.[12]

The religious pluralism of the Caribbean is not an issue of tolerance but a reflection of the nature of Caribbean culture and religiosity. Writing about this aspect of Caribbean religion, Patrick Taylor examines the different aspects of Caribbean religion and culture. This multidisciplinary study focuses on the spirituality and religio-historical aspect of Caribbean culture and the relationship between religion and politics.[13]

The interdisciplinary approach of this work and the paradigmatic usage of the term "dance," however, are reflective of Caribbean religious pluralism.[14] Dance is a means of communication that interprets and reflects the social and spiritual entities that are operative in a particular context.[15] In this case, it is in the context of the Caribbean people. After a genealogical usage of the term, Taylor concludes that in the general religious life of Caribbean people, it is customary to dance.[16] He argues:

> If God is a guarantor of meaning, meaning is contextualized and experienced in a multiplicity of evolving divine, ancestral and spiritual forces. When different peoples come into contact with each other, their differing spiritual forces enter into relationships.[17]

In Caribbean Christian theology, pluralism is understood as an expression of an ecumenical faith. As one of the many religions, George Mulrain is careful to show this distinctive element in Caribbean Christianity.

> Given the present climate with its increasing interest in popular religiosity, there is slowly emerging a new understanding of ecumenism. No longer is it a word which refers to things that are done only within the Christian church… The word suggests the entire household of God, the earth with all its inhabitants consists of men, women and children of various religious beliefs. They are all part of the family of God.[18]

This pluralistic interpretation of Caribbean Religion is a creative attempt to understand and practice faith or one's relationship with God in a diverse religious culture. It expresses the ecumenical nature and engenders the inclusive character of the Christian faith. The pluralistic culture shapes and informs the faith of the people so that they are able to not only live out but to embody the inclusive character of the Christian Religion. It is a faith that is grounded in the gospel that declares: "There is neither Jew nor Greek, slave nor free, male nor female, for you are all one in Christ Jesus" (Gal. 3:28; NIV).

Originating out of this heritage, the Caribbean diasporan church is not an ethnic enclave garrisoned by nationalistic sentiments but an inclusive community of faith called by God to be an expression of the One Church in a particular context. The task of the Caribbean diasporan church, therefore, is to determine the centrality of the Christian faith among world religions. While the church engages the culture, she must not lose her identity. As such, Caribbean theologian Winston Persuad provides this instruction:

> Because it is the crucified and risen Jesus Christ whom it follows, the church cannot but be involved in the alleviation of human suffering. The crucified Lord is to be found in the hungry, the naked, the sick, the imprisoned. The individual Christian and the church as a whole bear the marks of suffering, Christ's ongoing suffering in the world. The church's role as fellow sufferer, as protestor against suffering, as advocate, as individual and institution that practices mercy and charity and work for justice and peace, is rooted in its identity as people of the cross.[19]

On this basis, it is necessary to develop an ecumenical organization to facilitate the moral, intellectual and socio-political development of the Caribbean diaspora. This should not be a difficult task given the rich ecumenical context and heritage of the Caribbean diaporan church and the other models of Black ecumenicalism. In the United States, for example, there was the National Council of Black Churchmen which has evolved into becoming the Congress of National Black Churches[20] and, in Britain,[21] there is the Black Majority Church.

The establishment of this kind of organization is not an issue of transplanting Caribbean ecumenism to the Caribbean diaspora but rather it is a matter of drawing on such resources to create a symbolic, collective entity of identity, solidarity and community expressing Caribbean diasporan peoplehood. Inherent in this model of peoplehood is also the task of creative thinking, intellectual guidance, strategic planning and nurturing of hope amidst the inevitable encounters of the inescapable realities of diasporan life.

Taking on Today's Goliath

As well as facing the challenges of gender and religious pluralism, the task of the Caribbean diasporan church includes offering a prophetic critique of global capitalism. The church has accommodated the culture. It has accepted and patterned itself on the materialistic culture of society. Writing of this practice, the University of Chicago professor of theology, Dwight Hopkins, chartered the course for the future direction of African American theology in his *Head and Heart: Black Theology Past, Present and Future*, which is also instructive for the Caribbean diasporan church and theology. He expresses the tasks that Black theology faces. The challenges of the twenty-first century demand an ongoing Black theology. The spirit of freedom continues to persist among Black people; consequently, Black theology responds to this positive and human relationship.[22]

Arguing that Black theology is a major player in providing both personal and global liberation, Hopkins discusses the meaning of Black theology for Womanist theology, spirituality, heterosexism, the oppressive character of globalization, and then offers his vision for a just society by making the claim for justice by insisting on God's preferential option for the poor.

The fact that Hopkins identifies globalization as a religion is both insightful and informative because the Caribbean diaspora could become unsuspecting adherents of this religion. After dissecting this religion, Hopkins insists that the task of an emancipatory theology is to empower the adherents to both resist and protest global capitalism. He makes this plain:

> …globalization of monopoly finance capitalist culture itself is a religion. Such a religious system feeds on the most vulnerable people in the world theater.

Consequently, a theology of liberation is one necessary response to the rapacious appetite of globalization qua religion.[23]

The direction for the Caribbean diasporan church that I propose must be emancipatory, asserting its counter-cultural identity and fulfilling its prophetic function. Acknowledging this responsibility, Dwight Hopkins reminds us of the pervasive and pernicious influences that intend to domesticate the prophetic voice of the Black Church:

> ...we find a growing number of black churches catering to conservative forces in the country. They emphasize the accumulation of wealth and a prosperity gospel: preserving the status-quo of elite white power, privileging the individual self at the expense of the community, and squeezing out whatever advancements possible for upper-income black people. They are seduced by and embrace the larger sinister culture of immediate gratification, the fairy-tale illusion of becoming an instant millionaire, or the never-ending quest to establish a start-up company to compete with Silicon Valley corporations. They foster a spirituality that removes the individual from this world in order to feel good in the midst of material suffering and psychological wounds, while avoiding Jesus' mandate to revolutionize systems on earth on behalf of those lacking the resources to impact the direction of the nation or lives on a daily basis.[24]

This direction of the church involves the theological task of critical interrogation of the past, a constructive analysis of the present and a comprehensive vision of the future for the transformation of society and the approximation of the "beloved community." Informing this undertaking is the theological presupposition that the oppression of Black people is related to global capitalism as detected in its anti-poor policies, xenophobic immigration policies and materialistic and Constantinian theology.[25] Addressing these issues may be an enormous challenge for the Caribbean diasporan church. But at the same time, this can be a great opportunity for the church to make a significant contribution to society. Unlike other organizations, this church has the immense freedom of institutional autonomy. It is not intellectually, culturally, financially, politically accountable to any institutional power. In this regard, if used constructively, the Caribbean diasporan church will have unparalleled power to effect social and systemic changes in the creation of a better world.

Finally, I believe that it is the task of my generation to lay the foundation for Caribbean diasporan theological studies. This study, therefore, is a modest beginning in contributing to the fulfillment of this task. Also, I hope that this will serve as a source of encouragement to the Caribbean diasporan church whose experience is a source for theological discourse and a resource for confronting the Goliaths of diasporan existence and life.

Notes

Introduction

1. The term Caribbean people in this study refers to the descendants of the people from Caribbean countries that were former colonies of Britain. For further discussion, see Elizabeth M. Thomas-Hope, *Perspective on Caribbean Regional Identity* (Liverpool: University of Liverpool, Centre for Latin American Studies, 1984); Franklin W. Knight and Colin A. Palmer, eds, *The Modern Caribbean* (North Carolina: University of North Carolina Press, 1989); Mary Waters, *Black Identities: West Indian Immigrant Dreams and American Realities* (Massachusetts: Harvard University Press, 1999), 1–43.

2. Richard Hart, *Slaves Who Abolished Slavery: Blacks in Rebellion* (Kingston: University of the West Indies Press, 2002). See also Philip M. Sherlock and Hazel Bennett, *The Story of the Jamaican People* (Kingston: Ian Randle Publishers, 1998); Werner Zips, *Black Rebels* (Kingston: Ian Randle Publishers, 1999). For a study on the Jamaican Maroons, see Carey Robinson, *The Fighting Maroons of Jamaica* (London: Collins, 1969); for a more detailed account see Mavis C. Campbell, *The Maroons of Jamaica, 1655–1796: A History of Resistance, Collaboration and Betrayal* (Trenton: Africa World Press, 1990). For works about the individual Freedom Fighters, see Milton C. McFarlane, *Cudjoe of Jamaica: Pioneer for Black Freedom in the New World* (New Jersey: R. Enslow, 1977); Kamau Brathwaite, *Nanny, Sam Sharp, and the Struggle for People's Liberation* (Kingston: National Heritage Week Committee, 1977); Karla Gottlieb, *Mother of Us All: A History of Queen Nanny, Leader of the Windward Jamaica Maroons* (New Jersey: Africa Third World Press, 2000).

3. Hugh Sherlock, "National Anthem of Jamaica," cited in *Jamaica Celebrating 43 Years* (New York: n.p., 2005), 2.

4. Caribamerican is the term I use to designate, identify and define the people of the Caribbean diaspora in the United States of America. The terms that have been historically and currently used are West Indians and Caribbean Americans. Regarding the former, it is the pre-independent self-designation when the identity of the people was defined in relationship to the colonial government. The latter is a post independent self-designation but it reflects a dual identity and not a distinct community. With the name Caribamerican, it incorporates the elements of the above mentioned two terms but it signifies a distinct community. As such, the term acknowledges Caribbean people as a constitutive element of American society. Formerly, the Caribbean people were not regarded as a diaspora. The community is now regarded as a diaspora which the term Caribamerican signifies. This is not a Caribbean community in America but an American community of Caribbean people.

5. Stokley Carmichael (Kwame Ture) has not been recognized as a Caribamerican although this identity was not the basis on which he was engaged in this emancipatory struggle. It is important, however, for this to be known to both establish and identify the involvement of the Caribbean diaspora in this struggle. For an exploration of the role Carmichael played in the Civil Rights Movement, see Kwame Ture and Charles V. Hamilton,

Black Power: The Politics of Liberation (New York: Vintage Books, 1992). See also Aldon D. Morris, *The Origins of the Civil Rights Movement: Black Communities Organizing for Change* (New York: The Free Press, 1984); Clayborne Carson, *In Struggle: SNCC and the Black Awakening of the 1960s* (Massachusetts: Harvard University Press, 1995).

6. James Cone, personal communication, New York, 1987.

7. Neville Callam, personal communication, New York, 1991.

8. Ira Reid, *Negro Immigrant: His Background Characteristics and Social Adjustments, 1899–1937* (New York: Arno Press and The New York Times, 1969).

9. Irma Watkins-Owens, *Blood Relations: Caribbean Immigrants and the Harlem Community, 1900–1930* (Indianapolis: Indiana University Press, 1996).

10. For a study of the Caribbean intellectual tradition, see Michelle Ann Stephens, *Black Empire: The Masculine Global Imaginary of Caribbean Intellectuals in the United States, 1914–1962* (Durham: Duke University Press, 2005); Bill Schwartz, ed., *West Indians in Britain* (Manchester: Manchester University Press, 2003); W. B. Burghardt Turner and Joyce Moore Turner, eds, *Richard B. Moore, Caribbean Militant in Harlem: Collected Writings* (Bloomington and Indianapolis: Indiana University Press, 1988).

11. Caribbean Council of Churches, *Fashion Me A People* (Nashville: Parthenon Press, 1981).

12. Rex Nettleford, *Inward Stretch Outward Reach: A Voice from the Caribbean* (London: Macmillan, 1993).

13. *The Oxford English Dictionary* (New York: Clarendon Press, 1989).

14. R. S. Sugirtharajah, *Postcolonial Criticism and Biblical Interpretation* (Oxford: Oxford University Press, 2002), 181.

15. Surgiratharajah, *Postcolonial Criticism*, 182–83.

16. Surgiratharajah, *Postcolonial Criticism*, 183.

17. Surgiratharajah, *Postcolonial Criticism*, 183.

18. Surgiratharajah, *Postcolonial Criticism*, 183.

19. Eric Williams, *Capitalism and Slavery* (North Carolina: University of North Carolina Press, 1944). See also Barbara L. Solow, ed., *Slavery and the Rise of the Atlantic System* (New York: Cambridge University Press, 1991).

20. Joseph M. Murphy, *Working the Spirit: Ceremonies of the African Diaspora* (Massachusetts: Beacon Press, 1994), 177–78.

21. Murphy, *Working the Spirit*, 178–79.

22. Khachig Tololyan, "The Nation State and its Others: In Lieu of a Preface," *Diaspora* 1.1 (1991): 4–5.

23. Tololyan, "The Nation State," 4–5.

24. William Safran, "Diasporas in Modern Societies: Myths of Homeland and Return," *Diaspora* 1.1 (1991): 83–99.

25. Safran, "Diasporas," 94.

26. The term exile is used in various ways. The biblical writers used it to interpret the Babylonian enslavement of the Jewish people. In a theological sense, exile is punishment for sins, a period of time, and the experience of desolation and hope. For an account of this, see P. R. Ackroyd, *Exile and Restoration* (Philadelphia: Westminster Press, 1968); R. W. Klein, *Israel in Exile* (Philadelphia: Fortress Press, 1979); the Church is also believed to be an exilic community. A number of contemporary theologians used this metaphor to express this identity of the church as well as to interpret the nature of the relationship between the church and contemporary society. The concern, however,

is the loss of male power and the influence and privilege of the historic denominational churches. For an exploration of this trend, see Walter Brueggemann, *A Commentary on Jeremiah: Exile and Homecoming* (Michigan: Eerdsmans, 1998) and his *Hopeful Imagination: Prophetic Voices in Exile* (Philadelphia: Fortress Press, 1986); Martin B. Copenhaver et al., *Good News in Exile: Three Pastors Offer a Hopeful Vision of the Church* (Michigan: Eerdmans, 1999); Erskine Clarke, ed., *Exilic Preaching: Testimony for Christian Exiles in an Increasingly Hostile Culture* (Pennsylvania: Trinity Press International, 1998). In the African American theological tradition, the term is used to interpret the experience of marginalization and oppression. Rather than being in hostility towards the dominant society, the African American church has a dialectical relationship with the society. For a detailed study on this subject, see Cheryl J. Sanders, *Saints in Exile: The Holiness-Pentecostal Experience in African American Religion and Culture* (New York: Oxford University Press, 1996).

27. George Lamming, *The Pleasures of Exile* (Michigan: University of Michigan Press, 1992), 56.

28. Lamming, *The Pleasures of Exile*, 24.

29. Joseph Aldred, "Paradigms for a Black Theology in Britain," *Black Theology: An International Journal* 2 (1999): 9–32.

30. Aldred, "Paradigms," 14–23.

31. Aldred, "Paradigms," 23.

32. Robert Beckford, *Dread and Pentecostal: A Political Theology for the Black Church in Britain* (London: SPCK, 2000), 8–9.

33. Beckford, *Dread and Pentecostal*, 9.

34. Beckford, *Dread and Pentecostal*, 9.

35. Beckford, *Dread and Pentecostal*, 9–18.

36. Beckford, *Dread and Pentecostal*, 18.

37. Textual critical approach is one of the approaches Black and Womanist theologians used in doing their theological work. For example, see James H. Cone, *Spiritual and the Blues* (New York: Orbis Books, 1972); Peter J. Paris, *The Social Teachings of the Black Churches* (Philadelphia: Fortress Press, 1985); Katie G. Cannon, *Black Womanist Ethics* (Atlanta: Scholars Press, 1988); Dwight Hopkins, *Shoes That Fit Our Feet: Sources for a Constructive Black Theology* (New York: Orbis Books, 1993); J. Deotis Roberts, *Bonhoeffer and King: Speaking Truth to Power* (Louisville: Westminster John Knox Press, 2005).

38. James Cone, *Black Theology of Liberation* (New York: J. B. Lippincott Co., 1970), 17–49; see also Leslie James, "Text and the Rhetoric of Change: Bible and Decolonization in Post-World War II Caribbean Political Discourse," in *Religion, Culture and Tradition*, eds Hemshand Gossai and Samuel Nathaniel Murrell (London: Macmillan, 2000), 143–66.

39. Daniel L. Migliore, *Faith Seeking Understanding: An Introduction to Christian Theology* (Michigan: Eerdmans, 1991), 193.

40. William G. Demas, *West Indian Nationhood and Caribbean Integration* (Barbados: CCC Publishing House, 1974).

41. Elizabeth Thomas-Hope, "Hope and Reality in West Indian Migration to Britain," *The Journal of the Oral History Society* 8, no. 1 (1979): 35.

Chapter 1

1. Ransford Palmer, *In Search of a Better Life: Perspective on Migration from the Caribbean* (New York: Praeger Publishers, 1990), 6–7.

2. James Cone, *My Soul Looks Back* (New York: Orbis Books, 1986), 94.

3. Cone, *My Soul Looks Back*, 110. For a critical, insightful and corrective critique of this aspect of Black theology, see Cornel West and Eddie S. Glaude Jr, eds, *African American Religious Thought* (Louisville: Westminster John Knox Press, 2003), 874–92. See also Cornel West, "Black Theology of Liberation as a Critique of Capitalist Civilization," in James H. Cone and Gayraud Wilmore, eds, *Black Theology: A Documentary History: 1980–1992* (New York: Orbis Books, 1993), 410–26. Alternatively to West's critique, the Christian faith is itself counter-cultural. It has its own norms that provide the resources which can guide and inform faith and practice. Otherwise put, Black theology does not have to resort to any other resources, although it should engage them, for insight on how to live and to carry out its role in society. The life and teaching of Jesus Christ is the norm for faith and practice. The church, which is called to follow him, is an alternative society.

4. Cone, *My Soul Looks Back*, 113. For a helpful discussion on the relationship between Black theology and the theologies of the developing world, see Gayraud Wilmore and James Cone, eds, *Black Theology: A Documentary History, 1966–1979* (New York: Orbis Books, 1979), 445–622; James Cone and Gayraud Wilmore, eds, *Black Theology: A Documentary History: 1980–1992* (New York: Orbis Books, 1993), 355–426.

5. James Cone, *Speaking the Truth: Ecumenism, Liberation and Black Theology* (Michigan: Eerdmans, 1986), 142, 154.

6. Cone recognizes that African Americans do not know much about Caribbean church and theology. He sees this as unfortunate. He also acknowledges the need for African American theology to learn from Caribbean theology and vice versa in order to be in relationship. For further discussion, see his *For My People: Black Theology and the Black Church. Where have we been and where are we going?* (New York: Orbis Books, 1984), 140–74.

7. Cone, *For My People*, 140–74. See also Cone and Wilmore, *Black Theology: A Documentary History, 1966–1979*, 349–424.

8. Cone, *My Soul Looks Back*, 104–108.

9. Cone, *My Soul Looks Back*, 103.

10. J. Deotis Roberts, *Black Theology in Dialogue* (Philadelphia: Westminster Press, 1987), 19.

11. Deotis Roberts, *Black Theology in Dialogue*, 14. Roberts' reference to people from the so-called Third World includes Caribbean immigrants. While he is concerned about the conflict this creates, he has not addressed the cause of the migration. In arguing for Black theology in dialogue, the point of departure is America's race problem and thus the dialogue he seeks is an internal issue. He also wants to establish the universality of the faith without relating to issues other than race. Migration raises a bigger issue than conflict. It raises the issue of Black theology addressing class and to extending itself beyond national issues. For perspectives on this issue see Michael Battle, ed., *The Quest for Liberation and Reconciliation: Essays in Honor of J. Deotis Roberts* (Kentucky: Westminster John Knox Press, 2005), 109–26.

12. Roberts, *Black Theology in Dialogue*, 14. Roberts proposes a contextual methodology. This is interdisciplinary, ecumenical, pluralistic, biblical, relevant, doxological, political, holistic, particular and passionate. See also David Emmanuel Coatley, ed., *Black Religion, Black Theology: The Collected Essays of J. Deotis Roberts* (New York: Trinity Press International, 2003), 97–165.

13. Dwight Hopkins, *Black Theology USA and South Africa: Politics, Culture, and Liberation* (New York: Orbis Books, 1989), 1.

14. Dwight Hopkins, *Being Human: Race, Culture, and Religion* (Minneapolis: Fortress Press, 2005), 160. Hopkins' works represent the most inclusive and global expressions of African American theology. See, for example, *We are One Voice: Essays on Black Theology in South Africa and the USA* (Braamfontein: Skotaville Publishers, 1989); Dwight Hopkins et al., eds, *Religious Globalization: Theories and Cases* (Durham: Duke University Press, 2001); Batistone Mandiete and Dwight Hopkins, eds, *Liberation Theologies, Post Modernity in the Americas* (New York: Routledge, 1997). However, he does not engage the faith and religious practices of the Black diaspora in American and British societies.

15. Anthony B. Pinn, *Varieties of African American Religious Experience* (Minneapolis: Fortress Press, 1998), 1. For further discussion on this idea, see his *Why Lord: Suffering and Evil in Black Theology* (New York: Continuum, 1995). Just as the Black church is not the only representation of Black religious life, so Black theology is not limited to African American interpretations of Black theology.

16. I agree that there is no homogenous Black theology but it is a mistake to believe that Black theology and Black religion are one and the same. Proponents of this position advance the notion that Black theology is the study of any religion that relates to the Black experience. See, for example, Frederick L. Ware, *Methodologies of Black Theology* (Ohio: Pilgrim Press, 2002), vii–27.

17. Delores Williams, *Sisters in the Wilderness: The Challenge of Womanist God-Talk* (New York: Orbis Books, 1993), xiv–xv. For further exploration of this subject, see Stephanie Y. Michem, *Introducing Womanist Theology* (New York: Orbis Books, 2002); Jacquelyn Grant, *White Women's Christ and Black Women's Jesus: Feminist Christology and Womanist Response* (Georgia: Scholars Press, 1989); Katie Canon, *Katie's Canon: Womanism and the Soul of the Black Community* (New York: Continuum, 1996); Marcia Riggs, *Awake, Arise, and Act: A Womanist Call for Black Liberation* (Cleveland: Pilgrim Press, 1994); Karen Baker-Fletcher, *A Singing Something: Womanist Reflections on Anna Julia Cooper* (New York: Crossroad, 1994); Karen Baker-Fletcher and Garth Baker-Fletcher, *My Sister, My Brother: Womanist and Exodus God-Talk* (New York: Orbis Books, 1997). Womanist theology is a rapidly developing field of study but these are some key texts worth mentioning so as to provide an understanding of its origin, character, challenges, strengths and weaknesses and future direction. One will observe the centrality of African American women's experience in its development but also a slow yet significant trend to be more inclusive of the experience of the Black diaspora. Although this is commendable, it remains to be seen if it will be de-African Americanized. What I suspect may happen is that Womanist theology will continue to express theological concerns through the prism of the African American women's experience but will it be inclusive of non-African American women's experience?

18. Williams, *Sisters in the Wilderness*, xiv.

19. Williams, *Sisters in the Wilderness*, xiv.

20. Williams, *Sisters in the Wilderness*, xiv.

21. Williams, *Sisters in the Wilderness*, xiv–xv.

22. It is clear to me that Womanist theology does not speak for all Black women, but only for African American women. This is so despite Jacquelyn Grant's "inclusive discipleship" in her *White Women's Christ and Black Women's Jesus: Feminist Christology and Womanist Response* (Atlanta: Scholars Press, 1989). See also Emilie M. Townes, "Holistic Spirituality," in her *A Blaze of Glory: Womanist Spirituality as Social Witness* (Nashville: Abingdon Press, 1995). It is believed, however, that Womanist theology does not speak for all African American women. Pastor-scholar, Cheryl Sanders, advocates the notion that Womanist theology is not Christian and consequently does not represent the Christian community. For a more extensive study, see her "Roundtable Discussion: Christian Ethics and Theology in Womanist Perspective," *Journal of Feminist Studies in Religion* 5.2 (Fall 1989): 83–91; *Living the Intersection: Womanism and Afrocentrism in Theology*, ed. Cheryl J. Sanders (Minneapolis: Fortress Press, 1995), 157–75. Notwithstanding this argument, Sanders needs to give an account to those Christians who embrace Womanist theology. This debate cannot be solved here but it demonstrates the tensions and diversity within Womanist theology as I pointed out elsewhere in this study pertaining to Caribbean diasporan women's experience.

23. Williams, *Sisters in the Wilderness*, 239.

24. Lewis premises her theology on the Jamaican national hero, Nanny of the Maroons. Nanny was one of the great Jamaican Freedom Fighters. The designation of the term resonates and reflects the vernacular of the Jamaican culture. For example, in the Jamaican creole, theology is pronounced t'eology.

25. Majorie Lewis, "Diaspora Dialogue: Womanist Theology in Engagement with Aspects of the Black British and Jamaican Experience," *Black Theology: An International Journal* 2:1 (2004): 85–109.

26. Lewis, "Diaspora Dialogue," 90.

27. Kate Coleman, "Black Theology and Black Liberation: A Womanist Perspective," *Black Theology in Britain: A Journal for Contextual Praxis* 1 (1998): 68.

28. Coleman, "Black Theology and Black Liberation," 68.

29. Coleman, "Black Theology and Black Liberation," 68.

30. Coleman, "Black Theology and Black Liberation," 68–69.

31. Dianne M. Stewart, *Three Eyes for the Journey: African Dimensions of the Jamaican Religious Experience* (New York: Oxford University Press, 2005), 165.

32. Stewart, *Three Eyes for the Journey*, 158.

33. Stewart, *Three Eyes for the Journey*, 163, 168.

34. The earliest major works on Caribbean diasporan life in the American context include: Claude McKay, *Banjo* (New York: Harper & Brothers, 1957); Paule Marshall, *Brown Girl Brownstones* (New York: Feminist Press, 1981). This study engages some of these works.

35. Ira Reid, *Negro Immigrant: His Background, Characteristics, and Social Adjustment, 1899–1937* (New York: Columbia University Press, 1939); Randall Burkett, *Garveyism as a Religious Movement: The Institutionalization of Black Religion* (New Jersey: Scarecrow Press, 1978); *Black Redemption: Churchmen Speak for the Garvey Movement* (Philadelphia: Temple University Press, 1978). These works among others are engaged throughout this study.

36. Irma Watkins-Owens, *Blood Relations: Caribbean Immigrants and the Harlem Community, 1900–1930* (Indianapolis: University of Indiana Press, 1996), 56.

37. Nancy Foner, ed., *Island in the Sun: West Indian Migration to New York City* (California: University of California Press, 2001), 17.

38. Elaine Bauer and Paul Thompson, *Jamaican Hands Across the Atlantic* (Kingston: Ian Randle Publishers, 2006), 169–79. See also Vilna Francine Bashi, *Survival of the Knitted: Immigrant Social Networks in a Stratified World* (Standford: University of California Press, 2007), 203–206.

39. Bauer and Thompson, *Jamaican Hands*, 179.

40. Mark Sturge, *Look What the Lord has Done: An Exploration of Black Christian Faith in Britain* (Bletchey, England: Scripture Union, 2005).

41. Anthony Reddie, *Black Theology in Transatlantic Dialogue* (New York: Palgrave Macmillan, 2006), 2–3.

42. Reddie, *Black Theology in Transatlantic Dialogue*, 8–12.

43. Reddie, *Black Theology in Transatlantic Dialogue*, 2–3.

44. Reddie, *Black Theology in Transatlantic Dialogue*, 82.

45. Reddie, *Black Theology in Transatlantic Dialogue*, 168–80.

46. Reddie, *Black Theology in Transatlantic Dialogue*, 169. For further discussion on this issue, see "An Interactive Odyssey," in Geoffrey Stevenson, ed., *Pulpit Journeys* (London: Darton, Longman and Todd, 2006), 149–65.

47. Reddie, *Black Theology in Transatlantic Dialogue*, 180.

48. Reddie, *Black Theology in Transatlantic Dialogue*, 8–10.

49. Reddie, *Black Theology in Transatlantic Dialogue*, 203.

50. Reddie, *Black Theology in Transatlantic Dialogue*, 8.

51. Reddie, *Black Theology in Transatlantic Dialogue*, 9.

52. Reddie, *Black Theology in Transatlantic Dialogue*, 203.

53. Idris Hamid, ed., *Out of the Depths* (San Fernando: St. Andrew's Theological College, 1977).

54. Kortright Davis, *Emancipation Still Comin': Explorations in Caribbean Emanicipatory Theology* (New York: Orbis Books, 1990).

55. Noel Erskine, *Decolonizing Theology* (New York: Orbis Books, 1981).

56. Michael N. Jagessar and Anthony G. Reddie, *Postcolonial Black British Theology: New Text and Themes* (Peterborough: Epworth, 2007).

57. Michael N. Jagessar and Anthony G. Reddie, eds, *Postcolonial Black British Theology: New Textures and Themes* (Peterborough: Epworth, 2007), xii, xviii–xxi.

58. Jagessar and Reddie, *Postcolonial Black British Theology*, xvi–xxiv.

59. Jagessar and Reddie, *Postcolonial Black British Theology*, xiv.

60. Jagessar and Reddie, *Postcolonial Black British Theology*, xvii.

61. Jagessar and Reddie, *Postcolonial Black British Theology*, xiv.

62. Jagessar and Reddie, *Postcolonial Black British Theology*, xiii.

63. Mukti Barton, *Rejection, Resistance and Resurrection: Speaking Out on Racism in the Church* (London: Darton, Longman and Todd, 2005), 7.

64. For a study on Black Atlantic Christianity, see Jon F. Sensbach, *Rebecca's Revival Creating: Black Christianity in the Atlantic World* (Massachusetts: Harvard University Press, 2005). The importance of this work lies in the role Caribbean Christians play in the making of a Black Atlantic Christianity and the central role of women. See also Rupert Lewis and Patrick Bryan, eds, *Garvey: His Work and Impact* (Kingston: Institute of

Social and Economic Research and the Department of Extra Mural Studies, 1988), 67–83; Ula Yvette Taylor, *The Veiled Garvey: The Life and Times of Amy Jacques Garvey* (Chapel Hill: University of North Carolina Press, 2002).

65. The emergence of the Caribbean diaspora changes the character of both African American and American Christianity. For a study on the role and impact of diasporan communities on American religion and society, see R. Stephen Warner, *A Church of our Own: Disestablishment and Diversity in American Religion* (New York: Rutgers University Press, 2005) and also his very informative article, "Immigrants and the Faith They Bring: Coming to America," *Christian Century* (February 10, 2004): 20–23; Benedicta Cipola, "Immigration in America: Religion and Assimilation," in *Religion and Ethics: News Weekly* (New York: Thirteen WNET New York, 2005): 2–4.

66. Neville Callam, "Ethnicity and the Church's Catholicity: Ministry to the Caribbean Diaspora in North America," *Grace Baptist Chapel Anniversary Lecture* (Bronx, New York, September 20, 2002). See also David T. Shannon and Gayraud S. Wilmore, *Black Witness to the Apostolic Faith* (Michigan: Eerdmans, 1985).

Chapter 2

1. I use the term Caribbeaners to identify the people of the Caribbean diaspora in countries other than the United States of America. Those in the United States I call Caribamericans in order to differentiate the particular diasporan context especially since each context is different. I maintain, however, that they are still Caribbean people. Another way of stating it is that they are one people but many diasporas.

2. Stuart Hall, "Myths of Caribbean Identity," *The Walter Rodney Memorial Lecture* (Warwick, UK: University of Warwick, 1991), 1.

3. Daniel Yon, "Identity and Differences in the Caribbean Diaspora: Case Study from Metropolitan Toronto," in *The Reordering of Culture: Latin America, the Caribbean and Canada*, eds Alvin Ruprecht and Cecelia Taiana (Canada: Carleton University Press, 1995), 482–87. Globalization is a very important and expanding field of study which is central to an understanding of diasporan identity. This subject will not detain us because it is not the purpose of this work, but for further exploration, see L. Bash et al., *Nations Unbound: Transnational Projects, Postcolonial Predicament and Deterriorialized Nation-states* (Amsterdam: Gordon and Beach, 1994); A. Appadurai, "Disjuncture and Difference in the Global Cultural Economy," in *Global Culture: Nationalism, Globalization and Modernity*, ed. M. Featherstone (London: Sage Publications, 1992); U. Hannerz, *Cultural Complexity: Studies in the Social Organization of Meaning* (New York: Columbia University Press, 1992).

4. Jana Evans Braziel and Anita Mannur, *Theorizing Diaspora* (Massachusetts: Blackwell, 2003), 1–18.

5. The Caribbean Basin Initiative was an economic initiative during the 1980s between the United States and the Caribbean territories.

6. Orlando Patterson, "Ecumenical America: Global Culture and the American Cosmos," in O. Nigel Bollard, ed., *The Birth of Caribbean Civilization: A Century of Ideas about Culture, Identity, Nation and Society* (Kingston: Ian Randle Publishers, 2004),

632–51; Christine G. T. Ho and Keith Nurse, eds, *Globalisation, Diaspora and Caribbean Popular Culture* (Kingston: Ian Randle Publishers, 2005).

7. Dennis Conway, "The Caribbean Diaspora," in *Understanding the Contemporary Caribbean*, eds Richard S. Hillman and Thomas J. D'Agostino (Kingston: Ian Randle Publishers, 2003), 234–51.

8. For an overview of the nature of Caribbean diasporan life, see Lorna Chessum, *From Immigrant to Ethnic Minority* (Burlington: Ashgate, 2000); George Gmelch, *Double Passage: The Life of Caribbean Migrants Abroad and Back Home* (Michigan: University of Michigan Press, 1992); Nancy Foner, ed., *Island in the City: West Indian Migration to New York* (Berkeley and Los Angeles: University of California Press, 2001); Nancy Foner, ed., *New Immigrants in New York* (New York: Columbia University Press, 1987); Ransford Palmer, ed., *In Search of a Better Life* (New York: Praeger Publishers, 1990); Keith S. Henry, "Caribbean Political Dilemmas in North America and in the United Kingdom," *Journal of Black Studies* 7:4 (June 1977): 373–86; Pri Thomas, "Down These Mean Streets," *Journal of Caribbean Studies* 19:1&2 (Fall 2004–2005): 43–61; Humphery E. Lamur and John D. Speckmann, eds, *Adaptation of Migrants from Caribbean in the European and American Metropolis* (Netherlands: University of Amsterdam, 1975); Roy S. Bryce-Laporte, "Black Immigrants: The Experience of Invisibility and Inequality," *Journal of Black Studies* 3:1 (September 1972): 29–55; Russell R. McCloud, *Providing a Health Sanctuary: Meeting the Need of the Undocumented Alien* (unpublished D. Min. thesis, Drew University, 2003).

9. Diaspora as a theological paradigm is one usage of the term. The term is also used as personal and political self-identity, as a mediator of culture and as an analytical or interpretive tool for intellectual engagement. For an exposition of these ideas, see William Safran, "Diasporas in Modern Societies: Myths of Homeland Return," *Diaspora* 1:1 (1991): 38–99; Waltraud Kokot, Khachig Tololyan and Carolin Alfonso, eds, *Diaspora, Identity and Religion: New Direction in Theory and Research* (London: Routledge, 2004); Avar Brah, *Cartographies of Diaspora: Contesting Identities* (London: Routledge, 1996), 128–210.

10. While identity is not the subject of this discussion and is beyond the scope of this study, I recognize its complex and problematic nature. For an insightful discussion on the subject, see Stuart Hall and Paul du Gay, eds, *Questions of Cultural Identity* (London: Sage Publications, 1996). For a study on models of Black identity, see Mark Christian, ed., *Black Identity in the 20th Century: Expressions of US and UK African Diaspora* (London: Hansib Publications, 2002).

11. Robin Cohen, "Cultural Diaspora: The Case of the Caribbean," in *Caribbean Migration Globalised Identities*, ed. Mary Chamberlain (New York: Routledge, 1998), 22. See also Rex. M. Nettleford, *Caribbean Cultural Identity: The Case of Jamaica* (Kingston: Institute of Jamaica, 1978).

12. Cohen, "Cultural Diaspora," 27–33.

13. Ransform Palmer, *Pilgrims From the Sun: West Indian Migration to America* (New York: Twayne Publishers, 1995), 1–43. For further discussion on the creation of Caribbean cultural identity, consult Currdella Forbes, *From Nation to Diaspora: Samuel Selvon, George Lamming and the Cultural Performance of Gender* (Kingston: University of the West Indies Press, 2005).

14. Safran, "Diasporas in Modern Societies," 83–89.

15. Robin Cohen, *Global Diasporas: An Introduction* (London: UCL Press, 1997), 22–26.

16. Cohen, *Global Diasporas*, 22–26.

17. Cohen, *Global Diasporas*, 180.

18. Mervyn C. Alleyne, *The Construction and Representation of Race and Ethnicity in the Caribbean and the World* (Kingston: University of the West Indies Press, 2002), 94.

19. Stuart Hall, "Cultural Identity and Diaspora," in Jana Evans Braziel and Anita Manur, eds, *Theorizing Dispora* (Massachusetts: Blackwell, 2003), 244.

20. Hall, "Cultural Identity and Diaspora," 234.

21. Hall, "Cultural Identity and Diaspora," 234–35.

22. Hall, "Cultural Identity and Diaspora," 235.

23. Hall, "Cultural Identity and Diaspora," 236.

24. Kortright Davis, *Emancipation Still Comin': Explorations in Caribbean Emancipatory Theology* (New York: Orbis Books, 1990), 17.

25. Davis, *Emancipation Still Comin'*, 17–21.

26. Rex Nettleford, *Inward Stretch Outward Reach: A Voice From the Caribbean* (London: Macmillan, 1993), 180.

27. Hall, "Cultural Identity and Diaspora," 237.

28. Hall, "Cultural Identity and Diaspora," 237; Maureen Warner-Lewis, *Central Africa in the Caribbean: Transcending Time, Transforming Cultures* (Kingston: University of the West Indies, 2003). The literature on the diverse origins of the Africans who were brought to the Caribbean by force is immense. For a general discussion on this diversity, see Colin A. Palmer, "Africa in the Making of the Caribbean," in Brian L. Moore, B. W. Higman, Carl Campbell and Patrick Bryan, *Slavery, Freedom and Gender: Dynamics of Caribbean Society* (Kingston: University of the West Indies, 2001), 40–56.

29. Franklin W. Knight and Colin A. Palmer, eds, *The Modern Caribbean* (North Carolina: University of North Carolina Press, 1989), 6.

30. Eric Williams, *From Columbus to Castro: The History of the West Indies* (New York: Vintage Books, 1984), 348.

31. Hall, "Cultural Identity and Diaspora," 238.

32. Hall, "Cultural Identity and Diaspora," 239–44.

33. Davis, *Emancipation Still Comin'* , 21.

34. Davis, *Emancipation Still Comin'*, 23.

35. Camille Hernandez-Ramdwar, "Raced Caribbeans: Disproving Myths of National Identity in the Great White North," Conference on Caribbean Culture, March 3–6, 1996, Kingston, Jamaica.

36. Mary Waters, *Black Identities: West Indian Immigrant Dreams and American Realities* (Massachusetts: Harvard University Press, 1991), 21

37. Aisha Kahn, *Callaloo Nation* (Kingston: University of the West Indies Press, 2005). For related interest, consult Tina K. Ramnarine, *Creating Their Own Space* (Kingston: University of the West Indies Press, 2001). For an excellent study on the Indo-Caribbean, see Brinda J. Mehta, *Diasporic (Dis)locations* (Kingston: University of the West Indies Press, 2004). On Chinese culture in the Caribbean, consult Walton Look Lai, *Chinese in the West Indies 1806–1995* (Kingston: University of the West Indies Press, 1998). For an example of a particular cultural expression that belongs to one nationality but embodies the Caribbean, see Philip Scher, *Carnival and the Formation of a Caribbean Transnation* (Florida: University of Florida Press, 2003).

38. Paul Gilroy, *The Black Atlantic: Modernity and Double Consciousness* (Massachussets: Harvard University Press, 1993), 4–5. Gilroy uses the metaphor Black Atlantic as an analytical tool to construct a cosmopolitan or transnational perspective of Black identity. Recent scholarship shows an emerging interest in Black cosmopolitan identity. Consult, for example, the informative study of Michelle Ann Stephens, *Black Empire: The Masculine Global Imaginary of Caribbean Intellectuals in the United States, 1914–1962* (Durham: Duke University Press, 2005). While Gilroy uses the metaphor "Black Atlantic" and Stephens uses "Black Empire," I contend that the metaphor can be used interchangeably. Both are theorizing about Black identity. Their point of departure, however, is the usage of the metaphor. The "Black Atlantic" is an intellectual tool for constructing identity; the "Black Empire" is a materialistic theory of identity. In the case of this study, identity is considered according to the former perspective.

39. Gilroy, *The Black Atlantic*, 2.

40. Gilroy, *The Black Atlantic*, 15; 99–103; quotation on 15.

41. Paul Gilroy, "It ain't where you're from, it's where you are at... The Dialectics of Diasporic Identification," in *Migration, Diasporas and Transnationalism*, eds Steven Vertovec and Robin Cohen (Northampton: Edward Elgar Publishing, 1999), 282.

42. Waters, *Black Identities*, 321.

43. James Clifford, "Diasporas," in *Migration, Diasporas and Transnationalism*, eds Steven Vertovec and Robin Cohen (Massachusetts: Edward Elgar Publishing, 1999), 228.

44. Jana Evans and Anita Mannur, eds, *Theorizing Diaspora* (Oxford: Blackwell, 2003),7.

45. Gilroy, *The Black Atlantic*, 3, 19.

46. Paul Gilroy, *There Ain't No Black in the Union Jack: The Cultural Politics of Race and Nation* (Chicago: University of Chicago Press, 1991), 353–59.

47. Gilroy, *The Black Atlantic*, 15. I agree with Gilroy but it is problematic in that he is dialoging with only one aspect of the Black diaspora yet claims to be speaking for the whole Black family. In arguing that there is no unitary notion of Black identity, he is at the same time promoting a universalist perspective. While African Americans do not speak for the Black diaspora, Gilroy is attempting to do so out of the particularity of his British context.

48. Winston James, *Holding Aloft the Banner of Ethiopia: Caribbean Radicalism in Early Twentieth-Century America* (London: Verso, 1998), 51. James points out the distinctiveness of Caribbean people in the United States which predisposed them to progress in political engagement. One of these distinctions is the minimal role of the Christian faith in their lives. It is unfortunate that James is not aware of the work of Ethelred Brown who established the first Black Unitarian church in America. The Garvey movement was essentially religious or at least it had a religious dimension. This movement was the single most influential socio-political religious movement of that time. Yet, James discusses Brown and Garvey later in his study but disregards their faith and ignores that they were Christians.

49. People of African descent have been living in Britain since the era of the slave trade but they were not recognized as Blacks but as British subjects. As such, their relationship to the British Empire rather than by their African heritage defines their identity.

50. Constance R. Sutton and Susan R. Makiesky-Barrow, "Migration and West Indian Racial and Ethnic Consciousness," in Constance R. Sutton and Elsa M. Chaney, eds, *Caribbean Life in New York City: Social and Cultural Dimensions* (New York: Center for Migration Studies of New York, 1992), 87–105. For a comparative study between the British and American Caribbean diasporas, see Nancy Foner, "West Indians in New York City and London: A Comparative Analysis," *International Migration Review* 13 (1979): 284–97; "Jamaican Migrants: A Comparative Analysis of New York and London Experience," *Occasional Paper No. 36* (New York: Center for Latin American and Caribbean Studies, New York University, 1983). The context of each diaspora is different from the other but another important factor is that each Caribbean country has its own particular history. This, too, plays a role in shaping their identity. For a helpful study, see Bonham C. Richards, *Caribbean Migrations: Environment and Human Survival on St. Kitts and Nevis* (Knoxville: University of Tennessee Press, 1993), 3–31.

51. Sutton and Makiesky-Barrow, "Migration," 95.

52. Sutton and Makiesky-Barrow, "Migration," 97.

53. Gilroy, *The Black Atlantic*, 1. It is questionable if this Duboisian claim of double consciousness refers to the Black people as a whole or only to African Americans. If this notion is understood within the context it was used, then Dubois was not speaking on behalf of the entire Black diaspora. Using it out of this context would be universalizing the Black experience. This is the issue Gilroy opposes. For further exploration of this issue, see W. E. B. Dubois, *The Souls of Black Folk* (New York: Bantam, 1989).

54. Gilroy, *The Black Atlantic*, 15.

55. Gilroy, *The Black Atlantic*, 72–223.

56. Gilroy, *The Black Atlantic*, 16.

57. Gilroy, *The Black Atlantic*, 19. The claim by Gilroy is a very problematic issue. Gilroy is basing his claim on the European connections and experiences of these figures. It raises the question of whether one is desiring to be other than Black or to validate self. The claim could be made that Gilroy is exploring the European origin of identity. But, in order to do this, does it have to be done at the expense of denying one's Black origin? This then means the elimination of the African origin of the Black Atlantic identity.

58. Gilroy, *The Black Atlantic*, 220.

59. Gilroy, *The Black Atlantic*, 27.

60. Gilroy, *The Black Atlantic*, 4.

61. Gilroy, *The Black Atlantic*, 16.

62. Gilroy, *The Black Atlantic*, 17.

63. Gilroy, *The Black Atlantic*, 17.

64. Michelle Stephens, *Black Empire: The Masculine Global Imaginary of Caribbean Intellectuals in the United States, 1914–1962* (Durham: Duke University Press, 2005), 1–3.

65. Stephens, *Black Empire*, 2.

66. Clifford, "Diasporas," 228–34.

67. Reuel Rogers, "Black Like Who?" in *Island in the City: West Indian Migration to New York*, ed. Nancy Foner (California: University of California Press, 2001), 165.

68. Rogers, "Black Like Who?" 167. By locating the difference in the American context, Rogers overlooks the fact that the social context shapes national identity. African Americans cannot claim national identity in the same sense as Caribbamericans. The

latter have a homeland other than the resident homeland. The former do not have this. The experience in both also differs.

69. Clifford, "Diasporas," 221–34.

70. Gilroy, *The Black Atlantic*, 38.

71. Gilroy, *The Black Atlantic*, 37–38.

72. Gilroy, *The Black Atlantic*, 38–39.

73. Gilroy, *The Black Atlantic*, 39.

74. Walter Rodney, *The Groundings with my Brothers* (London: Bogle-L'Ouverture Publications, 1969), 62–63. See also his *Walter Rodney Speeches: The Making of an African Intellectual* (New Jersey: African World Press, 1990). For a detailed study on Rodney as an intellectual, see Rupert Lewis, *Walter Rodney's Intellectual and Political Thought* (Kingston: The Press University of the West Indies, 1998). Further exploration of the Caribbean intellectual tradition is provided by Dennis Benn, *The Caribbean: An Intellectual History 1774–2003* (Kingston: Ian Randle Publishers, 2004). See also George Lamming, *Coming Coming Home: Conversations II: Western Education and the Caribbean Intellectual Coming, Coming, Coming Home* (St. Martin: House of Nehesi Publishers, 1995). For a brief discussion on this subject, see Burchell Taylor, *Free For All: A Question of Morality and Community* (Kingston: Grace Kennedy Foundation, 1992).

Chapter 3

1. William G. Demas, *West Indian Nationhood and Caribbean Integration* (Barbados: CCC Publishing House, 1974).

2. Noel Erskine, *Decolonizing Theology: A Caribbean Perspective* (New York: Orbis Books, 1981), 81–86. The two best representative works on this subject dealing with the African American church are E. Franklin Frazier and C. Eric Lincoln, *The Negro in America: The Black Church Since Frazier* (New York: Schocken Books, 1974) and C. Eric Lincoln and Lawrence H. Mamiya, *The Black Church in the African American Experience* (Durham: Duke University Press, 1990). For works on the church in the British context, see M. J. Calley, *God's People: West Indian Pentecostal Sets in England* (London: Oxford University Press, 1965); Roslyn Gerloff, *A Plea for British Black Theologies: The Black Church Movement in Britain in its Transatlantic Cultural and Theological Interaction. Vol. 1* (Frankfurt: Peter Lang, 1992); Mark Sturge, *Look What The Lord Has Done: An Exploration of Black Christian Faith in Britain* (Bletchley, England: Scripture Union, 2005).

3. Nicole Rodriguez Toulis, *Believing Identity: Pentecostal and the Mediation of Jamaican Ethnicity and Gender in England* (New York: Berg, 1997), 2.

4. Toulis, *Believing Identity*, 210.

5. Mary Waters, *Black Identities: West Indian Immigrant Dreams and American Realities* (Massachusetts: Harvard University Press, 1999), 19–43. For an excellent examination of the formation of the Caribamerican identity, see Franklin W. Knight, "Migration, the Plantation Society and the Emergence of a Pan-Caribbean Culture," in *Caribbean Migration Program* (Gainesville: Center for Latin American Studies, University of Florida, 1982).

6. Ethnicity is a complex issue and is understood in a variety of ways. While there is no common understanding, I am using the term to identify and describe the people of

Caribbean origin in terms of commonalities in culture and interest. Culture must also be understood to mean history, experience, religion, customs or way of life as well as values and world-view. For a helpful discussion, representing two different perspectives on ethnicity, see Mervyn C. Alleyne, *The Construction and Representation of Race and Ethnicity in the Caribbean and the World* (Kingston: University of the West Indies Press, 2002), 9–12; Waters, *Black Identities*, 44–49. See also Rex M. Nettleford, *Identity, Race and Protest in Jamaica* (New York: William Morrow & Co., 1972). This text, however, addresses identity in the Jamaican context but is relevant to this study. It shows how identity is understood within one Caribbean nation.

7. Constance R. Sutton and Susan R. Makiesky-Barrow, "Migration and West Indian Racial and Ethnic Consciousness," in Constance R. Sutton and Elsa M. Chaney, eds, *Caribbean Life in New York City: Social and Cultural Dimensions* (New York: Center for Migration Studies of New York, 1992), 97.

8. Sutton and Makiesky-Barrow, "Migration," 98.

9. Waters, *Black Identities*, 6.

10. Waters, *Black Identities*, 6–7. For a study on the peculiarities of the Caribbean diasporan people, although the concern is about their predisposition to political involvement, see Winston James, *Holding Aloft the Banner of Ethiopia: Caribbean Radicalism in Early Twentieth-Century America* (London: Verso, 1998), 50–91.

11. Waters, *Black Identities*, 7–8. These can be described as the Caribbean diasporan moral values and ethics but they can become too individualistic and achievement oriented. Seen within its context, these values are not only organic to the Caribbean experience but counter to Euro-American, even African American, moral values.

12. Ransford W. Palmer, *In Search of a Better Life: Perspective on Migration from the Caribbean* (New York: Praeger Publishers, 1990).

13. Palmer, *In Search of a Better Life*, 6. The classic view of migration is what is called the "push pull theory." This topic will not detain us here as it is not the subject of this study. For clarity, however, I want to state how it is defined. The "Push" are factors from the home country, such as unemployment, education and other circumstances that create the need for people to leave their country. "Pull" are the forces that attract the immigrant to the host countries such as greater opportunities for accomplishing personal and family needs. This may include higher income, jobs and a standard of living that the home country cannot provide. For a helpful study on this issue, see Barry Levine, ed., *The Caribbean Exodus* (New York: Praeger Publishers, 1987). See also William Green, "Push Factors: Nineteenth-Century Background to the Caribbean Diaspora," *University of London Institute of Commonwealth Studies: Caribbean Migration and the Black Diaspora: A Comparative Study* (June, 1987).

14. Palmer, *In Search of a Better Life*, 9.

15. Bonham Richardson, *Caribbean Migrants: Environment and Human Survival on St. Kitts and Nevis* (Knoxville: University of Tennessee Press, 1983), 3. Any study on this migration tradition must include: Eric Williams, *Capitalism and Slavery* (North Carolina: University of North Carolina Press, 1944); Elizabeth Thomas-Hope, *Caribbean Migration* (Kingston: University of the West Indies Press, 1992). For a study on migration to Britain, see Mike Phillips and Trevor Philips, *Windrush: The Irresistible Rise of Multi-Racial Britain* (London: HarperCollins, 1998); Alan Cobley, ed., *Crossroads of Empire: The Europe-Caribbean Connections 1492–1992* (Barbados: University of the West Indies

Press, 1994). For an excellent study of Caribbean migration to the United States, see Winston James, *Holding Aloft the Banner of Ethiopia*, 9–49.

16. Waters, *Black Identities*, 44–93; 285–325.

17. Milton Vickerman, *Crosscurrents: West Indian Immigrants and Race* (New York: Oxford University Press, 1999), 12. The Jamaican motto "Out of Many One People" makes it very easy for them to have a deep sense of kinship with other Caribbean nationalities.

18. For a study on this issue, see Christine G. T. Ho and Keith Nurse, *Globalisation, Diaspora and Caribbean Popular Culture* (Kingston: Ian Randle Publishers, 2005).

19. Vickerman, *Crosscurrents*, 11.

20. Vickerman, *Crosscurrents*, 11. The point of departure of all three identity theories is different but they are formed by the same process. This difference is the framework that informs and shapes the identity. For a discussion on the nature of the Caribbean diasporan life, see *Virginia R. Dominguez, From Neighbor to Stranger: The Caribbean Peoples in the United States* (Connecticut: Antilles Research Program, Yale University, 1975); Barry Levine, ed., *The Caribbean Exodus* (New York: Praeger Publishers, 1987); Palmer, *In Search of a Better Life*; Constance Sutton, "Transnational Identities and Cultures: Caribbean Immigrants in the United States," in *Immigration and Ethnicity: American Society – "Melting Pot" or "Salad Bowl"*, ed. Michael D' Innocenzo and Josef P. Sirefman (Connecticut: Greenwood Press, 1992); Nancy Foner, ed., *New Immigrants in New York* (New York: Columbia University Press, 1987) and *Island in the Sun* (New York: Columbia University Press, 2001). Popular culture, although not the subject of this study, plays a pivotal role in forming identity. For an informative study of this subject, see Philip Scher, *Carnival as the Formation of a Caribbean Transnation* (Florida: University Press of Florida, 2003).

21. Vickerman, *Crosscurrents*, 11.

22. Vickerman, *Crosscurrents*, 26. A number of scholars have written about the experience of Caribbean people in the American experience with reference to the relationship to African Americans. Interestingly, the relationship has not changed after more than fifty years since the earliest study was done. For an exploration of this issue, see Ira Reid, *The Negro Immigrant* (New York: Columbia University Press, 1939). Noteworthy are Lennox Raphael, "West Indians and Afro-Americans," *Freedomways* (Summer 1964): 438–45; Roy S. Bryce-Laporte, "Black Immigrants, the Experience of Invisibility and Inequality," *Journal of Black Studies* 3, no. 1 (1972): 29–56; Philip Kasinitz, The Minority Within: The New York Black Immigrants," *New York Affairs* 10, no. 1 (Winter 1987): 44–58.

23. Vickerman, *Crosscurrents*, 36–39. For further discussion on the origin of race and its relationship with ethnicity, see Alleyne, *Construction*.

24. This position is contested. Walter Rodney argues otherwise. He thinks that this notion of a non-racial Caribbean is a myth. It is then the task of the Caribbean intellectual not only to attack it but to expose it as such. For an acquaintance with his thought, see his *The Groundings with my Brothers* (London: Bogle-L'Ouverture Publications, 1969); see also Eric Williams, *The Negro in the Caribbean* (New York: A & B Publishers, 1994).

25. Reuel Rogers, "'Black Like Who?' Afro-Caribbean Immigrants, African Americans, and the Politics of Group Identity," in *Island in the City: West Indian Migration to New York*, ed. Nancy Foner (California: University of California Press, 2001), 181.

26. Caribamericans and African Americans are siblings. For a discussion on this relationship, see Irma Watkins-Owens, *Blood Relations: Caribbean Immigrants and the Harlem Community, 1900–1930* (Indiana: Indiana University Press, 1996).

27. Barry Chevannes, *Betwixt and Between: Explorations in an African-Caribbean Mindscape* (Kingston: Ian Randle Publishers, 2006), 7.

28. Vickerman, *Crosscurrents*, 139.

29. Vickerman, *Crosscurrents*, 139.

30. Vickerman, *Crosscurrents*, 137–60. The complex and disturbing relationship between the Caribbean diasporan community and African Americans cannot be examined in this study. For a detailed study, see Ira Reid, *The Negro Immigrant*; Claude McKay, *Home to Harlem* (Boston: Northeastern University Press, 1987); Lennox Raphael, "West Indians and African Americans," *Freedomways* 4, no. 3 (Summer 1964): 438–45; Orde Coombs, "West Indians in New York: Moving Beyond the Limbo Pole," *New York Magazine*, July 13, 1970, 28–32.

31. Vickerman, *Crosscurrents*, 140.

32. Vickerman, *Crosscurrents*, 142.

33. Vickerman, *Crosscurrents*, 147–54. African Americans and Caribamericans have always worked together. Vickerman's claim is a recent phenomenon. In the earliest years, there were too few Caribbean people and thus the size of the Caribbean community was too small to engender a distinct identity. The issue is not so much about the relationship between these two groups of Black people but the diversity within the Black community. The Black community in America comprises more than African Americans. The challenge lies in how to foster the peaceful co-existence of each sector of the Black community while maintaining their distinct identities.

34. Vickerman, *Crosscurrents*, 155.

35. Noel Erskine, *Decolonizing Theology: A Caribbean Perspective* (New York: Orbis Books, 1981), 41–45.

36. Erskine, *Decolonizing Theology*, 41–42. The life of George Liele has not been sufficiently studied. For a brief but informative work on this great figure, see Clement Gayle, *George Liele: Pioneer Missionary to Jamaica* (Kingston: Jamaica Baptist Union, 1982).

37. Erskine, *Decolonizing Theology*, 42.

38. Kortright Davis, *Emancipation Still Comin': Explorations in Caribbean Emancipatory Theology* (New York: Orbis Books, 1990), 126.

39. Davis, *Emancipation Still Comin'*, 126.

40. Davis, *Emancipation Still Comin'*, 50–67.

41. Davis, *Emancipation Still Comin'*, 105–16.

42. Davis, *Emancipation Still Comin'*, 117–29. See also Orville W. Taylor, "Globalization, Racism and the Terrorist Attack: Incorporating an Afro-Caribbean Response," in Jullianne Malveaux and Reginna A. Green, eds, *The Parodox of Loyalty: An African American Response to the War on Terrorism* (Chicago: Third World Press, 2002), 210–20.

43. Davis, *Emancipation Still Comin'*, 126.

44. Davis, *Emancipation Still Comin'*, 127.

45. Cornel West, *Race Matters* (Boston: Beacon Press, 1993), x.

46. Waters, *Black Identities*, 340. For a discussion on aspiration to whiteness, see David R. Roediger, *Working Toward Whiteness: How America's Immigrants Became White* (New York: Basic Books, 2005).

47. Waters, *Black Identities*, 340.

48. Vickerman, *Crosscurrents*, 92. For an examination of how Caribbean people deal with racism, see James, *Holding Aloft the Banner of Ethiopia*, 92–121; Waters, *Black Identities*, 140–91.

49. Winston James and Clive Harris, eds, *Inside Babylon: The Caribbean Diaspora in Britain* (London: Verso Press, 1983), 233.

50. James and Harris, *Inside Babylon*, 243.

51. James and Harris, *Inside Babylon*, 233–34.

52. For a brilliant study on the genealogy of racism, see Cornel West, *Prophecy Deliverance: An Afro-American Revolutionary Christianity* (Philadelphia: Westminster Press, 1982), 47–65. For a general analysis with particular reference to a Caribbean perspective on race consult Alleyne, *Construction*.

53. G. Lewis, "Race Relations in Britain: A View from the Caribbean," *Race Today* 1, no. 3 (July 1969): 80. See also James and Harris, *Inside Babylon*, 234. They borrow the term pigmentocracy and find it pertinent to describe this racist ideology.

54. Emile Townes, *In a Blaze of Glory: Womanist Spirituality as Social Witness* (Nashville: Abingdon, 1995), 101.

55. Davis, *Emancipation Still Comin'*, 24.

56. Townes, *In a Blaze of Glory*, 101.

57. Davis, *Emancipation Still Comin'*, 24.

58. James and Harris, *Inside Babylon*, 235.

59. Vickerman, *Crosscurrents*, 92–94.

60. Vickerman, *Crosscurrents*, 98–112.

61. Vickerman, *Crosscurrents*, 112.

62. For a detailed study of how the Caribbean struggle is linked to the universal Black struggle, consult Michelle Ann Stephens, *Black Empire: The Masculine Global Imaginary of Caribbean Intellectuals in the United States 1914–1962* (Durham: Duke University Press, 2005). See also Scott McLemee, *C. L. R. James: On the 'Negro Question'* (Mississippi: University of Mississippi Press, 1996).

63. Vickerman, *Crosscurrents*, 168–69. Caribbean people are reluctant to become citizens of their host county although they have the opportunity to do so after living for years in the United States. The reasons are many but essentially it is the sense of giving up their national identity. Many are unaware that they do not need to give up their citizenship because their native country accepts dual citizenship. In recent times churches and civic organizations have sponsored citizenship drives. The governments of the various Caribbean countries realize that one of the best ways to access the power of their foreign citizens is to encourage them to become citizens of the host country.

64. Vickerman, *Crosscurrents*, 141. These are great virtues but they reflect individual interests. As they are practiced by the Caribbean diaspora, they are not practiced as communal ethics. For a study on Black ethics, see Peter Paris, *Spirituality of African Peoples: The Search for a Common Moral Discourse* (Minneapolis: Augsburg Fortress Press, 1995); Theodore Walker, Jr., *Empower the People: Social Ethics for the African American Church* (New York: Orbis Books, 1991); Cheryl L. Sanders, *Empowerment Ethics for a Liberated People: A Path to African American Social Transformation* (Minneapolis: Fortress Press, 1995); Joan Martin, *More Than Chains and Toil: A Christian Work Ethic of Enslaved Women* (Louisville: Westminster John Knox Press, 2000). If Caribbean intellectual thought is to be authentically Caribbean, it must be rooted in its heritage. In

the Black religious tradition, the pursuit of life was always for the common good. For a detailed study see Winston Lawson, *Religion and Race* (New York: Peter Lang, 1996); Albert Raboteau, *Slave: "The Invisible Institution" in the Antebellum South* (New York: Oxford University Press, 1978). It is important that he specifically notes the African origin of the practice of the common good and how it informed the total life of the community.

65. Peter J. Paris, *The Spirituality of African Peoples: The Search for a Common Moral Discourse* (Minneapolis: Augsburg Fortress Press, 1995), 51. Although Paris claims to be writing a social ethic for the Black Diaspora, the study is more about African Americans. Taking his intent in mind, as expressed in the title of the book, it is a spirituality for African peoples which includes the Caribbean diaspora. Even if it were for and about African Americans, the work would still be relevant to the Caribbean diaspora.

66. Cornel West, *Prophesy Deliverance: An Afro-American Revolutionary Christianity* (Philadelphia: Westminster Press, 1982), 17. It is unfortunate that there has not been much thought given to individualism in Black religious and theological thought. It is only recently that Black theologians have been addressing this as a theological issue but it is more a reactive attempt rather than as a proactive intellectual pursuit. For a critique of this position, see Dale Andrews, *Practical Theology for Black Churches: Bridging Black Theology and African American Folk Religion* (Louisville: Westminster John Knox Press, 2002), 50–105. He provides a critique of the apparently insidious sanitizing of individualism in contemporary Black culture. Individualism is characteristic of contemporary society especially of Black Christianity. The roots of individualism are in the Enlightenment and Protestant theology. Its justification is in the American Constitution and the United Nations document on Human Rights. This, however, does not mean an uncritical acceptance. In fact, this issue and practice need to be interpreted in light of the gospel of Jesus Christ by Black theologians. For a discussion on individualism in American society, see Robert N. Bellah et al., *Habits of the Heart: Individualism and Commitment in American Life* (California: University of California Press, 1985). For an analysis on religious individualism, consult Wade Clark Roof, *Spiritual Market Place* (New Jersey: Princeton University Press, 1999).

67. Paris, *Spirituality of African Peoples*, 117.

68. Paris, *Spirituality of African Peoples*, 118. Paris calls for individuals and community to work together to achieve Black liberation. The cause is bigger and greater than any one person. Paris is speaking, however, of the African American pursuit for justice. This call must be connected to the Black struggle for justice; it is truly about and for African peoples. For a fuller examination of this issue, see Amy Jacques Garvey, *Garvey and Garveyism* (New York: Macmillan, 1970); Rupert Lewis, *Marcus Garvey: Anti-Colonial Champion* (London: Karia Press, 1987); John Henrik Clark, ed., *Marcus Garvey and the Vision of Africa* (New York: Vintage Books, 1974).

69. Sam Selvon, *Lonely Londoners* (New York: Longman, 1994), 138.

70. James and Harris, *Inside Babylon*, 255.

71. Rex Nettleford, *Inward Stretch Outward Reach: A Voice From the Caribbean* (London: Macmillan, 1993), 173.

72. Nettleford, *Inward Stretch Outward Reach*, 173–81.

73. Rex Nettleford, "Migration, Transmission and Maintenance of the Intangible Heritage," in *Rex N: Select Speeches*, ed. Kenneth O. Hall (Kingston: Ian Randle Publishers, 2006), 23.

74. The issue of African retentions and change in the Black diaspora is not the focus of this study so it will not detain us here. I have made reference to the debate in Chapter 2 of this study. For a general discussion on this issue in the Caribbean context, see Winston James, *Religion and Race: African and European Roots in Conflict – a Jamaican Testament* (New York: Peter Lang, 1996). For further exploration, see Colin A. Palmer, "Africa in the Making of the Caribbean," in *Slavery, Freedom and Gender: The Dynamics of Caribbean Society*, eds Brian L. Moore, B. W. Higman, Carl Campbell and Patrick Bryan (Kingston: University of the West Indies Press, 2003), 40–56. An excellent study on this subject is Maureen Warner-Lewis's *Central Africa in the Caribbean: Transcending Time, Transforming Cultures* (Kingston: University of the West Indies Press, 2003). See also her essay "The Character of African-Jamaican Culture," in *Jamaica in Slavery and Freedom: History, Heritage and Culture*, eds Kathleen E. A. Monteith and Glen Richards (Kingston: University of the West Indies Press, 2002), 89–114.

75. James and Harris, *Inside Babylon*, 255.

76. George Lamming, *The Emigrants* (London: Allison and Busby, 1990).

77. George Lamming, *Coming, Coming Home: Conversations II: Western Education and the Caribbean Intellectual Coming, Coming, Coming Home* (St. Martin: House of Nehesi Publishers, 1995), 25.

Chapter 4

1. O. Nigel Bollard, "Creolisation and Creole Societies: A Cultural Nationalist View of Caribbean Social History," *Caribbean Quarterly* 44, nos. 1–2 (1998): 25.

2. C. Eric Lincoln and Lawrence H. Mamiya, *The Black Church in the African American Experience* (Durham: Duke University Press, 1990), 10–19. Lincoln and Mamiya use the term dialectic as a model of the African American Church. I use the term as a theological tradition of the Caribbean diasporan church to reflect the collective identity of the Caribbean diaspora. As will be detected throughout this study, the Caribbean diaspora is diverse. Although I argue that this dialectical tradition consists of African and European religions, it must be noted that each of these religions is diverse. Thus, diversity is implied in both of the religions and, consequently, the dialectical tradition reflects the diversity of Caribbean society and culture. As to the question of the place of Caribbean people of Asian decent in the dialectical tradition, these people arrived after the tradition was established. The dialectical tradition, therefore, preceded the arrival of the Asian people in the Caribbean. Notwithstanding their late arrival, Caribbeaners of Asian descent have influenced Caribbean Christianity. The impact of these influences is a subject outside the scope of this study.

3. Shirley C. Gordon, *Our Cause for His Glory: Christianisation and Emancipation in Jamaica* (Kingston: University of the West Indies Press, 1998), 9.

4. Dianne Stewart, *Three Eyes for the Journey: African Dimensions of the Jamaican Religious Experience* (New York: Oxford University Press, 2005), 90–137. See also Mervyn Alleyne, *Roots of Jamaican Culture* (London: Pluto Press, 1988), 76–105; Wallace W. Zane, *Journeys to Spiritual Lands: The Natural History of a West Indian Religion* (New York: Oxford University Press, 1999).

5. Stewart, *Three Eyes for the Journey*, 3.

6. Stewart, *Three Eyes for the Journey*, 101.

7. Stewart, *Three Eyes for the Journey*, 91–137.

8. Stewart, *Three Eyes for the Journey*, 100.

9. Stewart, *Three Eyes for the Journey*, 4.

10. Diane J. Austin-Broos, *Jamaica Genesis: Religion and the Politics of Moral Orders* (Kingston: Ian Randle Publishers, 1997), 4.

11. Austin-Broos, *Jamaica Genesis*, 4.

12. Austin-Broos, *Jamaica Genesis*, 43–71.

13. Austin-Broos, *Jamaica Genesis*, 5.

14. Winston Lawson, *Religion and Race: African and European Roots in Conflict – A Jamaica Testament* (New York: Peter Lang, 1996). Lawson writes primarily about Christianity in Jamaica but it can also be considered as representative of the Caribbean society. For a similar study, see Gordon, *Our Cause for His Glory*.

15. Lawson, *Religion and Race*, 1–200.

16. Lawson, *Religion and Race*, 158.

17. Noel Erskine, *Decolonizing Theology: A Caribbean Perspective* (New York: Orbis Books, 1981), 70. See also Robert Stewart, *Religion and Society in Post Emancipation Jamaica* (Knoxville: University of Tennessee Press, 1992), 1–65; Lewis Williams, *Caribbean Theology* (New York: Peter Lang, 1994), 1–56; Keith Hunte, "Protestantism in the British Caribbean," in *Christianity in the Caribbean: Essays on History*, ed. Armando Lampe (Kingston: University of the West Indies Press, 2001), 86–125.

18. Stewart, *Religion and Society*, 101–102.

19. Arthur Charles Dayfoot, *The Shaping of the West Indian Church 1492–1962* (Kingston: University Press of the West Indies, 1999), 6. This work is regarded as the major text on Caribbean church history. See also Armando Lampe, ed., *Christianity in the Caribbean* (Kingston: University of the West Indies Press, 2001).

20. Dayfoot, *Shaping of the West Indian Church*, 1–4.

21. Dayfoot, *Shaping of the West Indian Church*, 2–4.

22. Dayfoot, *Shaping of the West Indian Church*, 11. Dayfoot is merely reflecting his lack of understanding of Black religion. The differences between Black religion and white do not make Black religion any less Christian. I would like to know the basis on which he determined the term African Traditional Religion was modern. The remarks are condescending and an affront to Black people.

23. Mary Turner, *Slaves and Missionaries: The Disintegration of Jamaican Slave Society, 1787–1834* (Kingston: University Press of the West Indies, 1998), 39.

24. Turner, *Slaves and Missionaries*, 65. See also Shirley C. Gordon, *God Almighty Make Me Free: Christianity in Pre-Emancipation Jamaica* (Indianapolis: Indiana University Press, 1996); Lampe, *Christianity in the Caribbean*. For an excellent study on European Christianity as an agent of British cultural and religious imperialism, see Brian L. Moore and Michelle A. Johnson, *Neither Led Nor Driven: Contesting British Cultural Imperialism in Jamaica, 1865–1920* (Kingston: University of the West Indies Press, 2004).

25. C. L. R. James, *Beyond a Boundary* (London: Hutchinson, 1963); Stephen Howe, "C.L.R. James: Visions of History, Visions of Britain," in *West Indian Intellectuals in Britain*, ed. Bill Schwartz (Manchester: Manchester University Press, 2003), 153–74. For a study of James as a Caribbean intellectual see Kent Worchester, "A Victorian with the Rebel Seed: C.L.R. James and Politics of Intellectual Engagement," Kenneth Surin, "C.L.R. James' Materialist Aesthetic of Cricket" and Alrick Cambridge, "C.L.R. James:

Freedom through History and Dialects" in *Intellectuals in the Twentieth-Century Caribbean: Volume 1. Specter of the New Class: the Commonwealth Caribbean*, ed. Alistair Hennessy (London: Macmillan Press, 1992), 131–78.

26. Selwyn R. Cudjoe and William E. Cain, eds, *C.L.R. James: His Intellectual Legacies* (Massachusetts: University of Massachusetts Press, 1995), 1. For an introduction to the life and work of James, see his excellent biography, Kent Worchester, *C.L.R. James: A Political Biography* (Albany: State University of New York, 1996). For an intellectual exploration of his works, see Grant Farred, ed., *Rethinking C. L. R. James* (Cambridge: Blackwell, 1996); Scott McLemee, ed., *C.L.R. James: On the 'Negro Question'* (Jackson: University Press of Mississippi, 1996); Anna Grimshaw, ed., *C.L.R. James Reader* (Cambridge: Blackwell, 1992); Paget Henry and Paul Buhle, eds, *C.L.R. James's Caribbean* (Durham: Duke University Press, 1992).

27. James, *Beyond a Boundary*, 20

28. James, *Beyond a Boundary*, 7.

29. C. L. R. James, *Beyond a Boundary* (London: Hutchinson, 1963), 27.

30. Justo L. Gonzalez, *The Story of Christianity vol. 2* (Massachusetts: Price Press, 1985), 185.

31. James, *Beyond a Boundary*, 11.

32. James, *Beyond a Boundary*, 15.

33. James, *Beyond a Boundary*, 65.

34. James, *Beyond a Boundary*, 26.

35. James, *Beyond a Boundary*, 7.

36. Neville Linton, "Some Aspects of Political Morality in the Caribbean," in *Perspectives on Political Ethics: An Ecumenical Enquiry* (Geneva: WCC Publications, 1983), 80. See, for example, Horace O. Russell, *Foundations and Anticipation: The Jamaica Baptist Story: 1783–1892* (Georgia: Brentwood Christian Press, 1993), 103–24; Ashley Smith, "Mainline Churches in the Caribbean: Their Relationship to Cultural and Political Process," *Caribbean Journal of Religious Studies* 9 (1989): 27–39; Uxmal Livio Diaz, "The Role of Third World Christians and Churches in the Struggle against Colonialism and Neo-Colonialism," in *Out of the Depths*, ed. Idris Hamid (San Fernando: St. Andrews Theological College, 1977), 127–45.

37. Robert Beckford, *Jesus is Dread: Black Theology and Black Culture in Britain* (London: Darton, Longman and Todd, 1998), 46–49.

38. Beckford, *Jesus is Dread*, 50.

39. Beckford, *Jesus is Dread*, 50–54.

40. Beckford, *Jesus is Dread*, 54. This is a claim Black Christians made as well. See Steven McKenzie, *All God's Children: A Biblical Critique of Racism* (Kentucky: Westminster John Knox Press, 1997); Joel Edwards, *Lord, Make us One – But Not All the Same: Seeking Unity in Diversity* (London: Hodder & Stoughton, 1999).

41. Beckford, *Jesus is Dread*, 54–56.

42. Beckford, *Jesus is Dread*, 57. On this aspect of Caribbean emancipatory tradition, see Mavis C. Campbell, *The Fighting Maroons of Jamaica 1655–1796: A History of Resistance and Collaboration and Betrayal* (New Jersey: Africa World Press, 1990); Richard Hart, *Slaves Who Abolished Slavery: Blacks in Rebellion* (Kingston: University of the West Indies Press, 1985). This is not limited to the church. It was a part of Black culture with women playing a central role. See Lucille Mathurin Mair, *Rebel Woman in the British West Indies During Slavery* (Kingston: University of the West Indies Press,

1995); Brian Moore et al., *Slavery, Freedom and Gender* (Kingston: University of the West Indies Press, 2002); Steve O. Buckridge, *The Language of Dress: Resistance and Accommodation in Jamaica, 1750–1890* (Kingston: University of the West Indies Press, 2004); Brian L. Moore and Michele A. Johnson, *Neither Led nor Driven: Contesting British Cultural Imperialism in Jamaica 1865–1920* (Kingston: University of the West Indies Press, 2004).

43. Samuel Sharpe, cited in C. S. Reid, *Samuel Sharpe: From Slave to National Hero* (Kingston: Bustamante Institute of Public and International Affairs, 1988), 93. In addition to Sharpe, there were other revolutions led by Christians such as the Morant Bay Rebellion in 1865, led by two Baptist deacons, Paul Bogle and George William Gordon. They too were executed for their work of liberation for the poor and the oppressed. For further reflection, see Philip Sherlock and Hazel Bennett, *The Story of the Jamaican People* (Kingston: Ian Randle Publishers, 1998), 246–61.

44. Mary Turner, *Slaves and Missionaries: The Disintegration of Jamaican Slave Society, 1787–1834* (Kingston: University of the West Indies Press, 1998), 200.

45. Lawson, *Religion and Race*, 82. See also Alleyne, *Roots of Jamaican Culture*, 76–104.

46. Albert J. Raboteau, *Slave Religion: The "Invisible Institution" in the Antebellum South* (New York: Oxford University Press, 1978), 8. Consult also Peter J. Paris, *The Spirituality of African Peoples: The Search for a Common Moral Ground* (Minneapolis: Fortress Press, 1995).

47. Raboteau, *Slave Religion*, 4–16. See also Alleyne, *Roots of Jamaican Culture*, 106–19; Maureen Warner-Lewis, *Central Africa in the Caribbean: Transcending Time, Transforming Cultures* (Kingston: University of the West Indies Press, 2003), 138–98.

48. Raboteau, *Slave Religion*, 16.

49. Dale Bisnauth, *A History of Religion in the Caribbean* (Kingston: Kingston Publishers, 1990), 83.

50. Bisnauth, *History of Religion*, 80–100.

51. Kortright Davis, *Emancipation Still Comin': Explorations in Caribbean Emancipatory Theology* (New York: Orbis Books, 1990), 51.

52. Davis, *Emancipation Still Comin'*, 59. It is important to note that Black religion is not Christianity. Black Christianity is one form of Black Religion. For an important discussion, see Gayraud Wilmore, *Black Religion and Black Radicalism* (New York: Orbis Books, 1999), 22–51. For works that deal with African American Religion, see Joseph R. Washington, Jr., *Black Religion: The Negro and Christianity in the United States* (Boston: Beacon Press, 1994); C. Eric Lincoln, ed., *The Black Experience in America* (New York: Anchor/Doubleday, 1994); Henry H. Mitchell, *Black Belief: Folk Beliefs of Blacks in America and West Africa* (New York: Harper and Row, 1975). For an important early work on the Black diaspora, see George Eaton Simpson, *Black Religions in the New World* (New York: Columbia University Press, 1978); William Watty, *From Shore to Shore* (Kingston: United Theological College of the West Indies, 1981), 69–79.

53. Davis, *Emancipation Still Comin'*, 60. I am aware of the debate about African retentions and loss known as the Frazier-Herskovits Debate but this is not the issue in question. Scholars have given much attention to this subject. Those interested can consult Meville J. Herskovits, *The Myth of the Negro Past* (Boston: Beacon Press, 1969). See also Alleyne, *Roots of Jamaican Culture*; Raboteau, *Slave Religion*; Will Coleman, *Tribal Talk: Black Theology, Hermeneutics, and African/American Ways of "Telling the*

194

Story" (Pennsylvania: Pennsylvania State University, 2000); Maureen Warner Lewis, "The Character of African-Jamaica Culture," in *Jamaica in Slavery and Freedom: History, Heritage and Culture,* eds Kathleen E. A. Monteith and Glen Richards (Kingston: University of the West Indies Press, 2002), 89–114.

54. George Eaton Simpson, *Black Religions in the New World* (New York: Columbia University Press, 1978), 1–220.

55. Simpson, *Black Religions in the New World,* 21.

56. Simpson, *Black Religions in the New World,* 22.

57. George Mulrain, "African Caribbean Christianity," *Journal of Interdenominational Theological Center* xvi 1 and 2 (Fall 1988, Spring 1989): 249.

58. Mulrain, "African Caribbean Christianity," 63.

59. Raboteau, *Slave Religion,* 15–16.

60. Lawson, *Religion and Race,* 38.

61. Barry Channeves, "Our Caribbean Reality," in *Caribbean Theology: Preparing for the Challenges Ahead,* ed. Howard Gregory (Kingston: Canoe Press, 1995), 66.

62. Mulrain, "African Caribbean Christianity," 59.

63. Stewart, *Three Eyes for the Journey,* 3.

64. Stewart, *Three Eyes for the Journey,* 6.

65. Stewart, *Three Eyes for the Journey,* 12.

66. Mulrain, "African Caribbean Christianity," 197.

67. Gordon, *Our Cause for His Glory,* 1–44. The respectability theory has been uncritically accepted by some of the leading Caribbean religious scholars. See, for example, Barry Chevannes, *Betwixt and Between: Explorations in an African-Caribbean Mindscape* (Kingston: Ian Randle Publishers, 2006), 1–61.

68. Maureen Warner-Lewis, *Central Africa in the Caribbean: Transcending Time, Transforming Cultures* (Kingston: University of the West Indies Press, 2003).

69. J. Deotis Roberts, *Africentric Christianity: A Theological Appraisal for Ministry* (Valley Forge: Judson Press, 2000), 59. For a study on Black Biblical heritage, see Kenneth L. Waters, Jr., *Afrocentric Sermons: The Beauty of Blackness in the Bible* (Valley Forge: Judson Press, 1993); Randall C. Bailey and Jacquelyn Grant, eds, *The Recovery of Black Presence: An Interdisciplinary Exploration* (Nashville: Abingdon Press, 1995).

70. Mary Turner, *Slaves and Missionaries: The Disintegration of Jamaican Slave Society, 1787–1834* (Kingston: University of the West Indies Press, 1998). For additional study on this subject, see Shirley C. Gordon, *God Almighty Made Me Free: Christianity in Preemancipation Jamaica* (Bloomington and Indianapolis: Indiana University Press, 1996).

71. Brian L. Moore and Michele A. Johnson, *Neither Led nor Driven: Contesting British Cultural Imperialism in Jamaica, 1865–1920* (Kingston: University of the West Indies Press, 2004), 203; see also Stewart, *Religion and Society,* 110–52.

72. Wilmore, *Black Religion,* 106, emphasis original.

73. Robert J. Stewart, *Role of Religion in Post Emancipation Jamaica* (Knoxville: University of Tennessee Press, 1992), 110.

Chapter 5

1. Fred Craddock, *Luke: Interpretation. A Commentary for Teaching and Preaching* (Louisville: John Knox Press, 1990), 62. See also Robert C. Tannehill, *Luke* (Nashville:

Abingdon Press, 1996), 91–92. For an alternative interpretation that advocates the mission of Jesus as personal salvation which is spiritualizing the meaning of the Lukan text, see John Noland, *Word Biblical Commentary: Luke 1-9:20* (Dallas: Word, 1989), 195–99.

2. Tannehill, *Luke*, 93. See also Joel B. Green, *The Gospel of Luke* (Grand Rapids: Eerdmans, 1977); Joseph A. Fitzmyer, SJ, *The Gospel According to Luke* (Garden City: Doubleday, 1985), 523–35.

3. Craddock, *Luke*, 62.

4. Samuel G. Simpson, personal communication, 1983.

5. Albert Godson, "We've Come this Far by Faith," in *Lift Every Voice and Sing: An African American Hymnal* (New York: The Church Hymnal Corporation, 1993), 208.

6. Godson, "We've Come this Far by Faith," 208.

7. Oscar L. Bolioli, ed., *The Caribbean: Culture of Resistance, Spirit of Hope* (New York: Friendship Press, 1993), 56. The Verdun Proclamation is the proceeding of the consultation sponsored by the Caribbean/African American (CAAD) and the Caribbean Conference of Churches (CCC) held in Verdun, Barbados, May 1–3, 1992. The representatives at the event were from the Caribbean, North America and the United Kingdom. It was not only an ecumenical reflection on the issue of racism. The purpose of the event was an attempt to implement the decisions of the First Inter Continental Consultation of Indigenous peoples of African decent on racism. I find it interesting that this event took place without the inclusion and involvement of the people of the Caribbean diaspora when they are members of the respective countries that were represented at the conference. It is significant, however, that such an event occurred. It symbolizes the recognition of the particularity of ethnicity as well as the diversity of the Black race. Beyond that, it is an historic effort to address the common issue of racism. Racism affects all peoples but Black people, regardless of their ethnicity and location, are its victims. This was also an effort to cultivate relationships among the various Black communities. For an exposition on Jesus Christ as Emancipator, see James H. Evans, *We Have Been Believers* (Minneapolis: Fortress Press, 1992), 77–98; Kortright Davis, "Jesus Christ and Black Liberation," *Journal of Religious Thought* 42, no. 1 (Summer-Fall, 1985), 51–67.

8. John S. Mbiti, *African Religions and Philosophy* (New York: Doubleday, 1970), 3. The role of faith, while central in Caribbean diasporan Christianity, must be considered in light of its African roots. For an examination of this issue, see Winston Lawson, *Religion and Race: African and European Roots in Conflict – A Jamaican Testament* (New York: Peter Lang, 1996). For a fascinating study see Mervyn Alleyne, *Roots of Jamaican Culture* (London: Pluto Press, 1988). The classic study on the subject is Albert Raboteau, *Slave Religion: The 'Invisible Religion' in the Antebellum South* (New York: Oxford University Press, 1978). For a significant theological treatment of this subject, see J. Deotis Roberts, *Black Theology in Dialogue* (Philadelphia: Westminster Knox Press, 1987), especially chapters 2 and 3.

9. Theological foundations are the theological principles that constitute the essential basis on which the Caribbean diasporan church is built.

10. I regard the earliest works on Caribbean theology as the classic texts. They constitute the academic study of Caribbean theology where the Caribbean experience is interpreted in light of the gospel of Jesus Christ. I also use these texts because later

works are built on them. As such, the classic texts are the foundational texts on study of Caribbean theology.

11. William Watty, *From Shore to Shore: Soundings in Caribbean Theology* (Kingston: United Theological College of the West Indies, 1981), ix.

12. Noel Titus, "Our Caribbean Reality," in Howard Gregory, ed., *Caribbean Theology: Preparing for the Challenges Ahead* (Kingston: Canoe Press, University of the West Indies, 1995), 63. For additional information on this subject, see Lewin L. William, *Caribbean Theology* (New York: Peter Lang, 1994). I must point out that Williams makes a case for a contextual theology but he has not demonstrated any evidence of it. He, in other words, talks about what the theology ought to be but has not shown what the theology is. The work is, however, useful because it points in the direction Caribbean theology is to go.

13. In this study, I use the term Caribbean emancipatory theology interchangeably with Caribbean theology. The former concerns both the place and function of theology but the latter describes the location of the theology. In this regard, Caribbean emancipatory theology is a more inclusive terminology for describing and interpreting the Caribbean experience according to the purpose of God as revealed in Jesus Christ.

14. Ashley Smith, *Emerging From Innocence: Religion, Theology and Development* (Mandeville: Eureka Press, 1991), 14.

15. William Watty, *From Shore to Shore: Soundings in Caribbean Theology* (Kingston: United Theological College of the West Indies, 1981), 8.

16. Kortright Davis, *Emancipation Still Comin': Exploration in Caribbean Emancipatory Theology* (New York: Orbis Books, 1990), 107.

17. Davis, *Emancipation Still Comin'*, 103.

18. Davis, *Emancipation Still Comin'*, x.

19. Noel L. Erskine, *Decolonizing Theology: A Caribbean Perspective* (New York: Orbis Books, 1981), 116.

20. Erskine, *Decolonizing Theology*, 1.

21. Lewin Williams, *Caribbean Theology* (New York: Peter Lang, 1994), 1. For a discussion on contextual theology, although they do not address the Caribbean context in particular, see Stephen B. Bevans, *Models of Contextual Theology* (New York: Orbis Books, 1992); Clements Sedmak, *Doing Local Theology* (New York: Orbis Books, 2002). For works about the Caribbean context, see also Smith, *Emerging From Innocence*; idem, *Real Roots and Potted Plants: Reflections on the Caribbean Church* (Mandeville: Eureka Press, 1984); Neville Callam, *Deciding Responsibly: Moral Dimensions of Human Action* (Kingston: Jamaica Baptist Union, 1985); Neville Callam, ed., *Moral Responsibility: Issues in Church and Society* (Kingston: Tarrant Baptist Church, 1993); Vivian Panton, *The Church and Common – Law Union* (Kingston: Ebony Printers, 1992); C. S. Reid, *Church, Morality and Democracy* (Kingston: Bustamante Institute of Public & International Affairs, 1986); Christine Barrow, "Living in Sin: Church and Common –Law Union in Barbados," *The Journal of Caribbean History* 29, no. 2 (1995): 47–70.

22. Williams, *Caribbean Theology*, 1.

23. Williams, *Caribbean Theology*, 50.

24. Robert Stewart, *The Role of Religion in Post Emancipation Jamaica* (Knoxville: University of Tennessee Press, 1992). For an excellent study on Black protest tradition, see Gayraud S. Wilmore, *Black Religion and Black Radicalism: An Interpretation of the Religious History of Afro-American People* (New York: Orbis Books, 1995).

25. Stewart, *Role of Religion*, 195.

26. Stewart, *Role of Religion*, 195–96.

27. Stewart, *Role of Religion*, 13.

28. Stewart, *Role of Religion*, xvi–xix.

29. Stewart, *Role of Religion*, xviii–xix.

30. Stewart, *Role of Religion*, 110.

31. Stewart, *Role of Religion*, 188.

32. Stewart, *Role of Religion*, 189.

33. Brian L. Moore and Michele A. Johnson, *Neither Led nor Driven: Contesting British Cultural Imperialism in Jamaica, 1865–1920* (Kingston: University of the West Indies Press, 2004), 167–204.

34. Moore and Johnson, *Neither Led nor Driven*, 169.

35. Philip Curtin, *Two Jamaicans: The Role of Ideas in a Tropical Colony, 1830–1865* (New York: Atheneum, 1970), 25.

36. Burchell Taylor, "Onesimus – The Voiceless Initiator of the Liberating Process," in *Caribbean Theology: Preparing for the Challenges Ahead*, ed. Howard Gregory (Kingston: Canoe Press, 1995), 17.

37. Taylor, "Onesimus," 20. See also Taylor's other articles in this volume. He is offering a new understanding of the commonly held biblical interpretation of this Pauline epistle. It is a new reading on oppression and freedom but inadequate documentation of sources undermines its potency. For additional resources see also Allan Callahan's *Embassy of Onesimus: The Letter of Paul to Philemon* (Valley Forge: Trinity Press International, 1997).

38. William Watty, *From Shore to Shore: Soundings in Caribbean Theology* (Kingston: United Theological College of the West Indies, 1981), 40–50.

39. Watty, *From Shore to Shore*, 45–46.

40. Watty, *From Shore to Shore*, 46.

41. Davis, *Emancipation Still Comin'*, x.

42. Lawson, *Religion and Race*, 40–41.

43. Lawson, *Religion and Race*, 150–98. See also Stewart, *Role of Religion*.

44. Lawson, *Religion and Race*, 41.

45. Taylor, "Onesimus," 77.

46. Taylor, "Onesimus," 73.

47. Taylor, "Onesimus," 73–78.

48. Taylor, "Onesimus," 76.

49. Neville Callam, "Ethnicity and the Church's Catholicity: Ministry to the Caribbean Diaspora in North America," Grace Baptist Chapel Anniversary Lecture, New York, September 15, 2002.

50. Callam, "Ethnicity," 11.

51. Callam, "Ethnicity," 13.

52. Callam, "Ethnicity," 13.

53. Katie Cannon, *Katie's Canon: Womanism and the Soul of the Black Community* (New York: Continuum, 1996), 54. These remarks are not limited to women's experience but to all the people, women and men of the Caribbean diaspora.

54. Robert Beckford, *Jesus is Dread: Black Theology and Black Culture in Britain* (London: Darton, Longman and Todd, 1998), 33.

55. See Howard Gregory, ed., *Caribbean Theology: Preparing for the Challenges Ahead* (Kingston: Canoe Press, University of the West Indies, 1995); Dwight Hopkins, *Shoes that Fit our Feet: Sources for a Constructive Black Theology* (New York: Orbis Books, 1993); Deloris Williams, *Sisters in the Wilderness: The Challenge of Womanist God-Talk* (New York: Orbis Books, 1993); James Cone, *The Spiritual and the Blues* (New York: Orbis Books, 1992); Romney M. Moseley, "Decolonizing Theology in the Caribbean: Prospects for Hermeneutical Reconstruction," *Toronto Journal of Theology* 6:2 (1990): 235–46; Valentina Alexander, "Afrocentric and Black Christian Consciousness: Towards an Honest Intersection," *Black Theology International Journey* 1 (1998): 11–18.

56. James Cone, *God of the Oppressed* (New York: Seabury Press, 1975), 103.

57. Joseph Harris, *Global Dimension of the African Diaspora* (Washington, DC: Howard University Press, 1982). See also E. David Cronon, *Black Moses: The Story of Marcus Garvey* (Madison: University of Wisconsin Press, 1955), 16–17.

58. Cone, *God of the Oppressed*, 101–106.

59. This belief was affirmed in the first ecumenical council of the church held in Nicea, 325 CE where the Nicene Creed was formulated and adopted. There was an attempt both to combat the Arian controversy and to have a commonly held set of doctrine that expressed the one Faith. See Timothy Barnes, *Constantine and Eusebius* (Massachusetts: Harvard University Press, 1981), 208–23. One of the most prominent, if not the most prominent thinker, of the church regarding the doctrine of the Incarnation is Anthanasius of Alexandria. He was highly revered and known as the "Black Dwarf." See his most significant writings on the doctrine of the Incarnation, *On the Incarnation* (New York: St. Vladimir's Orthodox Theological Seminary, 1989); "Discourses Against the Arians" in *The Nicene and Post Nicene Fathers*, series, vol. IV., ed. Philip Schaff and Henry Wace (Michigan: Eerdsmans, 1957). For a study on the Incarnation as it is understood in Black theology, consult Howard Thurman, *Jesus and the Disinherited* (Nashville: Abingdon Press, 1949); George Kesley, *Racism and the Christian Understanding of Man* (New York: Charles Scribner's and Sons, 1965); James Evans, *We Have Been Believers* (Minneapolis: Fortress Press, 1992).

60. J. Deotis Roberts, *The Prophethood of Black Believers: An African American Political Theology for Ministry* (Kentucky: Westminster/John Knox Press, 1994), 1–8. Roberts is articulating primarily an African American theological interpretation of Black theology.

61. Roberts, *Prophethood of Black Believers*, 1–4.

62. Roberts, *Prophethood of Black Believers*, 1. I agree with Roberts' view but he fails to point out that the doing of God's will is not limited to the church. Black theologians argue that God's will has been carried by the Black Freedom Fighters, the Civil Rights Movement and contemporary liberation movements. For a study on this issue, see Gayraud Wilmore, *Black Religion and Black Radicalism: An Interpretation of the Religious History of Afro-American People* (Maryknoll: Orbis Books, 1983); James Cone, *Black Theology and Black Power* (New York: Seabury Press, 1967).

63. Gayraud Wilmore, *Black and Presbyterian: The Heritage and the Hope* (Philadelphia: Geneva Press, 1983). The ethnicity of Jesus is a very controversial issue. There are two schools of thought that deal with this issue, the literal and the existential. The former supports the idea that Jesus was a literally Black person. The major representative of this school is Albert Cleage, Jr. as delineated in his classic work, *The*

Black Messiah (Kansas: Sheed and Ward Inc., 1968). See also his *Black Christian Nationalism: New Directions for the Black Church* (New York: Marrow Quill, 1992). The latter view advocates a second perspective that Jesus was existentially Black. For further examination see James Cone, *God of the Oppressed* (New York: Seabury Press, 1995); Jacqueline Grant, *White Women's Christ and Black Women's Jesus: Feminist Christology and Womanist Response* (Atlanta: Scholars Press, 1998); see also her "Black Christology: Interpreting Aspects of the Apostolic Faith," in *Black Witness to the Apostolic Faith*, eds David T. Shannon and Gayraud S. Wilmore (Michigan: Eerdmans, 1985); Kelly Brown Douglas, *The Black Christ* (New York: Orbis Books, 1995); Kenneth L. Waters, Sr., *Afrocentric Sermons: The Beauty of Blackness in the Bible* (Valley Forge: Judson Press, 1993); Tom Skinner, *How Black is the Gospel* (New York: J. B. Lippincott, 1970); Randall Bailey and Jacquelyn Grant, eds, *The Recovery of the Black Presence: An Interdisciplinary Exploration* (Nashville: Abingdon Press, 1975); Ashley Smith, "The Religious Significance of Black Power in Caribbean Churches," in *Troubling of the Waters*, ed. Idris Hamid (Trinidad: Rahaman Printery, 1973), 83–103; Earl August, "The Spiritual Significance of Black Power," in Hamid, *Troubling of the Waters*, 109–13.

64. Eugene R. Fairweather, "The Kenotic Christology," in F. W. Beare, *The Epistle to the Philippians* (London: Adam and Charles Black, 1959), 159–74. The kenosis is the theological term used to describe God becoming human in Jesus of Nazareth or the self-emptying of Jesus Christ. Theologians and New Testament scholars are uncertain about the meaning of the term "kenosis" but the consensus is that it speaks of the Incarnation of Jesus Christ. See also Peter T. O'Brien, *Commentary on Philippians* (Michigan: Eerdmans, 1991), 186–269; Ralph Martin, *Philippians* (London: Marshall, Morgan & Scott, 1976), 94–102.

65. Fred B. Craddock, *Philippians: A Bible Commentary for Teaching and Preaching* (Atlanta: John Knox Press, 1985), 40. Craddock makes a significant observation. The idea of Jesus' pre-existence was not a problem in the East, Near East and to Jewish New Testament Christians. It is a problem for contemporary people because the idea of pre-existence is new to us. This, however, does not negate the paradoxical nature of the idea but Craddock is correct: the Christian faith always affirms this but not without difficulty.

66. Watty, *From Shore to Shore*, 61. For a discussion on the meaning of the Incarnation in Black British theology and culture, see Joseph Daniel Aldred, "Respect: A Caribbean British Theology" (Ph.D. dissertation, Sheffield University, 2003), 191–209.

67. F. F. Bruce, *The Acts of the Apostles* (Michigan: Eerdmans, 1965), 53–64. Bible scholars do not agree with this notion of diversity. One school of thought teaches that the gathering of the Jewish people in Jerusalem on the Day of Pentecost was not a gathering of diasporan Jews but those who resided in Jerusalem. For a further examination, see E. Earnest Haenchen, *The Acts of the Apostles* (Philadelphia: Westminster John Knox Press, 1971), 161–78.

68. Robert Beckford, *Dread and Pentecostal: A Political Theology for the Black Church in Britain* (London: Society for Promoting Christian Knowledge, 2000), 3. This study is a significant text on the Caribbean diasporan church. While the primary concern is the Black church in Britain, the study represents the Caribbean diasporan Christian community and, above all, the Black British Church as a Caribbean diasporan church. For a valuable study on the Pentecost church in the Caribbean although it is based on Pentecostalism in Jamaica, see Dianne J. Austin-Broos, *Jamaica Genesis: Religion and*

the Moral Orders (Kingston: Ian Randle Publishers, 1997). For a study on Black Pentecostalism in Britain, see Nicole Rodrigues Toulis, *Believing Identity: Pentecostalism and the Mediation of Jamaican Identity and Gender in England* (Oxford: Berg, 1997); Valentina Alexander, "'Breaking Every Fetter?' To what Extent has the Black Led Church in Britain Developed a Theology of Liberation?" (Ph.D. thesis, University of Warwick, 1997); Ian MacRobert, "Black Pentecostalism: Its Origins, Functions and Theology" (Ph.D. thesis, University of Birmingham, 1989). For works dealing with Pentecostalism as a movement, see W. J. Hollenweger, *Pentecostalism: Origins and Developments Worldwide* (Peabody: Hendrickson, 1997); Harvey Cox, *Fire From Heaven: The Rise of Pentecostal Spirituality and the Reshaping of Religion in the Twenty-First Century* (London: Cassell, 1996); Allan Anderson, *An Introduction to Pentecostalism* (Cambridge: Cambridge University Press, 2004); Allan Anderson and Walter J. Hollenweger, ed., *Pentecostals after a Century: Global Perspective on a Movement in Transition* (Sheffield: Sheffield Academic Press, 1999).

69. Beckford, *Dread and Pentecostal*, 174–76.

70. Beckford, *Dread and Pentecostal*, 161–68; 176–82. Beckford is careful to define this usage of the term. He observes its multiple usages in Black intellectual discourses. His particular usage is a subjective theological construct. I question, however, if this is not an attempt to relate aspects of Rastafarianism to Black Pentecostalism which would be an imposition of Beckford's presupposition on his notion of Pentecostalism. Dread as a theological construct is still more than revisionism but a contextual interpretation of aspects of a Black diasporan faith.

71. Beckford, *Dread and Pentecostal*, 176.

72. William H. Willimon, "Acts," in *Interpretation Bible Commentary*, ed. James Luther Mays (Atlanta: John Knox Press, 1988), 27–28. Willimon agrees that Pentecost is the birth of the church but thinks that it is more accurate to attribute it to Easter which is also the birth of Pentecost. Interestingly, he addresses the issue of the formation of the church without considering its diversity. For a study on this issue, see Justo Gonzalez, *Acts: The Gospel of the Spirit* (New York: Orbis Books, 2001), 33–48.

73. David Rhoads, *The Challenge of Diversity: The Witness of Paul and the Gospel* (Minneapolis: Fortress Press, 1996), 15. See also his *From Every People and Nation: The Book of Revelation in Intercultural Perspective* (Minneapolis: Fortress Press, 2005); James Dunn, *Unity and Diversity in the New Testament: An Inquiry into the Character of Earliest Christianity*, 2nd ed. (Philadelphia: Trinity Press International, 1990); Justo Gonzalez, ed., *Out of Every Tribe and Nation: Christian Theology at the Ethnic Roundtable* (Nashville: Abingdon Press, 1992); Steven McKenzie, *All God's Children* (Kentucky: Westminster John Knox Press, 1997); Joel Edwards, *Lord, Make us One: Seeking Unity in Diversity* (London: Hodder & Stoughton, 1999); David T. Shannon and Gayraud S. Wilmore, *Black Witness to the Apostolic Faith* (Michigan: Eerdmans, 1985).

74. The origin of this term is unknown. It is commonly used in ordinary conversations, especially during times of celebration and crises among Caribbean people to express their unity.

75. This is one of the national symbols of Jamaica and an expression that shapes its national identity being a country of diverse people groups. The motto is printed on Jamaican currency notes.

76. Randall K. Burkett, *Garveyism as a Religious Movement* (New Jersey: Scarecrow Press and The American Theological Library Association, 1978), 33.

Chapter 6

1. James Cone, *God of the Oppressed* (New York: Seabury Press, 1975), 45.

2. Cone, *God of the Oppressed*, 39.

3. Robert Beckford, *Dread and Pentecostal: A Political Theology for the Black Church in Britain* (London: SPCK, 2000), 210.

4. Beckford, *Dread and Pentecostal*, 210.

5. The term Caribbeaners is the self-designated term I use for the Caribbean diaspora in general as opposed to Caribamericans which identifies the North American Caribbean diaspora. The former, therefore, signifies the global Caribbean diaspora while the latter defines a geographical and specific Caribbean diaspora.

6. Winston James, *Holding Aloft the Banner of Ethiopia: Caribbean Radicalism in Early Twentieth-Century America* (New York: Verso, 1998), 92.

7. James, *Holding Aloft the Banner of Ethiopia*, 92–100.

8. James, *Holding Aloft the Banner of Ethiopia*, 94. This law was instituted in 1896.

9. James, *Holding Aloft the Banner of Ethiopia*, 92–96.

10. James, *Holding Aloft the Banner of Ethiopia*, 96.

11. Heather Hathaway, *Caribbean Waves* (Indianapolis: Indiana University Press, 1991), 12–28.

12. Hathaway, *Caribbean Waves*, 20.

13. Lilian Brandt, "The Make-up of Negro City Groups," *Charities* xv (October 7, 1905), 8.

14. *The New York Amsterdam News*, March 1938.

15. Philip Kasinitz, *Caribbean New York: Black Immigrants and the Politics of Race* (Ithaca: Cornell University Press, 1992), 24. See Ransford W. Palmer, *Pilgrims from the Sun: West Indian Migration to America* (New York: Twayne Publishers, 1995); Ransford W. Palmer, *In Search of a Better Life: Perspectives on Migration from the Caribbean* (New York: Praeger Publishers, 1990); Dawn Marshall, "A History of West Indian Migrations: Overseas Opportunities and 'Safety-Valve' Policies," in *The Caribbean Exodus*, ed. Barry Levine (New York: Praeger Publishers, 1987), 15–29.

16. Kasinitz, *Caribbean New York*, 24. See Palmer, *Pilgrims from the Sun*, 6–7.

17. Palmer, *Pilgrims from the Sun*, 11–12.

18. Kasinitz, *Caribbean New York*, 26. See also Dawn Marshall, "International Politics of Caribbean Migration," in *The Restless Caribbean: Changing Patterns of International Relations*, eds Richard Millett and W. Marvin Will (New York: Praeger Publishers, 1979), 42–50; Palmer, *Pilgrims from the Sun*, 10–13.

19. Kasinitz, *Caribbean New York*, 26–27.

20. Joel Edwards, "The British Afro-Caribbean Community," in *Britain on the Brink: Major Trends in Society Today*, ed. Martyn Eden (Nottingham: Crossway Books, 1993), 109. Edwards' concern is the historical development of the Caribbean diasporan church in the British context. See also Mark Sturge, *Look What The Lord Has Done: An Exploration of Black Christian Faith in Britain* (Bletchley: Scripture Union, 2005); Roswith Gerloff, *A Plea for British Black Theologies: The Black Church Movement in Britain and its Transatlantic Cultural and Theological Interactions, Part 1* (Frankfurt am Main: Peter Lang, 1982); Malcolm J. C. Calley, *God's People: West Indian Pentecostal Sects in Britain* (London: Oxford University Press, 1965).

21. Kasinitz, *Caribbean New York*, 27–28.

22. Kasinitz, *Caribbean New York*, 26–37.

23. Roy Simon Bryce-Laporte, "Black Immigrants: The Experience of Invisibility and Insecurity," *Journal of Black Studies* 3 (September 1972): 39–56.

24. Palmer, *Pilgrims from the Sun* and his *In Search of a Better Life*.

25. Elsa Chaney, "The Context of Caribbean Migration," in *Caribbean Life in New York: Social Cultural Dimensions*, eds Constance Sutton and Elsa M. Chaney (New York: Center for Migration Studies of New York, 1992), 2–12.

26. This issue has been discussed previously in Chapter 5 on "Theologizing Diaspora" as a social factor in the formation of the pan-Caribbean identity.

27. Palmer, *Pilgrims from the Sun*, 22.

28. Palmer, *Pilgrims from the Sun*, 8. For additional information about this issue, see Aaron Segal, "Caribbean Exodus in a Global Context," in *The Caribbean Exodus*, ed. Barry Levine (New York: Praeger Publishers, 1987), 44–61.

29. For a study on Caribbeaners' economic success with particular reference to home ownership, see Kyle D. Crowder and Lucky M. Tedrow, "West Indians and the Residential Landscape of New York," in *Island in the Sun: West Indian Migration to New York*, ed. Nancy Foner (Berkeley: University of California Press, 2001), 81–114. More information can be found in Palmer, *In Search of a Better Life*.

30. Palmer, *Pilgrims from the Sun*, 29.

31. Bonham C. Richardson, *Caribbean Migrants: Environment and Human Survival on St. Kitts and Nevis* (Knoxville: University of Tennessee Press, 1983), 18.

32. I am using the term respect to interpret the meaning of the Caribbean diasporan experience. The experience is interpreted as a pilgrimage where the search for respect is one expression of the meaning. This usage of the term differs from how it is being used in Black British theology where the term is employed to define Black British theology as a theology of respect. See Joseph Aldred, *Respect: A Caribbean British Theology* (Ph.D. dissertation, Sheffield University, 2003), 211–33.

33. Kortright Davis, "Living the Faith in a Strange Land," *Grace Baptist Chapel Anniversary Lecture*, New York, September 21, 2002, 10.

34. Davis, "Living the Faith in a Strange Land," 6.

35. Davis, "Living the Faith in a Strange Land," 11.

36. Davis, "Living the Faith in a Strange Land," 11.

37. Davis, "Living the Faith in a Strange Land, 10–11.

38. Anthony Harvey, ed., *Theology in the City: A Theological Response to Faith in the City* (London: SPCK, 1989), 108–12.

39. Ira Reid, *The Negro Immigrant: His Background, Characteristics and Social Adjustments, 1899–1937* (New York: Arno Press and The New York Times, 1969), 124–28.

40. Robert Stewart, *Religion and Society in Post Emancipation Jamaica* (Knoxville: University of Tennessee Press, 1992); Winston Lawson, *Religion and Race: African and European Roots in Conflict – A Jamaican Testament* (New York: Peter Lang, 1996), 57–93; Sylvia R. Frey and Betty Wood, *Shouting to Zion: African American Protestantism in the American South and British Caribbean to 1830* (Chapel Hill: University of North Carolina Press, 1998); Omar M. McRoberts, *Streets of Glory: Church and Community in a Black Urban Neighborhood* (Chicago: University of Chicago Press, 2003); Jon F. Sensbach, *Rebecca's Revival: Creating Black Christianity in the Atlantic World* (Massachusetts: Harvard University Press, 2005).

41. Irma Watkins-Owens, *Blood Relations: Caribbean Immigrants and the Harlem Community, 1900–1930* (Indianapolis: Indiana University Press, 1996), 57.

42. Adelaide Cromwell, *The Other Brahmins: Boston's Black Upper Class, 1750–1950* (Fayetteville: University of Arkansas Press, 1994), 224.

43. Watkins-Owens, *Blood Relations*, 59.

44. Reid, *Negro Immigrant*, 126.

45. Reid, *Negro Immigrant*, 26.

46. James, *Holding Aloft the Banner of Ethiopia*, 50.

47. Lennox Raphael, "West Indians and Afro-Americans," *Freedom Ways* 4 (1964): 441.

48. Watkins-Owens, *Blood Relations*, 60.

49. Watkins-Owens, *Blood Relations*, 60.

50. Omar M. McRoberts, *Streets of Glory: Churches and Community in a Black Urban Neighborhood* (Chicago: University of Chicago Press, 2003), 41.

51. McRoberts, *Streets of Glory*, 41.

52. McRoberts, *Streets of Glory*, 41.

53. Mark D. Morrison-Reed, *Black Pioneers in a White Denomination* (Boston: Beacon Press, 1984), 33–79.

54. Morrison-Reed, *Black Pioneers*, 31.

55. Morrison-Reed, *Black Pioneers*, 3.

56. Morrison-Reed, *Black Pioneers*, 1.

57. Morrison-Reed, *Black Pioneers*, 1.

58. Morrison-Reed, *Black Pioneers*, 1, 31.

59. Egbert Ethelred Brown Papers, Box 1, Folder 1. Schomburg Center in Research and Black Culture.

60. Brown Papers. Box 1, Folder 1.

61. Brown, Papers. Box 1, Folder 1.

62. Robert Hill and Barbara Blair, eds, *Marcus Garvey and Lessons* (Berkeley: University of California Press, 1987), 189.

Chapter 7

1. Cheryl Shanks, *Immigration and the Politics of American Sovereignty, 1890–1990* (Ann Arbor: University of Michigan Press, 2001), 96–186. See also Ransford W. Palmer, *Pilgrims from the Sun: West Indian Migration to America* (New York: Twayne Publishers, 1995); Roger Daniels and Otis Graham, *Debating America Immigration, 1882–Present* (Maryland: Rowan & Littlefield, 2001).

2. Palmer, *Pilgrims from the Sun*, 18.

3. Palmer, *Pilgrims from the Sun*, 1–30; Dawn Marshall, "A History of West Indian Migrations: Overseas Opportunities and 'Safety-Valves' Policies," in *The Caribbean Exodus*, ed. Barry B. Levine (New York: Praeger Publishers, 1987), 15–31; Robert Pastor, "The Impact of U.S. Policy on Caribbean Emigration: Does It Matter?" in *The Caribbean Exodus*, ed. Barry Levine (New York: Praeger Publishers, 1987), 259.

4. Constance R. Sutton, "The Caribbeanization of New York City and the Emergence of a Transnational Socio-Cultural System," in *Caribbean Life in New York City: Sociocultural*

Dimensions, eds Constance R. Sutton and Elsa M. Chancey (New York: Center for Migration Studies of New York, 1987), 21.

5. Palmer, *Pilgrims from the Sun*, 20.

6. F. Dionne Forde, *Images of America: Caribbean Americans in New York 1895–1975* (Charleston: Arcadia Publishing, 2002).

7. Frances Henry, *The Caribbean Diaspora in Toronto: Learning to Live with Racism* (Toronto: University of Toronto Press, 1994), 148.

8. Guy S. Notice, *If We Could Begin Again: A Retrospective Glance at One's Past Life with a Desire for a New Beginning* (Minneapolis: Braun Press, 1980), 86.

9. David J. Bosch, *Transforming Mission: Paradigm Shifts in Theology of Mission* (New York: Orbis Books, 1991), 56–79. Bosch argues that there are different interpretations of the Great Commission as represented by each gospel writer. He also offers a contextual theology of mission. For an alternate view, see Donald Senior and Carrol Stuhlmueller, *The Biblical Foundations for Mission* (New York: Orbis Books, 1995), 233–54.

10. Neville Callam, "Understanding Mission: A Global Perspective" (Paper presented at the Jamaica Baptist Union Mission Conference, Ocho Rios, November 2003).

11. Inclusivity is another term for Catholicity. I prefer the former because it gives a more contextual understanding and does not carry the theological baggage of the latter. The term also connotes diversity which is a characteristic of the Caribbean diasporan church. Catholicity does not convey such meanings. For an important discussion on this issue, see Stephen B. Bevans, *Models of Contextual Theology* (New York: Orbis Books, 2002), 14–15; Robert J. Schreiter, *The New Catholicity: Theology between the Global and the Local* (New York: Orbis Books, 1997), 116–33.

12. Idris Hamid, ed., *Out of the Depths* (San Fernando: St Andrews Theological College, 1977), ix. This attempt at inclusivity must be understood in the larger framework of the liberation movement of the time. This includes the Civil Rights Movement of the 1960s and Black Liberation Theology in the United States, Latin American Liberation Theology and the spread of Socialism in the Caribbean and Latin America. These events are not the direct influence of the origins of Caribbean liberation. The foundation for this development is the anti-colonial movement that is expressed through the various quests for independence. This development in Caribbean Theology is largely influenced by these various social and political events rather than an intentional theological belief. In any case, this was an attempt to decolonize theology. The major study on this subject is Noel Erskine's *Decolonizing Theology* (Maryknoll: Orbis Books, 1991). Kortright Davis, however, in his *Emancipation Still Comin'* (Maryknoll: Orbis Books, 1990) argues that the issue is not the decolonization of theology but the need for an emancipatory theology. The issue in question also demonstrates the various theological interpretations of Caribbean life as well as the different approaches and traditions in Caribbean theological and religious thought. For a pioneering study in Caribbean Theology, see David I. Mitchell, ed., *With Eyes Wide Open* (Trinidad: Christian Action for Development in the Caribbean, 1973); Idris Hamid, ed., *Troubling of the Waters* (San Fernando: Rahaman Printery, 1973); William Watty, *From Shore to Shore: Soundings in Caribbean Theology* (Barbados: Cedar Press, 1981). The most recent text is Howard Gregory, ed., *Caribbean Theology: Preparing for the Challenges Ahead* (Kingston: Canoe Press, 1995). See, as well, some major essays on this development in Burchell Taylor, ed., *Looking at the Theology of Liberation Together: An Ecumenical Reflection within the Caribbean* (Kingston: Jamaica Council of Churches, 1994). *Caribbean Journal of Religious Studies* is also a resource for material on this subject.

13. Hamid, *Out of the Depths*, x. For an example of the inclusive nature of a Caribbean understanding of mission, see Kortright Davis, *Mission for Caribbean Change: Caribbean Development as Theological Enterprise* (Bern: Peter Lang, 1982).

14. Hamid, *Out of the Depths*, ix.

15. Philip Potter and Barbel Wartenberg-Potter, *Freedom is for Freeing: A Study Book on Paul's Letter to the Galatians* (New York: The United Methodist Church, 1990), 73.

16. William Watty, "The New Missiology: A Biblical Perspective," in *Out of the Depths*, ed. Idris Hamid (San Fernando: Rahaman Printery, 1977), 91–112.

17. Watty, "The New Missiology," 99.

18. Watty, "The New Missiology," 110.

19. Carlos F. Cardoza Orlandi, "Conspiracy Among Idols: A Critique of Deconstruction from the Afro-Caribbean Religions," *Koinonia: Princeton Theological Seminary Graduate Forum* iv, no. 1 (Spring 1992): 27–41.

20. Ashley Smith, "Mission and Evangelism in an Age of Colonization," in *Out of the Depths*, ed. Idris Hamid (San Fernando: Rahaman Printery, 1977), 117–18.

21. Michael Jagessar, *Full Life for All: The Work and Theology of Philip Potter: A Historical Survey and Systematic Analysis of Major Themes* (Zoetermeer: Boekencentrum, 1997), 227–50; see also Jagessar's "Cultures in Dialogue: The Contribution of a Caribbean Theologian," *Black Theology: An International Journal* 1.2 (2003): 139–60.

22. Keith Hunte, "Protestantism and Slavery in the British Caribbean," in *Christianity in the Caribbean: Essays in Church History*, ed. Armando Lampe (Kingston: University of the West Indies Press, 2001), 112–15.

23. Hunte, "Protestantism and Slavery," 113.

24. Michael Jagessar, *Full Life for All*, 191.

25. Philip Potter, "Christ's Mission and Ours in Today's World," *International Review of Mission* 62/246 (April 1973): 150.

26. Jürgen Moltmann, *The Church in the Power of the Spirit* (New York: Harper & Row, 1977), 10–11. See also Jagessar, *Full Life for All*, 186–204. My work is a study on and about Caribbean mission. While I do not limit my interpretation to the Caribbean theological tradition, I want to interpret it within that framework. The use of non-Caribbean sources is not to legitimize this perspective but to facilitate conversations. This is a study about and for Caribbean people. I use, however, other sources where necessary and appropriate. For too long and too frequently, we depend on other resources; in most cases, those different and foreign to our history, culture, heritage and experience to define our theology. For an example of work that proposes to offer a general theology of mission, see Bosch, *Transforming Mission*, 83, 389–93.

27. Horace O. Russell, *The Missionary Outreach of the West Indian Church: Jamaica Baptist Missions to West Africa in the Nineteenth Century* (New York: Peter Lang, 2000).

28. Russell, *Missionary Outreach*, 8.

29. Russell, *Missionary Outreach*, 251.

30. Russell, *Missionary Outreach*, 8.

31. Clement Gayle, *George Liele: Pioneer Missionary to Jamaica* (Kingston: Jamaica Baptist Union, 1982), 3–17. Prior to the arrival of George Liele in Jamaica, there was no Baptist witness. Mission work among the Black population was carried out by the Anglicans and Catholic churches but they had very little success. For a study on the origin of the Black church in the Caribbean, see Robert Stewart, *Religion and Society in Post-Emancipation Jamaica* (Knoxville: University of Tennessee Press, 1992), 1–65,

110–52; Shirley C. Gordon, *Our Cause for His Glory: Christianization and Emancipation in Jamaica* (Kingston: University of the West Indies Press, 1998). The Baptists were the liberators from the oppression of Caribbean people. They saw the inconsistencies between the conditions of oppression and the gospel and decided to resist and protest against oppression. For a pioneering interpretation of this issue, see C. S. Reid, *Samuel Sharpe: From Slave to National Hero* (Kingston: Bustamante Institute of Public and National Affairs, 1988); see also Winston Lawson, *Religion and Race: African and European Roots in Conflict – A Jamaican Testament* (New York: Peter Lang, 1996).

    32. Russell, *Missionary Outreach*, 253–64.

    33. Russell, *Missionary Outreach*, 253.

    34. Russell, *Missionary Outreach*, 253.

    35. Brian Stanley, *The History of the Baptist Missionary Society, 1792–1992* (Edinburgh: T&T Clark, 1992), 68. For an account about the life and work of the founder of the Baptist Missionary Society, see S. Pearre Carey, *William Carey* (London: Wakeman Trust, 1993).

    36. Orlandi, "Conspiracy Among Idols," 30–31.

    37. Gayle, *George Liele*, 1–19. This study is a creative attempt to construct the life and work of a central person in the history of Caribbean Christianity. For a critical analysis of George Liele, see Noel Erskine, *Decolonizing Theology* (New York: Orbis Books, 1981).

    38. Gayle, *George Liele*, 3.

    39. Gayle, *George Liele*, 13–14. Gayle is proposing the view that Blacks were already involved in their own evangelization and this was not the initiative of the white church. This challenges the view that the English clergyman, William Carey, is the father of the modern missionary movement.

    40. Hunte, "Protestantism and Slavery," 113.

    41. Hunte, "Protestantism and Slavery," 113–15.

    42. Arthur Charles Dayfoot, *The Shaping of the West Indian Church 1492–1962* (Kingston: University of the West Indies Press, 1999), 219.

    43. Gayle, *George Liele*, 23–24. Gayle describes Liele as a pioneering missionary because he was the first Black Baptist preacher to preach in Jamaica, to win the greatest number of the enslaved Blacks to Christianity and to establish and lead the Black church in the Caribbean.

    44. Dayfoot, *Shaping of the West Indian Church*, 218–19. See also Ira V. Brooks, *Where Do We Go From Here?* (London: Charles Raper, 1982); *Another Gentleman to the Ministry* (Birmingham: Compeer Press, 1986). More study has been done on the Caribbean diasporan church in the British context. In the American context, the study is in its infancy and it is one of the first that focuses on the church in the American context.

    45. Ashley Smith, "Mission and Evangelization in an Age of De-colonization," in *Out of the Depths*, ed. Idris Hamid (San Fernando: Rahaman Printery, 1977), 117.

    46. Dayfoot, *Shaping of the West Indian Church*, 218–22.

    47. Dayfoot, *Shaping of the West Indian Church*, 218.

    48. Dayfoot, *Shaping of the West Indian Church*, 218.

    49. Inez Knibb Sibley, *The Baptists of Jamaica* (Kingston: Jamaica Baptist Union, 1965), 24–30. For an exploration in Jamaican Baptist history, see Horace Russell, *Foundations and Anticipations: The Jamaica Baptist Story: 1783–1892* (Georgia: Brentwood Christian Press, 1993); Devon Dick, "Diaspora and Church," *Jamaica Daily Gleaner*, June 27, 2006.

50. Personal communication, February 2005. The Jamaica Baptist Union appointed Audley Reid to work with Caribbean nationals in Canada.

51. Personal communication. The United Church of Jamaica and Grand Gayman appointed Marjorie Cooper Lewis to work in the United Kingdom with Caribbeaners.

52. Baptist Missionary Society, Minutes of General Meeting, January 23–24, 1962.

53. Horace Russell, "Jamaica Baptist Missionary Society in Mission: The Lessons and the Legacy" (Paper presented at the Jamaica Baptist Union Mission Conference, Ocho Rios, November 2003), 8. The Jamaica Baptist Missionary Society (JBMS) was too deeply committed to British colonialism. The reasons for taking the integrative approach were political and theological. In the first instance they did not want to rock the boat. Doing so would be going against the system that was literally feeding the organization. The JBMS may have sincerely believed that they were doing the right thing which goes to show the depths of their colonization. The second reason was theological. There is one church and the establishing of ethnically based congregations was contrary to their ecclesiology. In retrospect, history has proven the JBMS wrong. There is now the emergence of the Black British church tradition which represents the fastest growing Christian movement in Britain today.

54. Baptist Missionary Society, Minutes of General Meeting, April 28–29, 1960.

55. Baptist Missionary Society, Minutes of General Meeting, January 23–24, 1962.

56. Russell, "Jamaica Baptist Missionary Society in Mission," 8.

57. Dayfoot, *Shaping of the West Indian Church*, 17–233; see also Lampe, *Christianity in the Caribbean*.

58. Charles W. Conn, *Like a Mighty Army: A History of the Church of God* (Tennessee: Pathway Press, 1977), 190.

59. Rodwell Morgan, *Meet Corn Island: The History of Corn Island in Relation to the Ebenezer Baptist Church* (Florida: Morris Publishing, 1996), 56–65.

60. David Morgan, "Southern Baptist Witness to Jamaicans in America" (unpublished MS), 2.

61. Morgan, "Southern Baptist Witness," 6.

62. Samuel G. Simpson, *To Dream the Impossible Dream: Planning and Planting Churches in the City* (Georgia: Armon Press, 2003), 52.

63. Bosch, *Transforming Mission*, 312.

64. Bosch, *Transforming Mission*, 262–345.

65. Bosch, *Transforming Mission*, 313.

66. Harold Sitahal, "Rethinking Mission for the Caribbean," in *Out of the Depths*, ed. Adris Hamid (San Fernando: Rahaman Printery, 1977), 29.

67. Sitahal, "Rethinking Mission," 45.

68. Jagessar, *Full Life for All*, 193.

69. Phillip Potter, "From Missions to Mission," *International Review of Mission* 76/302 (April 1987): 166.

70. Neville Callam, *Perspective on Ministry* (Kingston: Jamaica Council of Churches, 1991). See also S. U. Hastings, *These Fifty Years* (Aruba: The Moravian Church Foundation, 1991), 18–23; James Earl Massey, *The Burdensome Joy of Preaching* (Nashville: Abingdon Press, 1998); Samuel D. Proctor and Gardner C. Taylor, *We Have this Ministry: The Heart of the Pastor's Vocation* (Valley Forge: Judson Press, 1996), 1–11.

71. Samuel Hines and Curtis Paul DeYoung, *Beyond Rhetoric: Reconciliation as a Way of Life* (Valley Forge: Judson Press, 2000), 125.

72. George H. W. Bush, Letter cited in *Celebrating God's Wonderful Works: Church's 80th Anniversary Pastor's 21st Anniversary* (Washington DC: Third Street Church of God, 1990), 9.

73. Richard C. Halverson, Letter cited in *Celebrating God's Wonderful Works*, 10.

74. Cheryl J. Sanders, *How Firm a Foundation: Eighty Years of History (1910–1990) Third Street Church of God* (Washington DC: Third Street Church of God, 1990), 38.

75. Samuel Hines, Letter cited in *Celebrating God's Wonderful Works*, 3.

76. Samuel G. Simpson, *To Dream the Impossible Dream: Planning and Planting Churches in the City* (Georgia: Orman Press, 2003), 53.

77. Simpson, *To Dream the Impossible Dream*, 11–20.

78. Simpson, *To Dream the Impossible Dream*, 11–20.

79. Karen L. Willoughby, "Churches Bloom in the Bronx Despite Years of Hard Times," *Baptist Press*, July 20, 2003.

80. Karen L. Willoughby, "In the Midst of Fire-devastated Bronx, N.Y. Church Rose to Provide Hope," *Baptist Press*, September 7, 2004.

81. Willoughby, "In the Midst."

82. Wesley Green, personal communication, February 2004. I will not question Green's sincerity but this reason for establishing a church reflects opportunism rather than a call. What is not clear is if the reason for establishing a church was the opportunity to do so or the call of God to do it. It can also be argued that the call comes through the opportunity. The issue is a call by God to establish a church. It must be clear, however, with the relationship between the call and opportunity, the call precedes the opportunity.

83. Peter J. Paris, *The Spirituality of African Peoples: The Search for a Common Moral Discourse* (Minnesota: Fortress Press, 1995), 51.

84. Paris, *Spirituality of African Peoples*, 57.

85. Jürgen Moltmann, *The Church in the Power of the Spirit* (New York: Harper & Row, 1977), 303. I find Moltmann's observation very pertinent to this study, although he is addressing the issue of the ministry of the church from a European perspective. He is, nonetheless, speaking of the ecumenical church which includes the Caribbean diasporan church. His discussion concerns the relationship between church and the tasks of individual members in the church. The tasks are not theirs but belong to the Christ whom they represent. This call to mission is fulfilled through the community of faith.

Chapter 8

1. Walter Brueggemann, *A Commentary on Jeremiah: Exile and Homecoming* (Michigan: Eerdmans, 1998), 256.

2. Brueggemann, *A Commentary on Jeremiah*, 257–58.

3. Brueggemann, *A Commentary on Jeremiah*, 158.

4. Brueggemann, *A Commentary on Jeremiah*, 258.

5. James Cone, "Theology's Great Sin," *Black Theology: An International Journal* 2:2 (July 2004): 142. See also Cornel West, "Black Theology of Liberation as a Critique of Capitalist Civilization," *Black Theology: A Documentary History Volume Two: 1980–1992*, eds James Cone and Gayraud Wilmore (New York: Orbis Books, 1993), 410–25.

6. Egbert Ethelred Brown, "I Have Two Dreams," 472, in Ethelred Brown Papers, Box 1, Folder 3, Schomburg Center for Research in Black Culture.

7. Brown, "I Have Two Dreams," 471.

8. Brown, "I Have Two Dreams," 471.

9. Brown, " I Have Two Dreams," 472

10. Egbert Ethelred Brown, "If Jesus Came to Harlem, Whom Would He Denounce?" Brown Papers, Box 4, Folder 2, Schomburg Center for Research in Black Culture.

11. Brown, "If Jesus Came to Harlem."

12. Mark D. Morrison-Reed, *Black Pioneers in a White Denomination* (Boston: Beacon Press, 1984), 61–62.

13. Morrison-Reed, *Black Pioneers*, 83–84.

14. Morrison-Reed, *Black Pioneers*, 84.

15. Brown, "If Jesus Came to Harlem."

16. Vincent P. Franklin, "Caribbean Intellectual Influences on Afro-Americans in the United States," in *Intellectuals in the Twentieth-Century Caribbean Volume 1 Spectre of the New Class: the Commonwealth Caribbean*, ed. Alistair Hennessy (London and Basingstoke: Macmillan, 1992), 179–90.

17. Bill Schwarz, *West Indian Intellectuals in Britain* (Manchester: Manchester University Press, 2003).

18. W. A. Roberts, *Six Great Jamaicans (Biographical Sketches)* (Kingston: Pioneer Press, 1951).

19. T. E. S. Scholes, *Glimpses of the Ages: or the 'Superior' and 'Inferior' Races So-called Discussed in Light of Science and History* (London: John Long, vol. I [1905]; vol. II [1908]).

20. Hollis Lynch, ed., *Edward Wilmot Blyden: Pan-Negro Patriot (1832–1912)* (New York: Oxford University Press, 1970).

21. Denis Benn, *The Caribbean: An Intellectual History 1774–2003* (Kingston: Ian Randle Publishers, 2004).

22. Winston James, *A Fierce Hatred of Injustice: Claude McKay's Jamaica and his Poetry of Rebellion* (New York: Verso, 2000).

23. Michelle Ann Stephens, *Black Empire: The Masculine Global Imaginary of Caribbean Intellectuals in the United States, 1914–1962* (North Carolina: Duke University Press, 2005).

24. W. Burghardt Turner and Joyce Moore Turner, eds, *Caribbean Militant in Harlem: Collected Writings 1920–1972* (Bloomington and Indianapolis: Indiana University Press, 1992).

25. Winston James, *Holding Aloft the Banner of Ethiopia: Caribbean Radicalism in Early Twentieth-Century America* (London: Verso, 1998).

26. James Cone, "Loving God with our Hearts, Soul and Mind," in *Blow the Trumpet in Zion: Global Vision and Action for the 21st-century Black Church*, eds Iva E. Carruthers, Fredrick D. Haynes III, and Jeremiah A. Wright, Jr. (Minneapolis: Fortress Press, 2005), 60.

27. Cone, "Loving God," 62.

28. Cone, "Loving God," 62.

29. Brown, "A Challenging Question," in Brown Papers, Box 2, Folder 3, Schomburg Center for Research in Black Culture.

30. Brown, "A Challenging Question."

31. Brown, "If Jesus Came to Harlem ." The Caribbean diasporan intellectual tradition has not been nurtured. For an interesting discussion, see Orlando Patterson, "Ecumenical America: Global Culture and the American Cosmos," in *The Birth of Caribbean Civilization: A Century of Ideas about Culture, Identity, Nation and Society*, ed. O. Nigel Bolland (Kingston: Ian Randle Publishers, 2004), 641–43.

32. Brown, "If Jesus Came to Harlem." See Mk 11:15–19 where Jesus expressed his anger at those who misused the purpose of the temple. It is this similar anger Brown expressed at the anti-intellectualism in the church of his time.

33. Cone, "Loving God," 60–61.

34. Cited in Cornel West, *Prophesy Deliverance! An Afro-American Revolutionary Christianity* (Philadelphia: Westminster Press, 1982), 62.

35. Richard H. Popkin, "Hume Racism," *The Philosophical Forum* 9:2–3 (Winter–Spring 1977–78): 213.

36. Brown, "The History of Harlem Unitarian Church," in Brown Papers, Box 1, Folder 6, Schomburg Center for Research in Black Culture.

37. "The Hubert Harrison Memorial Church: Statement of Purpose," in Brown Papers, Box 1, Folder 6, Schomburg Center for Research in Black Culture.

38. "A Statement and an Invitation," in Brown Papers, Box 1, Folder 6, Schomburg Center for Research in Black Culture.

39. Morrison-Reed, *Black Pioneers*, 37–41.

40. Brown, Brown Papers, Box 1, Folder 1, Schomberg Center for Research in Black Culture.

41. Brown, "I Have Two Dreams," 471.

42. Cone, "Theology's Great Sin," 142.

43. Cone, "Theology's Great Sin," 142.

44. James Cone, *For My People: Black Theology and the Black Church: Where have we been and where are we going?* (New York: Orbis Books, 1984), 40.

45. Cone, "Loving God," 62.

46. Egbert Ethelred Brown, "The Search for Truth," Box 3, Folder 5, "The Quest for Truth," Box 3, Folder 4, in Brown Papers, Schomburg Center for Research in Black Culture. One cannot appeal continually to non-white sources to defend an idea. The issue is using non-Black sources for validation which is characteristic of Brown as detected throughout his writings especially his sermons. Brown was learned enough to know of Black sources and it is very unfortunate that he did not engage with these in his work. This inconsistency between his theory and content still shows the depth of his enslavement to white culture although he was an advocate of emancipation. No excuse must be made for Brown because he was a contemporary of Marcus Garvey and was very aware of the influence of the United Negro Improvement Association. One would wonder if his lack of identity with Garveyism is also a reflection of his enslavement to white culture. For an examination of this issue, see the Ethelred Brown Papers, Box 1, Folder 6–7.

47. James Cone, "Strange Fruit: The Cross and the Lynching Tree," *Harvard Divinity Bulletin* (Winter 2007): 50.

48. West, *Prophecy Deliverance*, 47–48.

49. I describe the Caribbean people as self-consciously independent because they are by nature an independent people. This is expressed in the numerous revolts against oppression, including slavery, to the present time. For a more detailed study on this tradition of autonomy, see Kathleen E. A. Montieth and Glen Richards, eds, *Jamaica in*

Slavery and Freedom: History, Heritage and Culture (Kingston: University of the West Indies Press, 2002); Karla Gottlieth, *"The Mother of Us All": A History of Queen Nanny, Leader of the Windward Jamaican Maroons* (New Jersey: Africa Third World Press, 2002); Brian Meeks, *Narratives of Resistance; Jamaica, Trinidad, the Caribbean* (Kingston: University of the West Indies Press, 2000); Sylvia R. Frey and Betty Wood, *Come Shouting to Zion: African American Protestantism in the American South and the British Caribbean to 1830* (North Carolina: University of North Carolina Press, 1998). The movement among Caribbean countries for self-government from West Indian Federation to Independence is another example of the Caribbean tradition of autonomy. For further exploration of this subject, see C. L. R. James, "The Case for West Indian Self-Government"; "Lincoln Carnival, George Padmore: Writings for the Nation" and "From Toussaint L'Ouverture to Fidel Castro" in *The C.L.R. James Reader*, ed. Anna Grimshaw (Massachusetts: Blackwell, 1992), 49–62; 281–314.

50. James, "The Case for West Indian Self-Government," 61. This remark is a serious attack on the incompetence of the colonial power to govern. James was making the case for Caribbean self-government. He was confident that this was not only about competent leadership but having a kind of government that was more competent than the colonial government. This same attitude of the colonial power is characteristic of Euro-American Christianity that is practiced by their mission agencies.

51. James, *Holding Aloft the Banner of Ethiopia*, 136.

52. James, *Holding Aloft the Banner of Ethiopia*, 122–94. The role Caribbean intellectuals played in the Harlem Renaissance is a neglected area of scholarly study but there are some preliminary studies that provide an overview of this concern. John C. Walter and Jill Louise Ansheles, "The Role of the Caribbean Immigrant in the Harlem Renaissance," *Afro-Americans in New York Life and History* (1977): 49–64; Winfred D. Samuels, "Hubert H. Harrison and the New Negro Manhood Movement," *Afro-Americans in New York Life and History* (January 1981): 29–40; John Runice, "Marcus Garvey and the Harlem Renaissance," *Afro-Americans in New York Life and History* (July 1986): 7–25.

53. Irma Watkins-Owens, "Early Twentieth Century Caribbean Women," in *Island in the City: West Indian Migration to New York*, ed. Nancy Foner (Berkeley: University of California Press, 2001), 43–44.

54. Watkins-Owens, *Island in the City*, 44–49.

55. Watkins-Owens, *Island in the City*, 70.

56. Cited in James, *Holding Aloft the Banner*, 84.

57. W. A. Domingo, "Gift of the Black Tropics," 344–45. See also James, *Holding Aloft the Banner of Ethiopia*, 83–85; Ira Reid, *The Negro Immigrant: His Background, Characteristics and Social Adjustment, 1899–1937* (New York: Arman Press, 1969), 122.

58. Samuel G. Simpson, *To Dream the Impossible Dream: Planning and Planting Churches in the City* (Georgia: Armon Press, 2003), 53.

59. Simpson, *To Dream the Impossible Dream*, 53.

60. Orlanzo Hyatt, personal communication, Florida, February 2005. Hyatt is one of the pioneering Caribbean diasporan pastors. He is a member of the New Testament Church of God.

61. Simpson, *To Dream the Impossible Dream*, 54.

62. Simpson, *To Dream the Impossible Dream*, 54.

63. Bronx Baptist Church, *35 Years: Hand in Hand with God* (New York: n.p., 2001).

64. Simpson, *To Dream the Impossible Dream*, 55.

65. Cited in "Draft No 5 Final: Policy and Procedure – AGA-USA," 1–5. The Reverend Russell McCloud, pastor of Olivet Gospel Church, graciously made this document available to me. Also, the Reverend Lloyd Bewery, during his tenure as pastor of the Olivet Church, had previously discussed the formation of this new denomination with me. It was during these discussions that I discovered this as a new development in Caribbean diasporan ecclesiology.

66. "Policy and Procedure," 2–3.

67. V. Seymour Cole cited in *Bronx Bethany Church of the Nazarene 1964–1999: 35 Years of Ministerial Excellence* (Bronx: New York, 1999), 2.

68. *Bronx Bethany Church*, 21.

69. *Bronx Bethany Church*, 21.

70. *Bronx Bethany Church*, 21.

71. Ashley Smith, "Mission and Evangelism in an Age of De-Colonisation," in *Out of the Depths*, ed. Adris Hamid (San Fernando: St Andrews Theological College, 1977), 116. See also Kortright Davis, *Serving with Power: Reviving the Spirit of Christian Ministry* (New Jersey: Paulist Press, 1999). Davis writes within the Anglican church tradition which has an Episcopalian form of church government whereas the Church of the Nazarene and others such as the Baptist have a congregational form of government.

72. *Bronx Bethany Church*, 21–22.

73. Simpson, *To Dream the Impossible Dream*, 52. Simpson's response is common among first-generation Caribbean immigrants. This generation was very naïve about racism and in many ways ignorant of the history of the African American struggle against this oppression. Also, Caribbean people were uninformed about Southern Baptist history. They did not know that this denomination supported slavery, segregation and opposed the Civil Rights Movement. It was not until the 1990s that this denomination began to make token attempts to correct this disgraceful history. In 1990 the Southern Baptist Convention made an apology to African Americans for the evil and cruelty they executed against them. Furthermore, Simpson claimed that all people, particularly Christians, being one people, is an excuse for not addressing the real issues. This reflects a theological understanding that divorces faith from human existential conditions. I would argue that this view does not represent the Caribbean diasporan church and it is a misrepresentation of the faith and an incorrect interpretation of Scripture.

74. Brian Stanley, *The History of the Baptist Missionary Society 1792–1992* (Edinburgh: T&T Clark, 1992); see also Winston Lawson, *Religion and Race: African and European Roots in Conflict – A Jamaican Testament* (New York: Peter Lang, 1996), 56–82; Robert Stewart, *Religion and Society in Post-Emancipation Jamaica* (Knoxville: University of Tennessee Press, 1992); Diane J. Austin-Broos, *Jamaica Genesis: Religion and the Politics of Moral Order* (Kingston: Ian Randle Publishers, 1997).

75. Harold Cruse, *The Crisis of the Negro Intellectual: A Historical Analysis of the Failure of Black Leadership* (New York: Quill, 1967), 115–46.

76. Vincent Franklin, "Caribbean Intellectual Influences on Afro-Americans in the United States," in *Intellectuals in Twentieth Century Caribbean*, ed. Alistair Henessy (London: Macmillan, 1992), 179–88; Cruse, *Crisis of the Negro Intellectual*, 115–46.

77. James, *Holding Aloft the Banner*, 1–8; 101–94; 259–91.

78. James, *Holding Aloft the Banner*, 76.

79. W. A. Domingo, "Gift to the Black Tropics," in *The American*, ed. Alain Lock (New York: Arno, 1968), 346.

80. Dennis Forsythe, "West Indian Radicalism in America: An Assessment of Ideologies," in *Ethnicity in the Americas*, ed. Frances Henry (The Hague: Mouton, 1976), 302–33.

81. Claude McKay, "He Who Gets Slap," *The Liberator* 5 (April 1922): 24–25.

82. Robert Hill and Barbra Blair, eds, *Marcus Garvey and Lessons* (Berkeley: University of California Press, 1987), 189.

Chapter 9

1. Justo I. Gonzalez, *The Story of Christianity Vol. 2* (Massachusetts: Harper Collins, 1984), 63–66, 162–65; see also Daniel L. Migliore, *Faith Seeking Understanding: An Introduction to Christian Theology* (Michigan: Eerdmans, 1991), 140–56.

2. Jurgen Moltmann, *The Church in the Power of the Spirit* (London: SCM Press, 1977), 337–42.

3. Moltmann, *Church in the Power of the Spirit*, 338–39.

4. Moltmann, *Church in the Power of the Spirit*, 340. For a very useful text on the developing of creeds, see Francis Young, *The Making of Creeds* (Philadelphia: Trinity Press International, 1991).

5. James H. Evans, *We Have Been Believers: An African American Systematic Theology* (Minneapolis: Fortress Press, 1992), 135–40.

6. Evans, *We Have Been Believers*, 135.

7. Moltmann, *Church in the Power of the Spirit*, 342.

8. Evans, *We Have Been Believers*, 140.

9. Winston James, *Holding Aloft the Banner of Ethiopia: Caribbean Radicals in Early Twentieth-Century America* (New York: Verso, 1998), 123. See also Wilfred D. Samuels, "Hubert H. Harrison and the New Negro Manhood Movement," *Afro-Americans in New York Life and History* (January 1981): 23–40.

10. Ethelred Brown Papers, Box 1, Folder 6, Schomburg Center for Research in Black Culture.

11. James, *Holding Aloft the Banner of Ethiopia*, 124.

12. James, *Holding Aloft the Banner of Ethiopia*, 79.

13. Brown Papers, "A Statement and an Invitation," Box 1, Folder 6.

14. Brown Papers, "The Resolution," Box 1, Folder 6.

15. Brown Papers, "The Resolution," Box 1, Folder 6.

16. John Lathrop, "Letter to Ethelred Brown," in Ethelred Brown Papers, Box 1, Folder 6.

17. Brown, "Brief History," Box 1, Folder 6.

18. Brown, "Brief History."

19. Brown, "Statement and an Invitation."

20. Brown, "The Resolution."

21. Cornel West, *Prophetic Fragments* (Grand Rapids: Eerdsmans, 1992), 271–72. West has written extensively on the Black intellectual. See the following articles in this same book: "Martin Luther King, Jr.: Prophetic Christian as Organic Intellectual" (3–12); "Christian Theological Mediocrity" (195–96); *Race Matters* (Boston: Beacon Press, 1993), 35–46.

22. West, *Prophetic Fragments*, 272. For a critical appraisal of the Black intellectual, see West's "Dilemma of the Black Intellectual," in his *Keeping Faith* (New York: Routledge, 1993), 67–85.

23. Mark Christian, ed., *Black Identity of the 20th Century: Expressions of the US and UK African Diaspora* (London: Hansib Publications, 2002), 120–33.

24. Kortright Davis, "Living the Faith in a Strange Land," *Grace Baptist Chapel Anniversary Lecture*, Bronx, New York, September 21, 2002.

25. Davis, "Living the Faith in a Strange Land," 17.

26. Davis, "Living the Faith in a Strange Land," 17. For an exploration of the church as community of learning in the Black Church tradition, see Anthony Reddie, *Nobodies to Somebodies: A Practical Theology for Education and Liberation* (Warrington: Epworth Press, 2003); J. Alfred Smith, Sr., "Black Theology and the Parish Ministry," in *Black Faith and Public Talk: Critical Essays on James H. Cone's Black Theology and Black Power*, ed. Dwight Hopkins (New York: Orbis Books, 1999), 89–95; James H. Cone, *For My People: Black Theology and the Black Church: Where have we been and where we are going?* (New York: Obis Books, 1996), 99–121; James H. Cone, 'Loving God with our Heart, Soul and Mind," in *Blow the Trumpet in Zion: Global Vision and Action for the 21st-century Black Church*, eds Iva E. Carruthers, et al. (Minneapolis: Fortress Press, 2005), 59–75.

27. Anthony Reddie, *Faith, Stories and the Experience of Black Elders: Singing the Lord's Song in a Strange Land* (London: Jessica Kingsley, 1988), 94.

28. Reddie, *Faith, Stories and the Experience of Black Elders*, 93–94.

29. Anthony Reddie, "Peace and Justice through Black Christian Education," *Black Theology in Britain: A Journal of Contextual Praxis* 6 (2001): 81. Reddie has written extensively on Black Christian education as a prophetic tool. For a detailed study see his *Nobodies to Somebodies; Acting in Solidarity: Reflections in Critical Christianity* (London: Darton, Longman and Todd, 2005); *Dramatizing Theology: A Participative Approach to Black God-Talk* (London: Equinox, 2006).

30. Walter Brueggemann, *The Prophetic Imagination* (Philadelphia: Fortress Press, 1978), 13. See also his *Theology of the Old Testament: Testimony Dispute, Advocacy* (Minneapolis: Augsburg Fortress, 1977); *An Introduction to the Old Testament: The Canon and Christian Imagination* (Louisville: Westminster John Knox Press, 2003). For the major theological works, see George A. Lindbeck, *The Nature of Doctrine: Religion and Theology in a Postliberal Age* (Philadelphia: Westminster Press, 1984); Stanley Hauerwas, *After Christendom* (Nashville: Abingdon Press, 1991).

31. Albert Raboteau, *Slave Religion* (New York: Oxford University Press, 1978).

32. E. Franklin Frazier, *The Negro Church in America* (New York: Schocken Books, 1964); see also Hart M. Nelson and Anne K. Nelson, *Black Church in the Sixties* (Kentucky: University of Kentucky Press, 1975); Benjamin E. Mays and Joseph W. Nicholson, *The Negro's Church* (New York: Russell & Russell, 1933).

33. Dale Andrews, *Practical Theology for Black Churches: Bridging Black Theology and African American Folk Religion* (Louisville: Westminster John Knox Press, 2002).

34. James, *Holding Aloft the Banner of Ethiopia*, 122–94; see also Calvin B. Holder, "The Rise of the West Indian Politician in New York City, 1900–1952," *Afro-American in New York Life and History* (January 1980): 45–59; Charles Green and Basil Wilson, "The Afro-American, Caribbean Dialectic: White Incumbents in Black Constituents and the 1984 Election in New York City," *Afro-Americans in New York Life and History* (January

1987): 49–65; Bert J. Thomas, "Historical Functions of Caribbean-American Benevolent/ Progressive Associations," *Afro-Americans in New York Life and History* (July 1988): 45–57.

35. Irma Watkins-Owens, *Blood Relations: Caribbean Immigrants and the Harlem Community, 1900–1930* (Indianapolis: Indiana University Press, 1996), 64–70.

36. Philip Kasinitz, *Caribbean New York: Black Immigrants and the Politics of Race* (Ithaca: Cornel University Press, 1992), 115.

37. Kasinitz, *Caribbean New York*, 119.

38. Elizabeth Thomas-Hope, "Caribbean Identity: A Matter of Perception," in *Perspective on Caribbean Regional Identity*, ed. Elizabeth Thomas-Hope (Liverpool: Center for Latin American Studies, University of Liverpool, 1984), 113. For discussion on forging Caribbean identity, see Shridath S. Ramphel, "Dialogue of Unity: A Search for West Indian Identity," Ecumenical Consultation for Development, Trinidad, 16 November 1971; William G. Demas, ed., *West Indian Nationhood and Caribbean Integration* (Barbados: CCC Publishing House, 1974).

39. Bert J. Thomas, "Historical Functions of Caribbean-American Benevolent/ Progressive Associations," *Afro-Americans in New York Life and History* (July 1988): 53–54.

40. Dennis Conway, "The Caribbean Diaspora," in *Understanding the Contemporary Caribbean*, eds Richard S. Hillman and Thomas J. D. Agostino (Kingston: Ian Randle Publishers, 2003), 349–50.

41. Mark Sturge, *Look What The Lord Has Done: An Exploration of Black Christian Faith in Britain* (Bletchley: Scripture Union, 2005). The Black Church in Britain has an umbrella organization, the African Caribbean Evangelical Association. The origin and membership are constituted primarily of the Caribbean people. The Caribbean diaspora church in North America does not have a similar organization. Instead, the churches exist as individual congregations and as members within a particular denomination such as the Episcopalian, Baptists, Presbyterian, Methodist, Church of the Nazarene or within one of the churches in the Pentecostal tradition such as the Apostolic, Church of God, Cleveland Tennessee or as Non-denominational church. See, for example, F. Diannie Forde, *Caribbean Americans in New York City 1895–1975* (South Carolina: Arcadia Press, 2002), 76–87. This aspect of the Caribbean diasporan church in North America is an unexplored area of theological study. In this regard, no documented account can be given about this church. However, there are organizations such as the Caribbean Ministers Fellowship which functions as an ecumenical clergy fellowship and the Caribbean Diaspora Baptist Clergy Association which is still in its formative existence.

42. Frances Henry, *The Caribbean Diaspora in Canada: Learning to Live with Racism* (Toronto: University of Toronto Press, 1994), 152–58. For an illustrative account, see the *Bronxwood International Church of God 1976–2000* (New York: Beehive Press, 2000). The membership of most Caribbean diasporan churches are comprised of people from the various Caribbean countries. The Bronxwood International Church of God is representative of this phenomenon. In order to reflect the national diversity, many of these churches observe Caribbean Day and/or International Day celebration. Also, the flag of each country, represented in the membership of the church, is posted permanently in the church.

43. Kasinitz, *Caribbean New York*, 122.

44. Hyacinth Thomas, personal communication, 1999. This was the common perception of the area where the church is located.

45. Omar McRoberts, *Streets of Glory: Church and Community in a Black Urban Neighborhood* (Chicago: University of Chicago Press, 2003), 102.

46. McRoberts, *Streets of Glory*, 86.

47. Jürgen Moltmann, *Theology of Hope* (New York: Harper & Row, 1977), 16. Moltmann's position resonates with that of Black liberation theology. See James H. Cone, *Black Theology and Black Power* (New York: Seabury Press, 1969); *God of the Oppressed* (New York: Seabury Press, 1975); James H. Cone and Gayraud Wilmore, eds, *Black Theology: A Documentary History*, 2 vols. (Maryknoll: Orbis Books, 1993); Robert Beckford, *Jesus is Dread: Black Theology and Black Culture in Britain* (London: Darton, Longman and Todd, 1998); George C. L. Cummings, "Slave Narratives as a Source of Black Theological Discourse," in *Cut Loose Your Stammering Tongue: Black Theology in the Slave Narratives*, eds Dwight N. Hopkins and George Cummings (New York: Orbis Books, 1991).

48. Jürgen Moltmann, *The Crucified God* (New York: Harper & Row, 1975), 43.

49. Andrews, *Practical Theology for Black Churches*, 47.

50. Andrews, *Practical Theology for Black Churches*, 47.

51. Moltmann, *Church in the Power of the Spirit*, 133–34.

52. Neville Callam, "Ethnicity and the Church's Catholicity: Ministry to the Caribbean Diaspora in North America," Grace Baptist Chapel Conference on the Caribbean Diasporan Church, New York, September 15, 2002.

53. Frances Henry, *The Caribbean Diaspora in Toronto*, 148–56. In addition, see F. Donnie Forde, *Caribbean Americans in New York City 1895–1975* (South Carolina: Arcadia Publishing, 2002), 87–96.

54. There is no unitary understanding of home. For an exploration of this view, see Barbara L. Shaw-Perry, "(Re)Imagining Home: Migration and Cultural Identity in Contemporary Africa-Caribbean/British Women's Literature," MA thesis, University of Birmingham, 2000. Although Shaw-Perry argues that home is not a fixed place and thus the meaning changes, her understanding is too individualistic. She argues that home is a personally created space. This view is clearly rooted in Euro-American thought and not in the Caribbean culture and heritage such as the community that is rooted in the Caribbean African heritage. Shaw-Perry also does not reflect a Christian understanding of home which means community. For different perspectives on the meaning of home but also representing the diversity of meanings, see Yvonne Bobb-Smith, *I Know Who I Am: A Caribbean Woman's Identity in Canada* (Toronto: Women's Press, 2003), 107–89.

55. The term "home" is a general motif in Caribbean diasporan thought. It has been interpreted in a variety of ways. Most notably is the meaning of home as a return to the ancestral homeland as seen in the thought of Marcus Garvey defined in his "Back to Africa movement." See E. David Cronon, *Black Moses: The Story of Marcus Garvey and the Universal Negro Improvement Association* (Madison: University of Wisconsin Press, 1955), 179–201; John Henrik Clarke, ed., *Marcus Garvey and the Vision of Africa* (New York: Vintage Books, 1974); Amy Jacques Garvey, *Philosophy and Opinions of Marcus Garvey*, 2 vols., rpt (New York: Antheneum, 1980); Judith Stein, *The World of Marcus Garvey: Race and Class in Modern Society* (Baton Rouge: Louisiana State University Press, 1986), 108–27 and 209–22.

56. The most recent use refers to returning to the native or national homeland which most immigrants seek to do. For further exploration of this issue, see William Safran, "Diasporas in Modern Societies: Myths of Homeland and Return," *Diaspora* 1.1

(Spring 1991): 83–99; George Gemelch, *Double Passage: The Lives of Caribbean Migrants Abroad and Back Home* (Ann Arbor: University of Michigan, 1992); Elliot P. Skinner, "The Dialectic between Diaspora and Homelands," in *Global Dimensions of the African Diaspora*, ed. Joseph E. Harris (Washington DC: Howard University Press, 1993), 11–40; Mary Chamberlain, *Narratives of Exile and Return* (London: Macmillan, 1997); Frances Henry and Dwaine E. Plaza, *Returning to the Source: The Final Stage of Caribbean Migration Circuit* (Kingston: University of the West Indies Press, 2006).

57. Heather Hathaway, *Caribbean Waves* (Indianapolis: Indiana University Press, 1999), 29.

58. Hathaway, *Caribbean Waves*, 29.

59. Hathaway, *Caribbean Waves*, 29. McKay represents the Caribbean diasporan experience not only because he is a Caribbeaner but because of the nature of his life. Hathaway's definition of migrant is another way of defining a pilgrim. The pilgrim is never settled. She is always seeking a better place, a home which resonates with the biblical understanding. See Hebrews 11:8–10.

60. Claude McKay, *Home to Harlem* (London: The X Press, 2000), 232.

61. McKay, *Home to Harlem*, 152–53.

62. Claude McKay, *A Long Way from Home* (New York: Harcourt, 1970).

63. Claude McKay, "I Shall Return," in *Selected Poems of Claude McKay*, ed. Max Eastman (New York: Harvest/HBJ Books, 1953), 32.

64. Samuel Selvon, *Lonely Londoners* (New York: Longman, 1956), 140–41.

65. Selvon, *Lonely Londoners*, 141–42.

66. Bobb-Smith, *I Know Who I Am*, 107–27.

67. Anthony Reddie, "Singing the Lord's Song in a Strange Land," *Black Theology in Britain* 4.2 (2002): 191.

Conclusion

1. Stuart Hall, "Introduction: Who Needs an Identity?" in *Questions of Cultural Identity*, eds Stuart Hall and Paul Du Gay (London: Sage Publications, 1996), 1–18; see also Waktraud Kokot, Khachig Tololyan and Carolin Alfonso, *Diaspora, Identity and Religion* (New York: Routledge, 2004).

2. Elizabeth Thomas-Hope, *Caribbean Migration* (Kingston: University of the West Indies Press, 2002); see also George L. Beckford, *Persistent Poverty: Underdevelopment in Plantation Economies of the Third World* (London: Zed Books, 1983); Alan Cobley, ed., *Crossroads of Empire: The Europe-Caribbean Connection 1492–1992* (Barbados: Department of History, University of the West Indies, 1994).

3. Hyacinth Booth, "The Place of Women in Christ's Church," in *The Caribbean Pulpit*, eds C. H. L. and W. W. Watty (Barbados: Cedar Press, 1983), 12–19. See also Barbel V. Wartenberg-Porter, "Women and the Ministry of the Church," in *The David Jellyman Lectures* (Kingston: Jamaica Baptist Union, 1989), 73–87.

4. Irma Watkins-Owens, "Early-Twentieth Century Caribbean Women: Migration and Social Networks in New York," in *Islands in the City: West Indian Migration to New York*, ed. Nancy Foner (Berkeley: University of California Press, 2001), 25–51.

5. Demetrius K. Williams, *An End to This Strife: The Politics of Gender in African American Churches* (Minneapolis: Fortress Press, 2004), 190.

6. Williams, *An End to This Strife*, 190.

7. Cheryl Townsend Gilkes, *If it Wasn't for the Women* (New York: Orbis Books, 2001), 7.

8. Kortright Davis, *Emancipation Still Comin': Explorations in Caribbean Emancipatory Theology* (New York: Orbis Books, 1990), 50. For a challenging account of African-based religion in the Caribbean, see Dianne M. Stewart, *Three Eyes for the Journey: African Dimensions of the Jamaican Religious Experience* (New York: Oxford University Press, 2005).

9. Davis, *Emancipation Still Comin'*, 52–53.

10. Oscar L. Bolioli, *The Caribbean: Culture of Resistance, Spirit of Hope* (New York: Friendship Press, 1993), 40.

11. George Mulrain, "African Caribbean Christianity," *Journal of Interdenominational Theological Center* XVI 1 and 2 (Fall 1988–Spring 1989): 1–2.

12. Davis, *Emancipation Still Comin'*, 53.

13. Richard Taylor, *Nation Dance: Religion, Identity and Cultural Difference in the Caribbean* (Ithaca: Cornell University Press, 1989), 1–13.

14. Taylor, *Nation Dance*, 1–2.

15. Taylor, *Nation Dance*, 1–2.

16. Taylor, *Nation Dance*, 2.

17. Taylor, *Nation Dance*, 1–2.

18. Mulrain, "African Caribbean Christianity," 4.

19. Winston Persuad, "Caribbean Response to the Globalization of Theological Education," in *Caribbean Theology: Preparing for the Challenges Ahead*, ed. Howard Gregory (Kingston: Canoe Press, University of the West Indies, 1995), 45.

20. James Cone, *For My People: Black Theology and the Black Church: Where have we been and where are we going?* (New York: Orbis Books, 1984), 11–18.

21. Mark Sturge, *Look What the Lord Has Done! An Exploration of Black Christian Faith in Britain* (Bletchley: Scripture Union, 2005), 39–59. While I call attention to these examples of Black ecumenism, the individual member organization may not necessarily be defined by nor subscribe to Black theology. For an excellent account of this perspective, see Anthony G. Reddie, *Black Theology in Transatlantic Dialogue* (New York: Palgrave Macmillan, 2006), 16–18.

22. Dwight N. Hopkins, *Head and Heart: Black Theology Past, Present and Future* (New York: Palgrave, 2002), 19. For an excellent resource on the direction and future of Black theology, see Linda E. Thomas, ed., *Living Stones in the Household of God: The Legacy and Future of Black Theology* (Minneapolis: Fortress Press, 2004).

23. Hopkins, *Head and Heart*, 129; see also Cornel West, *Democracy Matters: Winning the Fight against Imperialism* (New York: Penguin Books, 2004).

24. Hopkins, *Head and Heart*, 19. For an insider account on the material prosperity religion, see Milmon F. Harrison, *Righteous Riches: The Word of Faith Movement in Contemporary African American Religion* (New York: Oxford University Press, 2005).

25. West, *Democracy Matters*, 145–72. For a vision of the "Just Society" from the perspective of American liberal Protestantism, see Gary Dorrien, *Soul in Society: The Making and Renewal of Social Christianity* (Minneapolis: Fortress Press, 1995). For a progressive Evangelical perspective, see Jim Wallis, *God's Politics: Why the Right Gets It Wrong and the Left Does Not Get It* (San Francisco: HarperCollins, 2005).

Select Bibliography

Aldred, Joseph. "Paradigms for a Black Theology in Britain." *Black Theology: An International Journal* 2 (1999).

Alexander, Valentina. "Afrocentric and Black Christian Consciousness: Towards an Honest Intersection." *Black Theology International Journal* 1 (1998).

———. "Breaking Every Fever?' To What Extent has the Black led Church in Britain Developed a Theology of Liberation?" PhD thesis. University of Warwick, 1989.

Alleyne, Mervyn. *Roots of Jamaican Culture*. London: Pluto Press, 1988.

Andrews, Dale. *Practical Theology for Black Churches: Bridging Black Theology and African American Folk Religion*. Louisville: Westminster John Knox Press, 2002.

Ascension Peace Presbyterian Church. *Tenth Anniversary Journal*. Florida, 2003.

Associated Gospel Assembly-USA. "Draft No. 5 Final: Policy and Procedure – AGA-USA."

Austin-Broos, Diane J. *Jamaica Genesis: Religion and the Politics of Moral Order*. Kingston: Ian Randle Publishers, 1997.

Baker-Fletcher, Karen. *A Singing Something: Womanist Reflections on Anna Julia Cooper*. New York: Crossroad, 1994.

Baker-Fletcher, Karen and Garth Baker-Fletcher. *My Sister, My Brother: Womanist and Exodus God-Talk*. New York: Orbis Books, 1997.

Baptist Missionary Society, Minutes of General Meeting, January 23–24, 1962.

Barrow, Christine. "Living in Sin: Church and Common-Law Union in Barbados." *The Journal of Caribbean History* 29, no. 2 (1995).

Barton, Mukti. *Rejection, Resistance and Resurrection: Speaking out on Racism in the Church*. London: Darton, Longman and Todd, 2005.

Battle, Michael, ed. *The Quest for Liberation and Reconciliation: Essays in Honor of J. Deotis Roberts*. Kentucky: Westminster John Knox Press, 2005.

Beckford, Robert. *Jesus is Dread: Black Theology and Black Culture in Britain*. London: Darton, Longman and Todd, 1998.

———. *Dread and Pentecostal: A Political Theology for the Black Church in Britain*. London: SPCK, 2000.

Bellah, Robert et al. eds. *Habits of the Heart: Individualism and Commitment in America*. New York: Harper and Row, 1985.

Benn, Denis. *The Caribbean: An Intellectual History 1774–2003*. Kingston: Ian Randle Publishers, 2004.

Bevans, Stephen B. *Models of Contextual Theology: Faith and Cultures*. New York: Orbis Books, 1992.

Bisnauth, Dale. *A History of Religion in the Caribbean*. Kingston: Kingston Publishers 1990.

Blount, Brian K. *Can I Get a Witness? Reading Revelation through African American Culture*. Louisville: Westminster John Knox Press, 2005.

Bob-Smith, Yvonne. *I Know Who I Am: A Caribbean Woman's Identity in Canada*. Toronto: Women's Press, 2003.

Bolioli, Oscar L. *The Caribbean: Culture of Resistance, Spirit of Hope*. New York: Friendship Press, 1993.

Bollard, O. Nigel. "Creolisation and Creole Societies: A Cultural Nationalist View of Caribbean Social History." *Caribbean Quarterly* 44, nos. 1–2 (1998).

Booth, Hyacinth. "The Place of Women in Christ's Church." In *The Caribbean Pulpit*, eds C. H. L. Gayle and W. W. Watty. Barbados: Cedar Press, 1983.

Bosch, David J. *Transforming Mission: Paradigm Shifts in Theology of Mission*. New York: Orbis Books, 1991.

Brandt, Lilian. "The Make up of Negro City Groups." *Charities*, xv (1905).

Brathwaite, Kamau. *Nanny, Sam Sharp and the Struggle for People's Liberation*. Kingston: National Heritage Week Committee, 1977.

Braziel, Jana Evans and Anita Mannur, eds. *Theorizing Diaspora*. Massachusetts: Blackwell, 2003.

Bronx Baptist Church. *The Constitution of the Bronx Baptist Church*. 1966.

———. *35 Years: Hand in Hand with God*. New York, 2001.

Bronx Bethany Church of the Nazarene. *Journal of Bronx Bethany Church of the Nazarene 1964–1999: 35 Years of Ministerial Excellence*. New York, 1999.

Bronxwood International Church of God. *Journal of Bronxwood International Church of God 1976–2000*. Bronx: Beehive Press, 2000.

Brown, Egbert Ethelred. "A Challenging Question." In Brown Papers, Box 2, Folder 3. Schomburg Center for Research in Black Culture.

———. "I Have Two Dreams." In Brown Papers, Box 1, Folder 3. Schomburg Center for Research in Black Culture.

———. "If Jesus Came to Harlem, Whom Would He Denounce?" In Brown Papers, Box 4, Folder 2. Schomburg Center for Research in Black Culture.

———. "The History of Harlem Unitarian Church." In Brown Papers, Box 1, Folder 6. Schomburg Center for Research in Black Culture.

———. "The Search for Truth." In Brown Papers, Box 4, Folder 2. Schomburg Center for Research in Black Culture.

Bruce, F. F. *The Acts of the Apostles*. Michigan: Eerdmans, 1965.

Brueggemann, Walter. *The Prophetic Imagination*. Philadelphia: Fortress Press, 1978.

———. *A Commentary on Jeremiah: Exile and Homecoming*. Michigan: Eerdmans, 1998.

Bryce-Laporte, Roy Simon. "Black Immigrants: The Experience of Invisibility and Insecurity." *Journal of Black Studies* 3 (September 1972).

Burkett, Randall. *Garveyism as a Religious Movement: The Institutionalization of Black Religion*. New Jersey: The Scarecrow Press Inc. and The American Theological Library Association, 1978.

———. *Church Advocate* 17, no. 5 (March 1908).

Bush, George H. W. Letter cited in *Celebrating God's Wonderful Works: Church's 80th Anniversary, Pastor's 21st Anniversary*. Washington DC, 1990.

Callahan, Allan. *Embassy of Onesimus: The Letter of Paul to Philemon*. Valley Forge: Trinity Press International, 1997.

Callam, Neville. *Deciding Responsibly: Moral Dimensions of Human Action*. Kingston: Jamaica Baptist Union, 1985.

———. "Ethnicity and the Church's Catholicity: Ministry to the Caribbean Diaspora in North America." Unpublished paper, Grace Baptist Chapel Anniversary Lecture, New York, 2002.

————. "Understanding Mission: A Global Perspective." Unpublished paper, Jamaica Baptist Union Mission Conference. Ocho Rios, November 2003.

Callam, Neville, ed. *Moral Responsibility: Issues in Church and Society*. Kingston: Tarrant Baptist Church, 1993.

Campbell, Mavis C. *The Maroons of Jamaica, 1655–1796: A History of Resistance, Collaboration and Betrayal*. Trenton: Africa Third World Press, 1990.

Cannon, Katie. *Katie's Canon: Womanism and the Soul of the Black Community*. New York: Continuum, 1996.

Carmichael, Stokely (Kwame Ture) and Charles B. Hamilton. *Black Power: The Politics of Liberation*. New York: Vintage Books, 1992.

Carrier, Herveé. *Evangelizing the Culture of Modernity*. New York: Orbis Books, 1993.

Carson, Clayborne. *In Struggle: SNCC and the Black Awakening of the 1960s*. Massachusetts: Harvard University Press, 1995.

Chaney, Elsa. "The Context of Caribbean Migration." In *Caribbean Life in New York: Social Cultural Dimensions*, eds Constance Sutton and Elsa M. Chaney. New York: Center for Migration Studies of New York Inc., 1992.

Chevannes, Barry. "Our Caribbean Reality." In *Caribbean Theology: Preparing for the Challenges Ahead*, ed. Howard Gregory. Kingston: Canoe Press, 1995.

————. *Betwixt and Between: Explorations in an African-Caribbean Mindscape*. Kingston: Ian Randle Publishers, 2006.

Christian, Mark, ed. *Black Identity of the 20th Century: Expressions of the US and UK African Diaspora*. London: Hansib Publications, 2002.

Christway Baptist Church. *Journal of Christway Baptist Church*. Florida.

Cipola, Benedicta. "Immigration in America: Religion and Assimilation." In *Religion and Ethics: News Weekly*. New York: Thirteen WNET, 2005.

Clark, Wayne C. *The Meaning of Church Membership*. Valley Forge: Judson Press, 1992.

Cleage, Albert. *The Black Messiah*. New York: Sheed and Ward, 1968.

Coatley, David Emmanuel, ed. *Black Religion, Black Theology: The Collected Essays of J. Deotis Roberts*. New York: Trinity Press International, 2003.

Cohen, Robin. *Global Diasporas: An Introduction*. London: UCL Press, 1997.

————. "Cultural Diaspora: The Case of the Caribbean." In *Caribbean Migration Globalised Identities*, ed. Mary Chamberlain. New York: Routledge, 1998.

Cole, Dorothy. "Interview," in *Journal of Bronx Bethany Church of the Nazarene 1964–1999: 35 Years of Ministerial Excellence*. New York, 1999.

Cole, V. Seymour. Statement cited in *Journal of Bronx Bethany Church of the Nazarene 1964–1999: 35 Years of Ministerial Excellence*. New York, 1999.

Coleman, Kate. "Black Theology and Black Liberation: A Womanist Perspective." *Black Theology in Britain: A Journal for Contextual Praxis* 1 (1998).

Cone, James. *Black Theology of Liberation*. New York: J. B. Lippincott Co., 1970.

————. *God of the Oppressed*. New York: Seabury Press, 1975.

————. *For My People: Black Theology and the Black Church: Where have we been and where are we going?* New York: Orbis Books, 1984.

————. *My Soul Looks Back*. New York: Orbis Books, 1986.

————. *Speaking the Truth: Ecumenism, Liberation and Black Theology*. Michigan: Eerdmans, 1986.

————. *The Spiritual and the Blues*. New York: Orbis Books, 1992.

————. "Theology: Great Sin: Silence in the Face of White Supremacy." *Black Theology in Britain: A Journal for Contextual Praxis* 2:2 (2004).

————. "Loving God with Our Heart, Soul and Mind." In *Blow the Trumpet in Zion: Global Vision and Action for the 21ˢᵗ-century Black Church*, eds. Iva E. Carruthers, Frederick D. Haynes III and Jeremiah A. Wright Jr. Minneapolis: Fortress Press, 2005.

————. "Strange Fruit: The Cross and the Lynching Tree." *Harvard Divinity Bulletin* (Winter 2007). Cone, James H. and Gayraud Wilmore, eds. *Black Theology: A Documentary History: 1966–1972, Vol. 1*. New York: Orbis Books, 1979.

————. *Black Theology: A Documentary History: 1980–1992, Vol. 2*. New York: Orbis Books, 1993.

Conn, Charles W. *Like a Mighty Army: A History of the Church of God*. Tennessee: Pathway Press, 1977.

Conway, Dennis. "The Caribbean Diaspora." In *Understanding the Contemporary Caribbean*, eds. Richard S. Hillman and Thomas J. D'Agostino. Kingston: Ian Randle Publishers, 2003.

Craddock, Fred. *Philippians: A Bible Commentary for Teaching and Preaching*. Atlanta: John Knox Press, 1985.

————. *Luke: Interpretation A Commentary for Teaching and Preaching*. Louisville: John Knox Press, 1990.

Cromwell, Adelaide. *The Other Brahmins: Boston's Black Upper Class, 1750–1950*. Fayettville: University of Arkansas Press, 1994.

Cronon, E. David. *Black Moses: The Story of Marcus Garvey*. Madison: University of Wisconsin Press, 1955.

Crummel, Alexander. "The Progress of Civilization along the West Coast of Africa." In *Classical Black Nationalism: From the American Revolution to Marcus Garvey*, ed. Wilson Moses. New York: New York University Press, 1996.

Cruse, Harold. *The Crisis of Negro Intellectuals: A Historical Analysis of the Failure of Black Leadership*. New York: Quill, 1967.

Cudjoe, Selwyn R. and William E. Cain, eds. *C.L.R. James: His Intellectual Legacies*. Massachusetts: University of Massachusetts Press, 1995.

Curtin, Philip. *Two Jamaicans: The Role of Ideas in a Tropical Colony, 1830–1865*. New York: Atheneum, 1970.

Davis, Kortright. "Jesus Christ and Black Liberation." *Journal of Religious Thought* 42, no. 1 (Summer–Fall 1985).

————. *Emancipation Still Comin': Explorations in Caribbean Emancipatory Theology*. New York: Orbis Books, 1990.

————. *Can God Save the Church: Living Faith While Keeping Church*. Missouri: Hodale Press Inc., 1994.

————. "Living the Faith in a Strange Land." Unpublished paper, Grace Baptist Chapel Anniversary Lecture. New York, September 21, 2002.

Dawes, Mark. "Mind and Spirit – Evangelical Alliance: A Model Organization." *Jamaica Gleaner*, January 7, 2006.

Dayfoot, Arthur Charles. *The Shaping of the West Indian Church 1492–1962*. Kingston: University of the West Indies Press, 1999.

Demas, William G. *West Indian Nationhood and Caribbean Integration*. Barbados: CCC Publication, 1974.

Domingo, W. A. "Gifts to the Black Tropics." In *The American*, ed. Alain Lock. New York: Arno Press, 1968.

Dulles, Avery. *Models of the Church*. Dublin: Gill and McMillan, 1974.

———. *Models of Revelation*. New York: Orbis Books, 1983.

Edwards, Joel. "The British Afro-Caribbean Community." In *Britain on the Brink: Major Trends in Society Today*, ed. Martyn Eden. Nottingham: Crossway Books, 1993.

Engel, Elliot. Letter cited in *25ᵗʰ Anniversary Journal of Wake Eden Community Baptist Church*. New York, 1997.

Erskine, Noel. *Decolonizing Theology: A Caribbean Perspective*. New York: Orbis Books, 1981.

Evans, James. *We Have Been Believers: An African American Systematic Theology*. Minneapolis: Fortress Press, 1992.

Evans, Jana and Anita Mannur, eds. *Theorizing Diaspora*. Oxford: Blackwell, 2003.

Fairweather, Eugene R. "The Kenotic Christology." In *The Epistle to the Phillipians*, ed. F. W. Beare. London: Adam and Charles Black, 1959.

Fitzmyer, Joseph A., SJ. *The Gospel According to Luke*. Garden City: Doubleday & Co., 1985.

Foner, Nancy, ed. *Island in the Sun: West Indian Migration to New York City*. California: University of California Press, 2001.

Foner, Phillip S., ed. *W.E.B. Dubois Speaks 1890–1999*. New York: Pathfinder Press, 1970.

Forde, F. Dionne. *Images of America: Caribbean Americans in New York 1895–1975*. Charleston: Arcadia Publishing, 2002.

Forsythe, Dennis. "West Indian Radicalism in America: An Assessment of Ideologies." In *Ethnicity in the Americas*, ed. Frances Henry. The Hague: Mouton, 1976.

Franklin, Vincent. "Caribbean Intellectual Influences on Afro-Americans in the United States." In *Intellectuals in Twentieth Century Caribbean*, ed. Alistair Henessy. London: Macmillan Press, 1992.

Frazier, E. Franklin. *The Negro Church in America*. New York: Schocken Books, 1964.

Garvey, Amy J. *Philosophy and Opinion of Marcus Garvey*. New Jersey: Frank Crass and Co., 1967.

Gaustad, Edwin Scott. *A Religious History of America*. New York: Harper & Row, 1990.

Gayle, Clement. *George Liele: Pioneer Missionary to Jamaica*. Kingston: Jamaica Baptist Union, 1982.

Gilkes, Cheryl Townsend. *If It Wasn't for the Women*. New York: Orbis Books, 2001.

Gilroy, Paul. *There Ain't No Black in the Union Jack: The Cultural Politics of Race and Nation*. Chicago: University of Chicago Press, 1991.

———. *The Black Atlantic, Modernity and Double Consciousness*. Massachusetts: Harvard University Press, 1993.

———. "It ain't where you're from, it's where you are at… The Dialectics of Diasporic Identification." In *Migration, Diasporas and Transnationalism*, eds Steven Vertovec and Robin Cohen. Northampton: Edgar Elgar, 1999.

Godson, Albert. "We've Come This Far by Faith." In *Lift Every Voice and Sing: An African American Hymnal*. New York: The Church Hymnal Corporation, 1993.

Gonzalez, Justo I. *The Story of Christianity Vol. 2*. Massachusetts: HarperCollins, 1984.

Gordon, Shirley. *God Almighty Make Me Free: Christianity in Pre-Emancipation Jamaica*. Indianapolis: Indiana University Press, 1996.

———. *Our Cause for His Glory: Christianization and Emancipation in Jamaica*. Kingston: University of the West Indies Press, 1998.

Gottlieb, Karla. *Mother of Us All: A History of Queen Nanny, Leader of the Windward Jamaica Maroons*. New Jersey: Africa Third World Press, 2000.

Grace Baptist Chapel. *Journal of Grace Baptist Chapel*. New York: Troy Printing, 2000.

Grant, Jacquelyn. *White Women's Christ and Black Women's Jesus: Feminist Christology and Womanist Response*. Atlanta: Scholars Press, 1989.

Green, Joel B. *The Gospel of Luke*. Grand Rapids: Eerdsmans, 1977.

Gregory, Howard, ed. *Caribbean Theology: Preparing for the Challenges Ahead* Kingston: Canoe Press, University of the West Indies, 1995.

Hall, Stuart. *Myths of Caribbean Identity: The Walter Rodney Memorial Lecture*. Warwick, UK: University of Warwick, 1991.

———. "Introduction: Who Needs an Identity?" In *Questions of Cultural Identity*, eds Stuart Hall and Paul Du Gay. London: Sage Publications, 1996.

———. "Cultural Identity and Diaspora." In *Theorizing Diaspora*, eds Jana Evans and Anita Mannur. Oxford: Blackwell, 2003.

Halverson, Richard C. Letter cited in *Celebrating God's Wonderful Works: Church's 80th Anniversary, Pastor's 21st Anniversary*. Washington DC, 1990.

Hamid, Idris, ed. *Out of the Depths*. San Fernando: St. Andrews Theological College, 1977.

Harris, James H. *Pastoral Theology: A Black Church Perspective*. Minneapolis: Fortress Press, 1991.

Harris, Joseph. *Global Dimension of the African Diaspora*. Washington DC: Howard University Press, 1982.

Harris, Winston and Clive, eds. *Inside Babylon: The Caribbean Diaspora in Britain*. London: Verso Press, 1983.

Hart, Richard. *Slaves Who Abolished Slavery: Blacks in Rebellion*. Kingston: University of the West Indies Press, 2002.

Harvey, Anthony, ed. *Theology in the City: A Theological Response to Faith in the City*. London: SPCK, 1989.

Hatch, Nathan. *The Democratization of American Society*. Connecticut: Yale University Press, 1989.

Hathaway, Heather. *Caribbean Waves*. Indianapolis: Indiana University Press, 1991.

Henry, Frances. *The Caribbean Diaspora in Canada: Learning to Live with Racism*. Toronto: University of Toronto Press, 1994.

Hernandez-Ramdwar, Camille. "Raced Caribbeans: Disproving Myths of National Identity in the Great White North." Paper presented at Conference on Caribbean Culture, Kingston, Jamaica, 1996.

Hill, Robert and Barbra Blair, eds. *Marcus Garvey and Lessons*. Berkley: University of California Press, 1987.

Hines, Samuel. Letter cited in *Celebrating God's Wonderful Works: Church's 80th Anniversary, Pastor's 21st Anniversary*. Washington DC, 1990.

Hines, Samuel and Curtis Paul DeYoung. *Beyond Rhetoric: Reconciliation as a Way of Life*. Valley Forge: Judson Press, 2000.

Holder, Calvin B. "The Causes and Composition of West Indian Immigration to New York City, 1900–1952." *Afro-Americans in New York Life and History*, 9–12 (1987).

Hopkins, Dwight. *Black Theology USA and South Africa: Politics, Culture and Liberation*. New York: Orbis Books, 1989.

———. *Shoes that Fit Our Feet: Sources for a Constructive Black Theology*. New York: Orbis Books, 1993.

———. *Head and Heart: Black Theology Past, Present and Future*. New York: Palgrave, 2002.

———. *Being Human Race: Culture and Religion*. Minneapolis: Fortress Press, 2005.

Howe, Stephen. "C.L.R. James; Visions of History, Visions of Britain." In *West Indian Intellectuals in Britain*, ed. Bill Schwartz. Manchester: Manchester University Press, 2003.

Hunte, Keith. "Protestantism and Slavery in the British Caribbean." In *Christianity in the Caribbean: Essays in Church History*, ed. Armando Lampe. Kingston: University of the West Indies Press, 2001.

Jackson, Anita. *Catching Both Sides of the Wind: Conversations with Five Black Pastors*. London: British Council of Churches, 1985.

Jagessar, Michael. *Full Life for All: The Work and Theology of Philip Potter – A Historical Survey and Systematic Analysis of Major Themes*. Zoetermeer: Boekencentrum, 1977.

———. "Cultures in Dialogue: The Contribution of a Caribbean Theologian." *Black Theology: An International Journal* 1.2 (2003).

Jagessar, Michael and Anthony G. Reddie. *Postcolonial Black British Theology: New Textures and Themes*. Peterborough: Epworth, 2007.

James, C. L. R. *Beyond a Boundary*. London: Hutchinson, 1963.

———. "The Case of West Indian Self-Government." In *The C.L.R. James Reader*, ed. Anna Grimshaw. Massachusetts: Blackwell, 1992.

James, Leslie. "Text and the Rhetoric of Change: Bible and Decolonization in Post World War II Caribbean Political Discourse." In *Religion, Culture and Tradition*, eds Hemshand Grossai and Samuel Nathaniel Murrell. London: Macmillan, 2000.

James, Winston. *Holding Aloft the Banner of Ethiopia: Caribbean Radicalism in Early Twentieth-Century America*. London: Verso, 1998.

———. *A Fierce Hatred of Injustice: Claude McKay's Jamaica and His Poetry of Rebellion*. New York: W.W. Norton & Co., Inc., 2001.

James, Winston and Clive Harris, eds. *Inside Babylon: The Caribbean Diaspora in Britain*. New York: Verso, 1993.

Kasinitz, Philip. *Caribbean New York: Black Immigrants and the Politics of Race*. Ithaca: Cornell University Press, 1992.

Knight, Franklin W. and Colin A. Palmer, eds. *The Modern Caribbean*. North Carolina: University of North Carolina Press, 1989.

Lamming, George. *The Emigrants*. London: Allison and Busby, 1990.

———. *Pleasures of Exile*. Michigan: University of Michigan Press, 1992.

———. *Coming Coming Home Conversations II: Western Education and the Caribbean Intellectual Coming, Coming, Coming Home*. St. Martin: House of Nehesi Publishers, 1995.

Lampe, Armanda, ed. *Christianity in the Caribbean*. Kingston: University of the West Indies Press, 2001.

Lathrop, John. "Letters to Ethelred Brown." In Ethelred Brown Papers, Box 1, Folder 6.

Lawson, Winston. *Religion and Race: African and European Roots in Conflict – A Jamaican Testament*. New York: Peter Lang, 1996.

Lewis, G. "Race Relations in Britain: A View from the Caribbean." *Race Today* 1, no. 3 (July 1969).

Lewis, Hortense, Statement cited in *Parkway Baptist Church Family Table Talk*. Florida, January 2004.

Lewis, Marjorie. "Diaspora Dialogue: Womanist Theology in Engagement with Aspects of the Black British and Jamaican Experience." *Black Theology: An International Journal* 2.1 (2004).

Lewis, Rupert and Patrick Bryan, eds. *Garvey: His Work and Impact*. Kingston: Institute of Social and Economic Research and the Department of Extra Mural Studies, 1988.

Lincoln, C. Eric and Lawrence H. Mamiya. *The Black Church in the African American Experience*. Durham: Duke University Press, 1990.

Linton, Neville. "Some Aspects of Political Morality in the Caribbean." In *Perspectives on Political Ethics: An Ecumenical Enquiry*. Geneva: WCC Publications, 1983.

Lynch, Hollis, ed. *Edward Wilmot Blyden: Pan-Negro Patriot (1832–1912)*. New York: Oxford University Press, 1970.

Marshall, Dawn. "A History of West Indian Migrations: Overseas Opportunities and 'Safety-Valves' Policies." In *The Caribbean Exodus*, ed. Barry Levine. New York: Praeger Publishers, 1998.

Marshall, Paula. *Brown Girl Brownstones*. New York: Feminist Press, 1981.

Maynard-Reid, *Diverse Worship: African-American, Caribbean and Hispanic Perspective*. Illinois: InterVarsity Press, 2000.

Mbiti, John S. *African Religions and Philosophy*. New York: Doubleday, 1970.

McFague, Sallie. *Speaking in Parables: A Study in Metaphor and Theology*. Philadelphia: Fortress Press, 1975.

———. *Models for God: Theology for an Ecological Nuclear Age*. Philadelphia: Fortress Press, 1987.

McFarlane, Milton C. *Cudjoe of Jamaica: Pioneer for Black Freedom in the New World*. New Jersey: R. Enslow, 1977.

McKay, Claude. "He who Gets Slap." *The Liberator*, April 5, 1922.

———. "I Shall Return." In *Selected Poems of Claude McKay*, ed. Max Eastman. New York Harvest/HBJ Books, 1953.

———. *Banjo: A Story Without a Plot*. New York: Harper & Brothers, 1957.

———. *A Long Way from Home*. New York: Harcourt, 1970.

———. *Home to Harlem*. London: The X Press, 2000.

McRoberts, Omar M. *Streets of Glory: Churches and Community in a Black Urban Neighborhood*. Chicago: University of Chicago Press, 2003.

Michem, Stephanie Y. *Introducing Womanist Theology*. New York: Orbis Books, 2002.

Migliore, Daniel L. *Faith Seeking Understanding: An Introduction to Christian Theology*. Michigan: Eerdmans, 1991.

Moltmann, Jurgen. *The Crucified God*. New York: Harper & Row, 1975.

———. *The Church in the Power of the Spirit*. London: SCM Press, 1977.

———. *Theology of Hope*. New York: HarperCollins, 1991.

———. *The Way of Jesus Christ: Christology in Messianic Dimensions*. Minnesota: Fortress Press, 1993.

Moore, Brian L., B. W. Higman, Carl Campbell and Patrick Bryan, eds. *Slavery, Freedom and Gender: The Dynamics of Caribbean Society*. Kingston: University of the West Indies Press, 2003.

Moore, Brian L. and Michele A. Johnson. *Neither Led Nor Driven: Contesting British Cultural Imperialism in Jamaica, 1865–1920*. Kingston: University of the West Indies Press, 2004.

Morgan, David. "Southern Baptist Witness to Jamaicans in America." Unpublished paper.

Morgan, Rodwell. *Meet Corn Island: The History of Corn Island in Relation to the Ebenezer Baptist Church*. Florida: Morris Publishing, 1996.

Morris, Aldon D. *The Origins of the Civil Rights Movement: Black Communities Organizing for Change*. New York: The Free Press, 1984.

Morrison-Reed, Mark D. *Black Pioneers in a White Denomination*. Boston: Beacon Press, 1984.

Moseley, Romney M. "Decolonizing Theology in the Caribbean: Prospects for Hermeneutical Reconstruction." *Toronto Journal of Theology* 6.2 (1990).

Moses, Wilson Jeremiah, ed. *Classical Black Nationalism: From the American Revolution to Marcus Garvey*. New York: New York University Press, 1996.

Mount Herman Baptist Church. *The Constitution and Laws of Mount Herman Baptist Church*. Florida: n.p.

Mulrain, George. "African Caribbean Christianity." *Journal of Interdenominational Theological Center* XVI 1 and 2 (Fall 1988–Spring 1989).

Murphy, Joseph M. *Working the Spirit: Ceremonies of the African People*. Massachusetts: Beacon Press, 1994.

Nettleford, Rex. *Inward Stretch Outward Reach: A Voice from the Caribbean*. London: Macmillan Press, 1993.

Noland, John. *Word Biblical Commentary: Luke 1–9:20*. Dallas: Word, 1989. Olivet Gospel Church. *The Laws of Olivet Gospel Church*. New York: n.p.

Palmer, Ransford W. *In Search of a Better Life: Perspective on Migration from the Caribbean*. New York: Praeger Publishers, 1990.

———. *Pilgrims from the Sun: West Indian Migration to America*. New York: Twayne Publishers, 1995.

Panton, Vivian. *The Church and Common-Law Union*. Kingston: Ebony Printers, 1992.

Paris, Peter. *The Spirituality of African Peoples: The Search for a Common Moral Discourse*. Minnesota: Augsburg Fortress Press, 1995.

Parkway Baptist Church. "Mission Statement." *Family Table Talk*. Miami, January 2004.

Persaud, Winston. "Caribbean Response to the Globalization of Theological Education." In *Caribbean Theology: Preparing for the Challenges Ahead*, ed. Howard Gregory. Kingston: Canoe Press, 1995.

Pinn, Anthony B. *Why Lord: Suffering and Evil in Black Theology*. New York: Continuum, 1995.

———. *Varieties of African American Religious Experience*. Minneapolis: Fortress Press, 1998.

Popkin, Richard H. "Hume's Racism." *The Philosophical Forum* 9.2–3 (Winter–Spring 1977).

Potter, Philip. "Christ's Mission and Ours in Today's World." *International Review of Mission* 62/246 (April 1973).

———. "From Missions to Mission." *International Review of Mission* 76/302 (April 1987).

Raboteau, Albert. *Slave Religion: The 'Invisible Religion' in the Antebellum South*. New York: Oxford University Press, 1978.

Raphael, Lennox. "West Indians and Afro-Americans." *Freedom Ways* 4 (1964).

Reddie, Anthony. *Faith, Stories, and the Experience of Black Elders: Singing the Lord's Song in a Strange Land*. London: Jessica Kingsley Publishers, 1998.

———. "Peace and Justice through Black Christian Education." *Black Theology in Britain: A Journal of Contextual Praxis* 6 (2001).

———. "Singing the Lord's Song in a Strange Land." *Black Theology in Britain* 4.2 (2002).

———. *Black Theology in Transatlantic Dialogue*. New York: Palgrave Macmillan, 2006.

Reid, C. S. *Church, Morality and Democracy*. Kingston: The Bustamante Institute of Public and International Affairs, 1986.

———. *Samuel Sharpe: From Slave to National Hero*. Kingston: Bustamante Institute of Public and National Affairs, 1988.

Reid, Ira. *The Negro Immigrant: His Background, Characteristics and Social Adjustments, 1899–1937*. New York: Arno Press and The New York Times, 1969.

Rhoads, David. *The Challenge of Diversity: The Witness of Paul and the Gospel*. Minnesota: Fortress Press, 1996.

Richardson, Bonham. *Caribbean Migrants: Environment and Human Survival on St. Kitts and Nevis*. Knoxville: University of Tennessee Press, 1983.

Riggs, Marcia. *Awake, Arise and Act: A Womanist Call for Black Liberation*. Cleveland: Pilgrim Press, 1994.

Roberts, J. Deotis. *Black Theology in Dialogue*. Philadelphia: Westminster Press, 1987.

———. *Liberation and Reconciliation: A Black Theology*. New York: Orbis Books, 1994.

———. *The Prophethood of Black Believers: An African American Political Theology for Ministry*. Kentucky: Westminster/John Knox Press, 1994.

Roberts, W. A. *Six Great Jamaicans (Biographical Sketches)*. Kingston: Pioneer Press, 1951.

Robinson, Carey. *The Fighting Maroons of Jamaica*. London: Collins, 1969.

Rodney, Walter. *The Groundings with my Brothers*. London: Bogle-L'Ouverture Publications, 1969.

Rogers, Reuel. "Black Like Who?" In *Island in the City: West Indian Migration to New York*, ed. Nancy Foner. California: University of California Press, 2001.

Russell, Horace O. *The Missionary Outreach of the West Indian Church: Jamaica Baptist Missions to West Africa in the Nineteenth Century*. New York: Peter Lang, 2000.

———. *JBMS in Mission: The Lessons and the Legacies*. Mission Conference Jamaica Baptist Union Mission Conference. Jamaica: Grande Hotel, Ocho Rios, November 2003.

Safran, William. "Diasporas in Modern Societies: Myths of Homeland and Return." *Diaspora* 1.1 (1991).

Sanders, Cheryl J. *How Firm a Foundation: Eighty Years of History (1910–1990) Third Street Church of God*. Washington, DC: Third Street Church of God, 1990.

Sanders, Cheryl J., ed. *Living the Intersection: Womanism and Afrocentrism in Theology*. Minneapolis: Fortress Press, 1995.

Schineller, Peter. "Christ and the Church: A Spectrum of Views." In *Why the Church?* eds Walter Burnhardt and William Thompson. New Jersey: Paulist Press, 1977.

Scholes, T. E. S. *Glimpses of the Ages: or the 'Superior' and Inferior Races so-called Discussed in Light of Science and History*. London: John Long, vol. I (1995); vol. II (1908).

Schwarz, Bill, ed. *West Indian Intellectuals in Britain*. Manchester: Manchester University Press, 2003.

Sedmak, Clements. *Doing Local Theology*. New York: Orbis Books, 2002.

Selvon, Samuel. *Lonely Londoners*. New York: Longman, 1994.

Sensbach, Jon F. *Rebecca's Revival: Creating Black Christianity in the Atlantic World*. Massachusetts: Harvard University Press, 2005.

Shanks, Cheryl. *Immigration and the Politics of American Sovereignty 1890–1990*. Ann Arbor: University of Michigan Press, 2001.

Shannon, David T. and Gayraud S. Wilmore. *Black Witness to the Apostolic Faith*. Michigan: Eerdmans, 1985.

Sherlock, Hugh. "National Anthem of Jamaica." In *Jamaica Celebrating 43 Years*. New York, n.p., 2005.

Sherlock, Philip M. and Hazel Bennett. *The Story of the Jamaican People*. Kingston: Ian Randle Publishers, 1998.

Sibley, Inez Knibb. *The Baptists of Jamaica*. Kingston: The Jamaica Baptist Union, 1965.

Simpson, George Eaton. *Black Religions in the New World*. New York: Columbia University Press, 1978.

Simpson, Samuel G. *To Dream the Impossible Dream: Planning and Planting Churches in the City*. Georgia: Armon Press, 2003.

Sitahal, Harold. "Mission and Evangelism in an Age of Colonization." In *Out of the Depths*, ed. Idris Hamid. San Fernando: Rahaman Printery, 1977.

———. "Rethinking Mission for the Caribbean." In *Out of the Depths*, ed. Idris Hamid. San Fernando: Rahaman Printery, 1977.

Smith, Ashley. "Mission and Evangelism in an Age of Colonization." In *Out of the Depths*, ed. Idris Hamid. San Fernando: Rahaman Printery, 1977.

———. *Real Roots and Potted Plants: Reflections on the Caribbean Church*. Mandeville: Eureka Press, 1984.

———. *Emerging from Innocence: Religion, Theology and Development*. Mandeville: Eureka Press, 1991.

Stanley, Brian. *The History of the Baptist Missionary Society, 1792–1992*. Edinburgh: T&T Clark, 1992.

Stephens, Michelle Ann. *Black Empire: The Masculine Global Imaginary of Caribbean Intellectuals in the United States, 1914–1962*. Durham: Duke University Press, 2005.

Stewart, Diane. *Three Eyes for the Journey: African Dimensions of the Jamaican Religious Experience*. New York: Oxford University Press, 2005.

Stewart, Robert. *Religion and Society in Post Emancipation Jamaica*. Knoxville: University of Tennessee Press, 1992.

———. *The Role of Religion in Post Emancipation Jamaica*. Knoxville: University of Tennessee Press, 1992.

Stuckey, Sterling. *Nationalist Theory and the Foundations of Black America*. New York: Oxford University Press, 1987.

Sturge, Mark. *Look What the Lord Has Done! An Exploration of Black Christian Faith in Britain*. Bletchley: Scripture Union, 2005.

Sugiratharajah, R. S. *Postcolonial Criticism and Biblical Interpretation*. Oxford: Oxford University Press, 2002.

Sutton, Constance R. "The Caribbeanization of New York City and the Emergence of a Transnational Socio-Cultural System." In *Caribbean Life in New York City: Socio-Cultural Dimensions*, eds Constance R. Sutton and Elsa M. Chaney. New York: Center for Migration Studies of New York, 1987.

Sutton, Constance R. and Susan R. Makiesky-Barrow. "Migration and West Indian Racial and Ethnic Consciousness." In *Caribbean Life in New York City: Social and Cultural Dimensions*, eds Constance R. Sutton and Elsa M. Chaney. New York: Center for Migration Studies of New York, 1992.

Tannehill, Robert C. *Luke*. Nashville: Abingdon Press, 1996.

Taylor, Burchell. *The Church Taking Sides*. Kingston: Bethel Baptist Church, 1995.

———. "Onesimus – The Voiceless Initiator of the Liberating Process." In *Caribbean Theology: Preparing for the Challenges Ahead*, ed. Howard Gregory. Kingston: Canoe Press, 1995.

Taylor, Patrick, ed. *Nation Dance: Religion, Identity and Cultural Difference in the Caribbean*. Indianapolis: Indiana University Press, 2001.

Taylor, Ula Yvette. *The Veiled Garvey: The Life and Times of Amy Jacques Garvey*. Chapel Hill: University of North Carolina Press, 2002.

Terry-Thompson, A. C. *The History of the African Orthodox Church*. New York: Beacon Press, 1956.

Thomas, Bert J. "Historical Functions of Caribbean-American Benevolent/Progressive Associations." *Afro-Americans in New York Life and History* (July 1988).

Thomas-Hope, Elizabeth. "Hopes and Reality in the West Indian Migration to Britain." *The Journal of the Oral History Society* 8, no. 1 (1980).

———. *Caribbean Migration*. Kingston: University of the West Indies Press, 2002.

Thomas-Hope, Elizabeth, ed. "Caribbean Identity: A Matter of Perception." In *Perspective on Caribbean Regional Identity*. Liverpool: University of Liverpool, Center for Latin American Studies, 1984.

Titus, Noel. "Our Caribbean Reality." In *Caribbean Theology: Preparing for the Challenges Ahead*, ed. Howard Gregory. Kingston: Canoe Press, University of the West Indies, 1995.

Tololyan, Khachig. "The Nation State and its Others: In Lieu of a Preface." *Diaspora* 1.1 (1991).

Toulis, Nicole Rodriguez. *Believing Identity: Pentecostalism and the Mediation of Jamaican Ethnicity and Gender in England*. New York: Berg, 1997.

Townes, Emile. *In a Blaze of Glory: Womanist Spirituality as Social Witness*. Nashville: Abingdon Press, 1995.

Tracey, David. *Blessed Rage for Order: The New Pluralism in Theology*. New York: Seabury Press, 1975.

Turner, Henry McNeal. "God is a Negro." *Voice of Missions* 1.1 (February 1898).

Turner, Mary. *Slaves and Missionaries: The Disintegration of Jamaican Slave Society, 1787–1834*. Kingston: University of the West Indies Press, 1998.

Turner, W. Burghardt and Joyce Moore Turner. *Richard B. Moore, Caribbean Militant in Harlem: Collected Writings 1920–1972*. Bloomington and Indianapolis: Indiana University Press, 1992.

Vickerman, Milton. *Crosscurrents: West Indian Immigrants and Race*. New York: Oxford University Press, 1999.

Victory Seventh Day Adventist Church. *Official Opening Souvenir Journal of Victory Seventh Day Adventist Church*. New York, May 1996.

Volf, Miroslav. *After our Likeness: The Church as the Image of the Trinity*. Michigan: Eerdsmans, 1998.

Wake Eden Community Baptist Church. *25ᵗʰ Anniversary Journal of Wake Eden Community Baptist Church*. New York: Waken Eden Community Baptist Church, 1997.

Ware, Frederick L. *Methodologies of Black Theology*. Ohio: Pilgrim Press, 2002.

Warner, R. Stephen. "Immigrants and the Faith They Bring: Coming to America." *Christian Century*, February 10, 2004.

———. *A Church of Our Own: Disestablishment and Diversity in American Religion*. New York: Rutgers University Press, 2005.

Warner-Lewis, Maureen. *Central Africa in the Caribbean: Transcending Time, Transforming Cultures*. Kingston: University of the West Indies Press, 2003.

Waters, Mary. *Black Identities: West Indian Immigrants' Dreams and American Realities*. Massachusetts: Harvard University Press, 1999.

Watkins-Owens, Irma. *Blood Relations: Caribbean Immigrants and the Harlem Community, 1900–1930*. Indianapolis: Indiana University Press, 1996.

———. "Early Twentieth Century Caribbean Women." In *Island in the City: West Indian Migration to New York*, ed. Nancy Foner. Berkeley: University of California Press, 2001.

———. "Early Twentieth Century Caribbean Women: Migration and Social Networks in New York." In *Islands in the City: West Indian Migration to New York*, ed. Nancy Foner. Berkeley: University of California Press, 2001.

Watty, William. "The New Missiology – A Biblical Perspective." In *Out of the Depths*, ed. Idris Hamid. San Fernando: Rahaman Printery, 1977.

———. *From Shore to Shore: Soundings in Caribbean Theology*. Kingston: United Theological College of the West Indies, 1981.

West, Cornel. *Prophesy Deliverance: An Afro-American Revolutionary Christianity*. Philadelphia: Westminster Press, 1982.

———. *Prophetic Fragments*. Grand Rapids: Eerdmans, 1982.

———. *Race Matters*. Boston: Beacon Press, 1993.

———. *Democracy Matters: Winning the Fight against Imperialism*. New York: Penguin, 2004.

West, Cornel and Eddie S. Glaude, Jr., eds. *African American Religious Thought*. Louisville: Westminster John Knox Press, 2003.

Wilkinson, John L. *Church in Black and White*. Edinburgh: St. Andrew Press, 1993.

Williams, Delores. *Sisters in the Wilderness: The Challenge of Womanist God-Talk*. New York: Orbis Books, 1993.

Williams, Demetrius K. *An End to this Strife: The Politics of Gender in African American Churches*. Minneapolis: Fortress Press, 2004.

Williams, Eric. *Capitalism and Slavery*. North Carolina: University of North Carolina Press, 1944.

———. *From Columbus to Castro: The History of the West Indies*. New York: Vintage Books, 1984.

Williams, Lewin. *Caribbean Theology*. New York: Peter Lang, 1994.

Willimon, William H. "Acts." In *Interpretation Bible Commentary*, ed. James Luther Mays. Atlanta: John Knox Press, 1988.

Wilmore, Gayraud. *Black and Presbyterian: The Heritage and the Hope*. Philadelphia: Geneva Press, 1983.

———. *Black Religion and Black Radicalism: An Interpretation of the Religious History of Afro-American People*. New York: Orbis Books, 1985.

Willoughby, Karen L. "Churches Bloom in the Bronx Despite Years of Hard Times." *Baptist Press*, July 20, 2003.

———. "In the Midst of Fire-devastated Bronx, N.Y. Church Rose to Provide Hope." *Baptist Press*, September 7, 2004.

Yon, Daniel. "Identity and Differences in the Caribbean Diaspora: Case Study from Metropolitan Toronto." In *The Reordering of Culture: Latin America, the Caribbean and Canada*, eds Alvin Ruprecht and Cecelia Taiana. Canada: Carleton University Press, 1995.

Zane, Wallace W. *Journeys to Spiritual Lands: The Natural History of a West Indian Religion*. New York: Oxford University Press, 1999.

Zips, Werner. *Black Rebels*. Kingston: Ian Randle Publishers, 1999.

Printed in the United Kingdom
by Lightning Source UK Ltd.
133962UK00001B/82-108/P